66 desire

Citizen Outsider

Citizen Outsider

Children of North African Immigrants in France

———

Jean Beaman

UNIVERSITY OF CALIFORNIA PRESS

University of California Press, one of the most distinguished university presses in the United States, enriches lives around the world by advancing scholarship in the humanities, social sciences, and natural sciences. Its activities are supported by the UC Press Foundation and by philanthropic contributions from individuals and institutions. For more information, visit www.ucpress.edu.

University of California Press
Oakland, California

Suggested citation: Beaman, Jean. *Citizen Outsider: Children of North African Immigrants in France.* Oakland: University of California Press, 2017. doi: https://doi.org/10.1525/luminos.39

Library of Congress Cataloging-in-Publication Data

Names: Beaman, Jean, 1980– author.
Title: Citizen outsider : children of North African immigrants in France / Jean Beaman.
Description: Oakland, California : University of California Press, [2017] | Includes bibliographical references and index.
Identifiers: LCCN 2017022042 (print) | LCCN 2017024014 (ebook) | ISBN 9780520967441 (ebook) | ISBN 9780520294264 (pbk. : alk. paper)
Subjects: LCSH: North Africans—France—Ethnic identity. | Children of immigrants—France
Classification: LCC DC34.5.N67 (ebook) | LCC DC34.5.N67 B395 2017 (print) | DDC 305.23089/92761044—dc23
LC record available at https://lccn.loc.gov/2017022042

26   25   24   23   22   21   20   19   18   17
10   9   8   7   6   5   4   3   2   1

CONTENTS

ILLUSTRATIONS

MAP

FIGURES

Why Paris?[1] Why France? I've been asked those questions more times I can remember—even before I entered graduate school. I always think my interest in France is a boring or ordinary story. I quickly fell in love with the French language as a middle school student, even though the language was somewhat difficult to master. I continued to study French throughout high school. I became very curious about visiting France and getting an opportunity to speak French with French people living in France. I finally got that chance when I enrolled in a study abroad program my junior year in college. And for someone who did not have the opportunity to travel much growing up, my world opened. Not only did I become fluent in French by living with a family in Paris and taking courses at Paris 7 (one of the University of Paris campuses in the Latin Quarter) and the Institut Catholique de Paris, I felt a new sense of independence.

I quickly realized that I was in France not only as an American citizen but also as a black American. I saw this in the way I was treated, the questions people asked me. I remember being one of the only African-Americans in my study abroad program. I remember struggling to find a salon where I could get my hair relaxed. And I thought about the complexity of my experiences—having simultaneously the privilege of being American and the complications of being black. The French, influenced by various stereotypes and images (both positive and negative) circulating in the media, asked me questions about being American, while shopkeepers followed me around in stores. One day when I was on one of my long walks across the city, I came across Tyler Stovall's *Paris Noir: African Americans in the City of Light* (1996) and began to appreciate how I was part of long line of African-Americans living in Paris for long periods, such as James Baldwin, Duke Ellington, and Richard Wright, and how being Black in Paris made apparent many of the contradictions of the French Republic.

My fascination and interest in Paris, and France more generally, only deepened as I started to apply my "sociological imagination" to my experiences and observations about race, ethnicity, and identity in France. Such observations stayed with me long after my study abroad experience, to when I entered graduate school and started to consider what other scholars had written related to these topics. I found my population to study—children of North African immigrants, or descendants of the French colonial empire in the Maghreb, who were born and had known only France yet were positioned outside of it. Through my ethnographic research, I learned about much more than this population. Among other things, I learned fundamentally about how race and ethnicity continue to separate and mark individuals as different in both the United States and France.

I hope that the following pages do justice to the long history of black scholars writing about other communities on the margins.

ACKNOWLEDGMENTS

It's incredibly humbling to write these acknowledgments and realize how blessed I am to have had so much support throughout the researching and writing of this book. I am thankful to God for all of those who helped me along this journey.

Although the research for this book began with my dissertation, my fascination and interest in race and identity in France began much earlier. I would like to thank the many people who nurtured and supported my interest in France and the French language throughout my life, including Margaret Sinclair and the French Department at Northwestern University and Carol Denis and the Sweet Briar College Junior Year Abroad in France Program. I am also fortunate that I learned what sociology was and how to be a sociologist at Northwestern University, both as an undergraduate and a graduate student. I am eternally grateful to Wendy Nelson Espeland and the late Allan Schnaiberg for helping me see that I could be a sociologist and that I had something worthwhile to contribute to the discipline. They both empowered me to pursue a Ph.D. in sociology. I first encountered them as an undergraduate student, and they continued to shape my development as a graduate student. I also thank the late Carla B. Howery of the American Sociological Association for being such a fantastic mentor. While in graduate school, I benefited from the mentorship of Celeste Watkins-Hayes, who provided an excellent model for how to survive graduate school while also maintaining your sanity.

As co-chairs of my dissertation committee, Mary Pattillo and Monica Prasad provided crucial guidance as I undertook the fieldwork for this project and tried to make sense of all my data. In addition to providing great models for conducting thorough and rigorous research, they both, in their own ways, pushed me to deepen my analyses, which only improved my writing and work. Mary provided an inspiring model for conducting thoughtful research on communities on the margins. And Monica's attention to both detail and the bigger scope of things was invaluable for understanding what was particular to France and what had broader implications. I also thank the other members of my dissertation committee— Tessie Liu and Wendy Griswold. Tessie has always been supportive of my work and thinking, and provided valuable expertise on the complexities inherent in French Republican society. Wendy helped shape my development as a cultural sociologist throughout graduate school. Many of the ideas in this book were fleshed out during Wendy's Culture Workshop. I am thankful to participants for their feedback, including Marcus Anthony Hunter, Mikaela Rabinowitz, Japonica Brown-Saracino, Corey Fields, Nicole Van Cleve, Zandria Robinson, Geoff Harkness, and Lori Delale O'Connor. I am thankful to have gone through graduate school with this kind of company. In short, I feel fortunate to have had so much formal and informal support at Northwestern University as I have developed as a sociologist. And this support has remained after graduate school.

I am enormously grateful to each of my interviewees, for giving their time and sharing their experiences with me, principally during my stay in Paris from 2008 to 2009. They invited me into their homes or offices, spent many hours in cafés with me, and often helped me form valuable connections that facilitated this research. Though I cannot identify them by name, there would not be a book without their generosity. Of course, the same can be said for those at the Nanterre Association. (The real name of this organization has been changed per Institutional Review Board guidelines. However, I chose to identify the banlieue, as I have with all the banlieues and geographical locations in this book.) From day one, the people there were incredibly welcoming of this "American visitor." My interactions with staff, students, and clients not only provided rich data but also a family away from my American one.

I am thankful to the Lebrun and Lepoutre families for helping to facilitate my stays in Paris. Engaging with Patrick Simon, Angeline Escafré-Dublet, Jules Naudet, Alexandre Biotteau, Elyamine Settoul, El Yamine Soum, Rokhaya Diallo, Cécile Coquet-Mokoko, Nacira Guénif Souilamas, Aurélien Gillier, and Pap Ndiaye was invaluable for further understanding the French side of things, particularly as I turned this dissertation into a book.

Writing this book has taken me to many places, and therefore there are many people to thank. The Erskine A. Peters Dissertation Fellowship at the University of Notre Dame provided me with a different intellectual environment in both the Africana Studies and Sociology Departments. I am thankful to Richard Pierce, Dianne Pinderhughes, Laurence Ralph, Nicole Ivy, Omar Lizardo, Jessica Collett, and Lyn Spillman for their various feedback and support. The Max Weber Fellowship at the European University Institute in Florence provided a beautiful location to begin transforming this dissertation into a book. I am thankful for the mentorship of Rainer Bauböck and Laura Lee Downs. In addition, friends including Gabrielle Clark, Heather Brundage, Konrad M. Lawson, Stefan Link, Anita Kurimay, Bridget Gurtler, Bilyana Petkova, Gregorio Bettiza, Swen Hutter, and Simon Jackson helped me face the various highs and lows of academic writing. I also spent a year at Duke University's Center for the Study of Race, Ethnicity and Gender in the Social Sciences and the Research Network on Racial and Ethnic Inequality as a postdoctoral associate. I thank William "Sandy" Darity, Kerry Haynie, Laurent Dubois, Jessica Barron, Dena Montague, Joseph Lariscy, Achim Edelmann, Steve Vaisey, and Eduardo Bonilla-Silva (who also provided helpful feedback on my book prospectus). Despite his multiple commitments, Sandy Darity always had time for me and continues to inspire me with his passion for empirical research's potential to shed light on and ameliorate racial and ethnic inequalities, particularly for black populations.

At Purdue University, I am thankful for the support of Rachel Einwohner, Candy Lawson, Dan Olson, Linda Renzulli, Kevin Stainback, Mangala Subramaniam, Bob Perrucci, Carolyn Perrucci, and Venetria Patton. I also am thankful to the community of friends and colleagues I've developed at Purdue, including Natasha Watkins, Wendy Kline, Margaret Tillman, Natasha Duncan, Dwaine Jengelley, Monica Trieu, Su'ad Abdul Khabeer, Evie Blackwood, Stacey Mickelbart, Robyn Malo, Nadia Brown, Valeria Sinclair-Chapman, Patti Thomas, Nadège Veldwachter, Silvia Mitchell, S. Laurel Weldon, Will Gray, Sandra Sydnor, Tithi Bhattacharya, Bill Mullen, and Megha Anwer.

I thank the University of California for publishing my first monograph. I thank Naomi Schneider for her supreme guidance and patience through this process and Renee Donovan and Jessica Moll for their editorial assistance and answers to my many questions. I also thank the reviewers of this book for their time and critical and helpful feedback. The book is better as a result.

I also thank Stacey Mickelbart for her editorial assistance. I appreciate the support of my writing accountability group (Dafney Dabach, Kaelyn Wiles, and Nicole Overstreet) at the National Center for Faculty Development and Diversity. I thank Melissa Weiner, Syed Ali, Deborah Reed-Danahey, Erik Bleich, Mounira Maya Charrad, Trica Keaton, Patricia McManus, Jennifer Fredette, Nasar Meer, Christine Barwick, Roger Waldinger, Ruben Hernandez-Leon, Rubén Hernández-León, Tara Zahra, Jens Schneider, Mayanthi Fernando, Crystal Fleming, Inés Valdez, Cathy Jean Schneider, Marc Hebling, Rhys Williams, Dorit Geva, Caitlin Killian, and Samir Meghelli for their engagement with and feedback on my research over the years. In particular Lyn Spillman and David S. Meyer have been fantastic sources of support over the years. Since my time at Notre Dame, Lyn has provided much-needed support when I struggled with different aspects of this project. David has been a great sounding board, especially related to publishing and academia more generally. I am very grateful to have crossed paths with them both.

I received funding for the research and writing of this book through the Northwestern University French Interdisciplinary Group; the Graduate School of Northwestern University; the University of Notre Dame Erskine A. Peters Dissertation Fellowship; Duke University; the European University Institute Max Weber Fellowship; Purdue College of Liberal Arts; and the Purdue Research Foundation. Parts of this research have been presented at conferences for the Council for European Studies; the American Sociological Association; the Association for Black Sociologists; the Association for the Sociology of Religion; International Migration, Integration, and Social Cohesion (IMISCOE); the Social Science History Association; and the International Sociological Association. This is in addition to presentations at Duke University; Georgia State University; Indiana University; Loyola University Chicago; the University of Cambridge; the University of Cincinnati; the University of California, Davis; the University of California, Los Angeles; the University of Notre Dame; and the University of Texas at Austin. I thank all participants for their feedback.

Finally, I feel especially blessed for the support of friends I've known for quite a long time, both inside and outside of academia, including LaShawnDa Pittman, Min Kyung Lee, Zandria Robinson, Japonica Brown-Saracino, Nicole Van Cleve, Lori Delale O'Connor, Jean-Yves Klein, Jessie Lan Kim, Esther Contreras, Dena Montague, and Jennifer Hobbs. I especially thank Marcus Anthony Hunter and Mikaela Rabinowitz, whom I met in graduate school and who have become great friends. They both engaged with my work and tolerated my neuroses at various stages (both during and after graduate school) and helped me tremendously when I was on the brink of giving up. I also thank Marcus for the book title idea. I could not have reached this stage without the support of my family, who always believed I could research and write this book and supported my various stays in Paris. Thanks to my siblings, Lauren, Leigh, and Kevin; my grandmother Maxine; my late grandfather, James; my godmother, Karen Rayfield, and her family; my niece McKenzie; my Aunt Joan and Aunt Fern; and my cousins Denise, Pete, and Evan. I especially thank my parents, Kellye Beaman and James Beaman Jr., for all their various sacrifices which allowed me to reach this stage of my life. I love you all.

1

North African Origins in and of the French Republic

The Republic makes no distinction among its children.
—MANUEL VALLS, *FORMER FRENCH PRIME MINISTER*[1]

Look at the Gare du Nord.[2] You no longer have the impression of being in France, you have the impression of being in Africa. No, really. . . . You arrive at Gare du Nord, it's Africa, it's no longer France. We don't have the right to say that, but I'll say it because it's true.
—NADINE MORANO, *LES RÉPUBLICAINS PARTY POLITICIAN*[3]

A tall, muscular man with tousled dark brown hair, Abdelkrim met me one afternoon in March of 2009 at a Starbucks in the *quartier* (neighborhood) of Montparnasse and told me he identifies with Bruce Lee, the Hong Kong–American martial artist and action-film star. "He was too American for the Chinese and too Chinese for Americans," he explained between sips of his espresso.[4,5] Despite his successes, Bruce Lee was caught between American and Chinese cultures, and never considered as belonging to either. Abdelkrim completely relates to this dualism; he too feels that he is too French for Maghrébins and too *maghrébin* for the French.[6]

Abdelkrim similarly told me about reading *The Autobiography of Malcolm X* as a teenager, and how Malcolm's struggles to be accepted as a black man in white America deeply resonate with him. A thirty-two-year-old with dual French and Algerian citizenship, Abdelkrim boasts that he was born in the same town in central France, Châteauroux, as French actor Gérard Depardieu and is just as French as Depardieu is.

The story of Abdelkrim's parents' immigration to France from Algeria is distinctive when compared with that of other North African immigrants. Whereas many maghrébin immigrants came to France primarily for economic reasons in the immediate postcolonial period, Abdelkrim's parents, who are bilingual in French and Arabic, came for political ones. They arrived in the late 1960s from Algiers, the capital city of Algeria, after the nation won its independence from France in 1962. His father was active in the Front de libération nationale, a socialist political party fighting for Algerian independence. After the war, he became disenchanted with living in Algeria because of the instability in the country brought about by Algeria's new political system. He eventually married Abdelkrim's mother and had five children, and the entire family then immigrated to France. Abdelkrim's father became a maintenance worker at a *habitation à loyer modéré* (subsidized housing, or HLM) complex, and his mother was a homemaker. They had three additional children after immigrating to France—including Abdelkrim, who is the youngest of the eight. Abdelkrim grew up in a Muslim household, and though as an adult he celebrates Ramadan with his family, he does not otherwise engage in Muslim practices. He also believes religion should be a private affair, per French Republican ideology.

When Abdelkrim was growing up, his parents actively engaged with his schooling and communicated with his teachers, thanks to their fluency in French. Though neither attended school past the age of fourteen, they engaged in self-education afterward. In their predominately immigrant neighborhood, it was Abdelkrim's parents who helped neighborhood residents who could not read or write with their "daily round" (Logan and Molotch 1987), whether it was going to doctor's appointments or having conferences with teachers.

In this context, Abdelkrim does not remember feeling particularly different from others because of his maghrébin origins growing up, until he attended a middle school outside his neighborhood, where there were fewer nonwhites and immigrant-origin individuals. "That is when everything changed," he recalls, "You discovered others and they discovered you. And we didn't have the same life." Sometimes he became friends with people different from him; oftentimes he did not. As Abdelkrim had more and more interactions with people outside his neighborhood, his visibility as a maghrébin-origin individual and how that marked him as different became increasingly apparent to him. Growing up as a nonwhite person in France, Abdelkrim has since struggled to come to terms with his identity.

He later attended a university in Tours, a town in central France's Loire valley, to please his mother, who wanted him to become a lawyer. He remembers there being only two other ethnic minorities there and feeling he had to stick with them to survive. On two separate occasions, he was physically attacked and called ethnic slurs by other students. Abdelkrim eventually left law school and has since become an accomplished freelance journalist, which he feels is his calling.

Still, despite his successes and his attainment of a middle-class status, he finds that many of his fellow citizens do not accept him as French. He usually has an acute sense of being French only when he is traveling internationally, as opposed to when he is in France. He remembers traveling to London when he was twenty-four years old and meeting some African Americans. Upon telling them that he was maghrébin and Algerian, they informed him that he was French. "They just kept telling me that I am from France, so I am French," he recalled. It seemed so logical to them, yet this logic is not so easily accepted in French society.

This disconnect between where he was born and how he is perceived is the reality for racial and ethnic minorities born in France to immigrant parents.

And that is the subject of this book, *Citizen Outsider: Children of North African Immigrants in the France*. Based on ethnographic research, including interviews, in the Paris metropolitan area, I address the following questions: How do ethnic minorities in France contend with implicitly race-based definitions of what it means to be French? How do upwardly-mobile and middle-class maghrébin-origin individuals perceive the possibilities for participating fully in the French mainstream? Decades after the end of France's brutal colonial empire in the North African countries of Algeria, Tunisia, and Morocco, what is the legacy of this empire for the immigrant-origin population, born and raised in France to parents who emigrated for better opportunities, and what are the everyday sociopolitical realities it faces? How do individuals who are citizens remain on the margins of mainstream society, and what does this reveal about how race and ethnicity, including differences based on them, operate in practice?

Despite former Prime Minister Manuel Valls and other French politicians' declarations that there is no differential treatment in France, the experiences of Abdelkrim and other children of North African immigrants reveal how this conclusion is wrong. Differential treatment and exclusion are based on racial and ethnic status; individuals like Abdelkrim are marginalized because they are nonwhite. Even if Abdelkrim and others like him feel French, claiming French identity rests in the degree to which individuals perceive them as French. They hit a glass ceiling: France's imagined community (Anderson 1991) does not include them. Much research on the second generation in Europe and the United States focuses on the degree to which they are assimilated, acculturated, or integrated, particularly in terms of specific outcomes, such as educational attainment or labor force participation (Alba and Foner 2015; Alba and Waters 2011; Crul and Mollenkopf 2012; Waters 2000; Waters et al. 2010; Zhou 1997; Zhou and Lee 2007). Yet while all these terms may apply to Abdelkrim—for example, in his educational attainment and achievement of a middle-class status—he is still alienated from mainstream French society because he is nonwhite. As such, a focus on the second generation through the lens of assimilation or integration is insufficient.

This book specifically focuses on the middle-class segment of the North African second generation—those individuals who have achieved upward mobility vis-à-vis their immigrant parents. This is the first ethnographic account of this segment of the second-generation population. It connects to a growing literature on middle-class subaltern minorities worldwide. Instead of just focusing on their outcomes, particularly relating to educational attainment and employment patterns, I focus on their experience as an ethnic minority, including the processes embedded within that experience, in a national context that does not recognize minorities based on ethnic origin or have a language or framework for making sense of them.

In doing so, I lay to rest the notion of a French exceptionalism regarding distinctions based on race and ethnicity. I examine how a population that is legally and technically French is not considered culturally French, and is therefore excluded from popular imaginations of who a French person is. This reveals how race, ethnicity, and culture intersect in determining who is a citizen of the nation-state and who can claim a French identity.

The continually reinforced rejection by mainstream society experienced by Abdelkrim and others belies previous conclusions about the salience of race and ethnicity as markers of difference in France. By traditional measures, many children of North African immigrants, or the North African second generation, as I also refer to them, are assimilated (Portes and Zhou 1993).[7] The individuals I discuss in this book were educated at French schools and universities. Their native tongue is French. They are French citizens. While their middle-class status might suggest a triumph of France's Republican model, which purports to downplay distinctions based on identity among citizens, this population's continued experiences of exclusion and discrimination challenge this straightforward conclusion.

I frame these individuals as "citizen outsiders"—a framework rooted in early works by black scholars such as Audre Lorde (2007), W. E. B. DuBois ([1903] 1994) and Frantz Fanon (1967) and recently coined by political scientist Cathy Cohen (2010)—in that they are simultaneously members of a society yet kept on the margins of that society. I further use the framework of "cultural citizenship" as a corrective to theories of immigrant incorporation and assimilation, as well as to illustrate how difference is implicitly marked among individuals without explicit designations by the state. Individuals who are technically citizens are not treated as full citizens because of their assigned otherness as racial and ethnic minorities. Members of this French-born population find that they cannot escape this assigned otherness. Because of their North African origins, they have been denied cultural citizenship, which signifies a claim to societal belonging that is accepted by others, enabling children of North African immigrants to traverse the cultural-symbolic boundaries of French identity and be considered truly French.

These individuals' marginalization reveals both how race and ethnicity remain significant in shaping life circumstances in French society and how citizenship status is not a sufficient boundary defining insiders and outsiders. Rather, acceptance as a fellow citizen is inextricably linked to boundaries around French identity marked by race and ethnicity. Despite promoting a colorblind ideology, France, at both the state level and through microlevel interactions, reinforces the

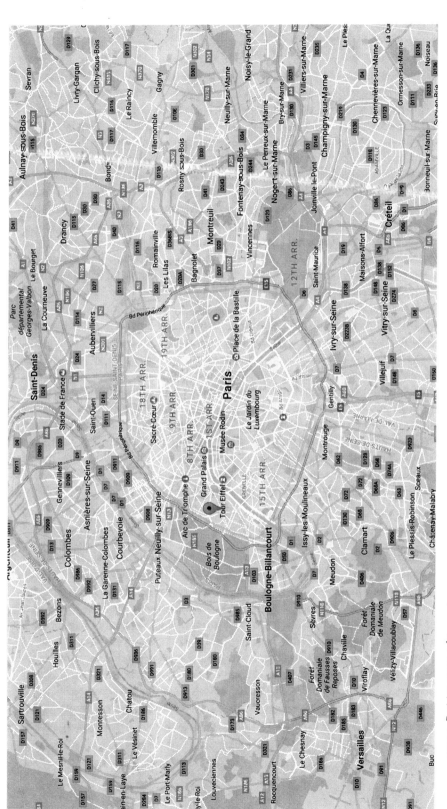

MAP 1. Parisian metropolitan region.

differentiation between nonwhite individuals and the rest of French society, no matter how much the North African second generation seeks to challenge that.

The question of who makes up a nation, the role of race and ethnicity in this definition, and what happens to those individuals excluded from that definition, is, of course, not limited to France. The experiences of children of North African immigrants have implications for other racial and ethnic minority populations worldwide, including, but not limited to, second-generation immigrants in the United States such as West Indians (Waters 2000) and Mexicans (Portes and Rumbaut 2001), middle-class African Americans (Carter 2005; Frazier 1957; Lacy 2007; Pattillo 2007; Pattillo-McCoy 1999), middle-class Dutch women of Surinamese descent in the Netherlands (Essed 1991), and the Turkish second generation in Western Europe (Fleischmann et al. 2011). Ultimately, for populations designated as "other" or treated as outsiders, including the North African second generation, citizenship, or being a citizen, does not sufficiently allow for traversing boundaries of full societal inclusion.

In this chapter, I present a historical background on French Republicanism and North African immigration to France that contextualizes the contemporary experiences of the middle-class adult children of North African immigrants whom I studied. I then provide an overview of our existing knowledge of the North African second generation. Next, I discuss how, despite the middle-class status of this population, its members remain marginalized because they are nonwhite. I further discuss France's "racial project" (per Omi and Winant's 1994 formulation) and how race and ethnicity operate in France, without state-level designations. Extending from this, I discuss the framework of cultural citizenship, the denial of which is evidence of France's racial project. I finally discuss the methods of this study and provide a brief overview of subsequent chapters.

FROM THE MAGHREB TO FRANCE

Despite a long history of immigration and colonialism, France rarely acknowledges that history, invoking its Republican ideology to preserve the status quo and promote a monolithic version of French identity and history (Barou 2014; Noiriel 1996; Thomas 2007). But France has never been the uniform entity that the Republican model would suggest (Chabal 2015). For example, about 25 percent of the French population has at least one parent or grandparent who immigrated to France (from any country) (Barou 2014). More recently, according to the Institut national de la statistique et des études économiques (National Institute of Statistics and Economic Studies, or INSEE), which conducts the census, as of 2014, immigrants comprise 8.6 percent of the total French population (Brutel 2015). Immigration has long been framed as a social problem that threatens French national identity (Tetreault 2013).

Under the Republican model, France emphasizes citizenship as the connecting factor among her citizens over any other characteristic and conceives of its identity in national and civic, rather than ethnic, terms, an emphasis dating from before the French Revolution (Bell 2003). The state interacts with individuals independent of any group categorization or special interest group (Amselle 2003; Chapman and Frader 2004; Oberti 2007; Tetreault 2013).[8] Republicanism in France is based on equality before the law, individual emancipation (or a rejection of *communautarisme*[9]), jus solis (based on place of birth) and jus sanguinis (based on parental origins) citizenship, *laïcité*, and cultural assimilation (d'Appollonia 2009).

Established by law in 1905, *laïcité* is the French term for the separation of church and state.[10] It has often been employed to stress the assimilation of immigrant-origin individuals (Bowen 2006; Kuru 2008). The French state cannot promote any individual religion, and individuals are encouraged to keep their religious affiliations to themselves (Bowen 2004b).[11] The distinction between the public and private spheres is emphasized; any difference should be relegated to the private sphere (Escafré-Dublet and Kastoryano 2012; Kastoryano and Escafré-Dublet 2012). Some scholars have noted the role that religion, particularly Catholicism, has played in the development of French Republican society (Gray 2008; Laborde 2008), despite France's emphasis on *laïcité*.[12]

Being French is supposed to supersede all other identities and identifications, including ethnic, racial, religious, linguistic, and regional. The creation of France as a nation rested in subsuming such identifications. French philosopher Ernest Renan's lecture at the Sorbonne famously asked the question, "Qu'est-ce qu'une nation?" (What is a nation?) ([1887] 1992). He emphasized the solidarity among individuals—and the sacrifices citizens make on behalf of that solidarity—over language, race, religion, or geography (Cartrite 2009). It is these commonalities that are supposed to constitute France as a nation and bring its members together. In this "indivisible" Republic, acknowledging differences regarding identity and recognizing racial and ethnic diversity threatens the disruption of the Republican model (Cooper 2014; Kastoryano and Escafré-Dublet 2012). Acknowledging difference is viewed as propagating difference. In fact, the United States is often framed as an example of this danger, in that an identity politics based on multiculturalism hinders the fostering of a unified and centralized national community (Chabal 2015).

Despite the Republican emphasis on the renunciation of racial and ethnic categorization, scholars have argued that France has long relied on racial and ethnic boundaries in constructing its national identity (Chapman and Frader 2004; Kastoryano 2004; Peabody and Stovall 2003; Wieviorka 1992). According to French historian Gérard Noiriel (1996), immigration has been an elemental feature of the construction of the distinction between "us" and "them" in the creation of the French nation.[13] The Republican model, in fact, marks difference, even without officially acknowledging it (Chapman and Frader 2004; Fernando 2009; Laborde 2008; Schneider 2008; Wilder 2007). Moreover, French identity has long been implicitly framed as white (Constant 2009; Peabody and Stovall 2003). Ideologies of racial inferiority were used to justify France's imperialism in the Maghreb and other regions. To give one example, aristocrat Arthur de Gobineau's 1884 *Essai sur l'inégalité des races humaines* (Essay on the Inequality of the Human Races) asserted the biological and cultural superiority of Europeans over blacks, who were described as animal-like subjects and belonging to the lowest racial category (Thomas 2007; Winant 2001; Wright 2004).[14]

France's colonial empire served to reify the boundary between French and "other" and highlighted the contradictions embedded within French Republicanism (Kastoryano and Escafré-Dublet 2012).[15] France's relationship with the Maghreb began with the colonization of Algeria in 1830, of Tunisia in 1831, and of Morocco in 1912. Tunisia and Morocco were French protectorates, while Algeria was considered an overseas territory of France. Tunisia and Morocco remained in French control until 1956, and Algeria remained in French control until 1962. Colonialism in the Maghreb created a differential status for those of North African origin, which has ramifications for descendants of immigrants from those French colonies today.[16] North Africans were framed as culturally distinct from the French colonialists, an attitude that persists in the postcolonial period (Kastoryano and Escafré-Dublet 2012).

Though emigration from the Maghreb to France began as early as the early 1900s, World War I brought immigrants from these French colonies en masse to France for work (Barou 2014; Kaya 2009).[17] It was expected that these immigrants would be temporary residents (Winant 2001). In many cities, including Paris, immigrant workers settled in the outlying *banlieues* (suburbs), owing to the presence of cheaper housing and factory employment (Esman 2009; Stovall 2003).[18] Often these immigrants "were marginalized and excluded from full participation in French society. Economically they frequently performed the dirtiest and most menial tasks; legally they were disadvantaged as they were not French citizens and therefore did not have the same rights as the French; socially and geographically they were confined to areas on the outskirts of major cities" (Silverman 1992, 46). Moreover, they were treated worse than immigrants from European countries (Barou 2014). The numbers of North African immigrants continued to increase after World War II, the end of the Fourth Republic in 1958, and the Algerian War of Independence in 1962.[19] Within a decade, by the early 1970s, there were more than 800,000 immigrants from Algeria alone (Silverstein 2008).

This growth in the number of North African immigrants saw more of them living in an HLM (subsidized housing) complex in the banlieues, as opposed to the *bidonvilles* (shantytowns), where they had lived previously (Dikeç 2007; Hargreaves 1996; Silverstein 2008; Weir 1993). As more and more middle-class Français de souche (white native French) moved from HLMs to private housing because of low-interest loans provided by the French government in the early 1970s, HLMs and banlieues became even more associated with North African and sub-Saharan African immigrant-origin individuals (Barou 2014; Simon 1998; Tissot 2008).[20,21,22] Owing to an economic recession and declining employment opportunities, the French government temporarily suspended immigration of non-European low-skilled workers in 1974 (Stovall 2003).[23] However, this led to migrant workers settling permanently with their families in France, as opposed to returning to their countries of origin (Barou 2014; Body-Gendrot 1993; Kaya 2009). According to INSEE, more than half of the immigrants who arrived before 1974 came for employment; one-third came to join their husbands or family. The North African second generation descended primarily from this population (Silberman et al. 2007).

Government policies and actions have targeted various aspects of the living conditions of immigrant-origin individuals.[24] The presidency of Socialist François Mitterrand in 1981 saw increased immigration-related legislation (Thomas 2007). In 1981 he granted equal rights of association to immigrants (Amara 2006; Body-Gendrot 1993). As a result, organizations such as SOS Racisme, an antiracist organization heavily influenced by Republican ideology, and France Plus, an activist group, were founded during the 1980s (Begag 1990; Silverman 1992). These and similar organizations were also influenced by the 1983 Marche des Beurs (also known as the March for Equality and against Racism), by children of North African immigrants from Marseille and Paris (Amara 2006; Begag 1990; Hajjat 2013).

A 1972 law banned collecting statistics related to race and ethnicity, including in the census. This law further codified the use of race-neutral policies in France and framed racism as an individual act, as seen in, for example, prohibitions against hate speech (Bleich 2004).[25] Because French government policies stress formal race neutrality, they are often perceived as ineffective in addressing discrimination in areas such as education, housing, and employment (see Bleich 2001, 2003, 2004; Calves 2004; Favell 2001; Hargreaves 2004; Lieberman 2004). Because of Republican ideology, government policies target particular geographical areas instead of identity-based communities, as in the United States, creating, for example, a territorial affirmative action instead of an ethnic or race-based affirmative action (Dikeç 2007).[26]

Understanding the presence of Islam in France is crucial for understanding the racism and marginalization the North African–origin population faces, even if all maghrébin-origin individuals do not automatically identify as Muslim. While I discuss Muslims throughout this book, I stress the distinction between Muslims and North African–origin individuals here. While many respondents are Muslims, which impacts their everyday lives and experiences of marginalization, the fact that they are maghrébin or North African is the basis of their exclusion.

Because of laws prohibiting categorization based on faith, statistics on Muslims in France are scarce and somewhat inconsistent (Bowen 2004c; Laurence 2001; Laurence and Vaisse 2006). Muslims are estimated to be about 6 to 8 percent of France's total population (including immigrants and those born in France) (d'Appollonia 2009; Gray 2008; Sebian 2007). France remains the country with the largest concentration of Muslims in Europe (Hargreaves et al. 2007; Keaton 2006), and most Français de confession musulmane (French Muslims) are of Algerian and Moroccan origin (Bowen 2004b; Laurence 2001). Much research on French Muslims has highlighted their heterogeneity, particularly in terms of identity and practices (which I discuss further in chapter 3, and has drawn a distinction between Muslim culture and Muslim religion or between believing versus practicing Muslims.[27]

Despite portrayals of French Muslims as adopting an oppositional Muslim identity and of Islam as fundamentally incompatible with French society (Foner and Alba 2008), recent research has challenged the prevailing notion of French Muslims as completely different from other French people (Klausen 2008; Laurence and Vaisse 2006), as well as the notion of Muslim status conflicting with national belonging to France (Beaman 2016; Maxwell and Bleich 2014).[28] Identifying as Muslim does not pose a barrier to identifying as French (Barou 2014; Beaman 2016; Nyiri 2007).[29] Whether or not they actually practice Islam or identify as practicing Muslims, North African–origin individuals are often considered or identified as Muslim by others because Islam is the major religion in their parents' country of origin (Hargreaves et al. 2007). As I discuss further in chapter 3, the marginalization that respondents experience as Muslims is emblematic of racial and ethnic exclusion, in a context in which Islam is an acceptable way to mark difference, and race and ethnicity are not. The use of Muslim as a category for maghrébin individuals is a way to subvert discussion of race and ethnicity.

The growing attention paid to immigration in France is not related to numbers, as the actual number of immigrants has remained constant since 1930, but rather to its changing demographics, as presently more immigrants are from former North African colonies than other regions (Gafaïti 2003; Noiriel 1996; Thomas 2007; Tribalat 2004a).[30] Recent immigration-related developments in France reveal how national identity remains under debate and how immigrants and their descendants are continually framed as disruptive to this constructed national identity (Silverstein 2008). In 2007 then-president Nicolas Sarkozy established the Ministère de l'immigration, de l'intégration, de l'identité nationale et du développement solidaire (Ministry of Immigration, Integration, National Identity and Codevelopment). The ministry's stated goals included controlling migration flows, favoring integration, and promoting French identity,[31] which illustrated how language relating to immigration and citizenship were tightened under his presidency (Barou 2014). To some, this ministry suggested that "immigrants don't suit French national identity. [It tells them] Integrate or else" (Green 2007). In November 2009, Sarkozy and then-minister of IIADS Eric Besson launched a public debate on French national identity, with the stated purpose of "constructing a better shared vision of what French national identity is today" and "reaffirming Republican values and pride in being French."[32] This debate was criticized as a cover for anti-immigrant sentiment toward and ignorance about ethnic and religious minorities (Cowell 2009; Erlanger 2009; Erlanger 2010).[33] Under controversy, IIADS was demolished in 2010 (Kastoryano and Escafré-Dublet 2012).

The complexities of nationality and citizenship status in France are crucial to understanding how postcolonial immigrants and their descendants were routinely left out of both the social and symbolic boundaries around France as a nation and French as an identity (Silverstein 2008).[34] The French census classifies its populations in three categories: French by birth, French by naturalization, and foreign (Kastoryano 2004). Citizenship is based on jus solis (place of birth) rather than jus sanguinis (parental origins); however, children of foreigners have long been an exception to this rule (see Bass 2014 for overview of policies and laws for children of foreigners). Part of this is due to the historical distinction between French citizenship and nationality, as nationality does not mean automatic citizenship and all the benefits it confers. Brubaker (1992) discusses how France has a civic conception of nationhood (in contrast to Germany, which has an ethnic conception of nationhood and citizenship based on jus sanguinis).

In this book, I discuss how, despite this conception of citizenship, descendants of colonialism in the Maghreb are kept from being full members of French society. Because Algeria was a French colony, Algerians had French nationality, but they were not considered French citizens and did not have all the rights conferred to French citizens, such as voting (Noiriel 1996).[35] During the period of French colonialism, Maghrébins had a second-class status because of this distinction between French nationality and French citizenship. Colonial relations therefore shaped French citizenship and belonging (Tetreault 2013).[36] This second-class status continued even after the end of colonialism (Kastoryano and Escafré-Dublet 2012).

The *carte d'identité* (national identity card) and the *code de la nationalité française* (French nationality code) have served to exclude immigrants from becoming full members of French society (Noiriel 1996). The *code de la nationalité* has increasingly shifted toward a more restrictive definition of citizenship amid concerns over increasing immigration from North African and sub-Saharan African countries (Feldblum 1999; Silverstein 2008).[37] Those born in France to maghrébin immigrants acquire "virtual citizenship at birth" (Simon 2012). They are considered foreigners at birth and generally become citizens when they are eighteen years old, or earlier by request (Bass 2014; Brubaker 1992; Keaton 2006). The French model of integration is an assimilationist one (Schnapper et al. 2003;

Tribalat 2004a).[38] Immigrants and their descendants are supposed to assimilate into France—to be and act as French as possible. Yet this is not sufficient for descendants of France's colonial empire to be included in France.

THE NORTH AFRICAN SECOND GENERATION

As questions regarding race and ethnic origin are not asked on the French census,[39] there is a paucity of statistics available about children of North African immigrants (Laurence and Vaisse 2006; Schnapper et al. 2003; Simon 1999; Tribalat 2004a). A few recent large-scale quantitative studies have begun to fill this gap by combining data on individuals' country of birth and their parents' country of birth. The 1999 *Étude de l'histoire familiale* (Study of family history, or EHF) determined that 22 percent of France's total foreign-origin population has origins in the Maghreb and 25.9 percent of second-generation immigrants in France are of maghrébin origin (Tribalat 2004a). To be more precise, about 14 percent are of Algerian origin, 9 percent Moroccan, and 4 percent Tunisian (Borrel and Simon 2005; Tribalat 2004a).[40]

Even though this population is statistically invisible, it is socially visible. Despite being born and raised in France, the maghrébin second generation is often made to feel different by their compatriots. This is evident in the lack of a common language or term to describe the North African second generation (Kastoryano 2006; Murray 2006). For example, the term *étranger* (foreigner) is often used to refer to the North African second generation (and immigrant-origin populations more generally), even though they were born in France (Ribert 2006; Silverman 1992; Stolcke 1995; Tin 2008). While I use the terms "second-generation North African immigrant," "second-generation maghrébin immigrant," "children of maghrébin immigrants," and "the French North African second generation" interchangeably throughout this book when referring to this population, there is no commonly agreed-upon term (such as an equivalent to African American, for example).[41] They are often distinguished from Français de souche, though they are also native French. They are also frequently referred to as Muslims, although this privileges a religious identification over other identifications and presumes that every North African origin individual claims a Muslim identity in an identical way, or even at all (Alba and Silberman 2002). The term *beur* has also been used, though it is historically complicated. *Beur*, a slang term that is a partial anagram of the word *arabe*, was conceived in the Parisian banlieues by children of North African immigrants to challenge the negative connotations associated with being Arab (Begag 1990). However, the term *beur* grew to have a negative connotation as well, as it became attached to negative representations of the banlieues and their residents (Hargreaves 2007).[42] Part of the complication regarding their simultaneous visibility and invisibility rests in the French colonial legacy in which the descendants of maghrébin immigrants were never supposed to be part of France (Sayad 2004; Silverstein 2008).

The largest survey of France's second generation, the 2009 joint Institut national d'études démographiques (National Institute of Demographic Studies, or INED) and INSEE study, *Trajectoires et origines*, found that 37 percent of second-generation Moroccan and Tunisian immigrants and 39 percent of second-generation Algerian immigrants, aged eighteen to fifty, had sometimes or often experienced unequal treatment or discrimination in the five years prior to the study. In addition, there exists a strong mismatch between individuals who feel French and those who perceive that others see them as French. When asked whether they feel French, about 70 percent of second-generation maghrébin immigrants indicated that they do, but about 43 percent also feel that their "Frenchness" is denied by others, as Frenchness is based on rather on a restricted vision of who "looks French" (Simon 2012, 13). This finding suggests the racial and ethnic parameters that define who is in fact accepted as French. This book is an ethnographic complement to this survey data. Moreover, I demonstrate how the source of the dissonance Simon (2012) identifies lies in how the North African second generation is denied cultural citizenship because of its racial and ethnic origins.

Other surveys have revealed the pervasiveness of discrimination facing the maghrébin second generation, which historian Tyler Stovall refers to as "a self-destructive threat to France's racial status quo" (2003, 354).[43] In 2008 the Centre national de la recherche scientifique (National Center for Scientific Research, or CNRS) conducted a study of ethnic profiling by the police in Paris and found that those who appeared to be of North African origin were at least 7.5 times more likely than whites to be stopped (OSI 2009).[44]

Other research on the North African second generation has focused on disadvantage inherited from the first generation, particularly in terms of specific outcomes, including educational attainment and employment prospects and relative disadvantage vis-à-vis whites. For example, many individuals of North African origin experience discrimination in employment, especially hiring, which they perceive as based on their name, skin color, or residential location—all seen as proxies for ethnic origin (Silberman 2011). The North African second generation is less likely than whites to have professional types of work and is to more likely to have a lower average annual income than whites (Lombardo and Pujol 2011). Overall, the quality of life of the North African second generation (as defined by poverty rate and unemployment) is worse than the quality of life of whites and children of European immigrants (Lombardo and Pujol 2011).[45]

Using data from the EHF, Meurs et al. (2006) compare the labor force participation of the first generation with the second generation. Based on measures such as access to employment, occupational status, and access to jobs in the civil sector, they find that although the second-generation experiences less occupational segregation overall than the first, they persist in experiencing high unemployment rates and low job security relative to whites.[46] According to Meurs et al. (2005), having a maghrébin background makes someone 2.5 times more likely to be unemployed than if someone is white (controlling for educational attainment). Similarly, according to a 2011 report by the Haut Conseil à l'intégration (High Council for Integration, or HCI),[47] second-generation immigrants of non-European origin were twice as likely to be unemployed as other citizens. This disparity exists even for those individuals who are skilled, qualified, and well educated (Barou 2014).

Moreover, even for those children of maghrébin immigrants who are gainfully employed, a glass ceiling still exists (Belmessous 2007). They are more likely than whites to hold jobs beneath their educational attainment level. The disadvantage that second-generation North African immigrants experience vis-à-vis whites cannot be explained entirely by differences in levels of educational attainment (Lutz et al. 2014; Silberman et al. 2007).[48]

As of 2003, about 15 percent of second-generation North African immigrant men, and about 23 percent of second-generation North African immigrant women, held salaried jobs. In this book, I focus on this population, or what some have termed the *beurgeoisie*, a play on the slang term for children of North African immigrants, *beur* (Hargreaves 1998; Wenden and Leveau 2001). These individuals have experienced upward mobility vis-à-vis their immigrant parents and have achieved middle-class status in terms of educational and professional accomplishments.

MIDDLE-CLASS, YET MARGINALIZED

By focusing on the middle-class, I argue that being incorporated into French society and being accepted as French by others is not a question of professional success, educational attainment, or adhering to Republican ideology. Rather, France has a growing group of citizens who, despite doing everything right, cannot achieve full membership in French society. This demonstrates the limitations of citizenship within a democratic context, wherein difference based on ethnic status reveals a more dynamic notion of who is included in the Republic and who is not. Focusing on the middle-class is both a theoretical and empirical contribution, as previous research has focused more heavily on how working-class and impoverished immigrants and their children are marginalized and less on how "successful" children of immigrants face similar issues despite their upward mobility. Middle-class status does not provide automatic inclusion into mainstream society.

By mainstream or mainstream society, I am applying Alba and Nee's (2003, 12) definition: "interrelated institutional structures and organizations regulated by rules and practices," as well as "practices that foster assimilation, that is, back-grounding ethnic origins of 'included' ethnic minority" members.[49] So in this context, mainstream society is hegemonic and refers to what is often outside of respondents' maghrébin cultural world—including what they learn in school, what and whom they see represented in the media, and whom they see represented at various levels of government. More generally, mainstream society may be thought of as where the majority population feels at home, or "where its presence is taken for granted and seen as unproblematic" (Alba and Foner 2015, 5).

In terms of middle-class status, I focus on respondents' educational attainment and professional employment. Following a Weberian perspective, social scientists have measured a middle-class status based on both objective and subjective factors, including income, education level, shared values and goals, and prestige (Feagin 1991; Stearns 1979; Urry 1973; Wacquant 1991). Middle-class status is not just a socioeconomic location, but also a social status (Weber [1922] 1978). Subjective factors related to class include the ideas "people have and hold about their own social positions, ideas that may not be systematically arrived at or as exclusively tied to hard and fast economic charts, ideas that can even give substantial weight to noneconomic criteria of social worth" (Jackson 2001, 128–29). The symbolic boundaries around middle-class as a category are also important, as the middle-class is also defined by what it is not (Wacquant 1991).

This echoes research measuring the African American middle-class and minority middle-class populations more generally (see Marsh et al. 2007). For example, Pattillo-McCoy (1999, 13) uses "a combination of socioeconomic factors (mostly income, occupation, and education) and normative judgments (ranging from where people live, to what churches or clubs they belong to, to whether they plant flowers in their gardens" in her exegesis of Chicago's black middle-class. Furthermore, Landry and Marsh (2011) emphasize a Weberian approach to measuring and understanding middle-class populations, which are therefore constituted by individuals with *white-collar* employment, a term coined by C. Wright Mills ([1951] 2002) (see also Feagin 1991).

In my focus on "middle-classness," I emphasize how respondents perceive themselves as middle-class individuals and make meaning in their everyday lives. Achieving a middle-class status, in France, the United States, and other societies, is a benchmark for having made it. Middle-class status, including being educated and holding a professional job, is often framed as an aspiration, a step closer to being an ideal citizen.

Middle-class minorities are often positioned as examples of successful assimilation, or full integration within mainstream society. As Landry and Marsh (2011, 374) point out: "For a minority group, the development of a middle-class marks a decisive moment in its development, affords access to improved life chances as well as membership in the class that provides the brain trust for industry and government. In addition, a minority middle-class serves the indispensable role of leadership in the struggle against discrimination and oppression that is often the experience of its members."

Yet the middle-class of a majority group differs from the middle-class of a minority group (Hout 1986), or a "subaltern middle-class," which Pandey (2009, 322) defines as "middle-class groups that emerge from, and remain in various ways closely tied to, long-stigmatized lower-class and underclass populations." Race and ethnicity remain salient regardless of socioeconomic position. Again, the black middle-class is an instructive referent, as its members remain distinct from their white middle-class counterparts in the United States. In the *Black Bourgeoisie,* African American sociologist E. Franklin Frazier (1957) highlighted the particular cultural and political circumstances of the black middle-class. And we now know that the black middle-class is not as stable as other middle-class populations, owing to continual systematic racism (S. Collins 1983; Gregg 1998; Pattillo-McCoy 1999). Journalist Ellis Cose highlights the "permanent vulnerability of status" (1994, 41), as black middle-class professionals find that their middle and upper-middle-class statuses do not shield them from race-based marginalization.[50]

As the black and white middle-classes remain distinct in the United States (Marsh et al. 2007), so, too, do the white and the North African–origin middle-classes in France.[51] Middle–class status does not confer the same advantages, both real and symbolic, on North African–origin individuals as it does on their white middle-class counterparts. The fact that socioeconomic status does not ameliorate the distinctions among individuals further reveals how France is permanently hindered by its racism and colonial past.

Their stigmatized ethnic and racial identity, in tandem with a middle-class, or economically advantaged, status, means that minority middle-class populations experience a particular tension. Their middle-class status and accomplishments take them only so far—because they are racial and ethnic minorities. They have to strategically navigate this insider-outsider position between stigma and status (Clerge 2014), or as Hicham, a twenty-nine-year-old of Moroccan origin who lives in the banlieue of Poissy, puts it, between "the two sets of codes—French and maghrébin. We understand them both."

Achieving middle-class status is thus not a panacea for resolving social exclusion. This is true for the North African second generation. Such status does not do the same work for these individuals as it does for their white counterparts. They realize their middle-class status mostly in relation to their working-class counterparts and immigrant parents, yet they feel excluded from the full privileges associated with a middle-class status. As I later discuss, the maghrébin second generation draws boundaries that, depending on the context, both distinguish them from and include them in the economically disadvantaged segment of the maghrébin second generation. Respondents are conscious of how their everyday lives are both similar and markedly different from those of their working-class counterparts (this is one example of how respondents make sense of their social locations).

French demographer Patrick Simon (2003) identified three paths for France's second generation: a reproduction of the positions of the first generation; a successful upward social mobility through education; or a mobility hindered by discrimination. In this book, I focus on the second category—individuals who have achieved upward mobility through education yet simultaneously feel hindered by discrimination and exclusion in terms of their actual place in mainstream society. This is different from positioning the maghrébin second generation as successfully assimilated, as Loïc Wacquant (2007) attests, which I discuss further in chapter 3.

By marginalization, I am referring not just to the denial of access to material resources, but also what Cathy Cohen (1999, 38) terms the "stigmatized or illegitimate social identity that such groups have in the larger or dominant society." Marginalized groups are distinguished by "the pervasive way in which ideologies or myths which explain, justify, and recreate their secondary position become institutionalized throughout society" (43).[52] This stigmatized or illegitimate identity is born out of the French colonial context. I posit here that children of North African immigrants—even those who are middle-class—are framed as stigmatized or illegitimate with respect to having a rightful place within France, and must develop a framing of their marginalization outside of a sanctioned language to discuss racial and ethnic difference. Throughout this book, I discuss how the secondary position of the maghrébin second generation is reinforced through both individual-level interactions and macrolevel structures and practices. Middle-class individuals often experience more discrimination or feel more marginalized than their working-class counterparts (Cose 1994; Tomaskovic-Devey et al. 2005). Educated and middle-class second-generation immigrants are more likely to report higher levels of discrimination than immigrants and less educated immigrant-origin individuals (Fleischmann et al. 2011). Research has shown that the more highly educated North African immigrant-origin individuals are, the more the complaints of discrimination (Silberman et al. 2007). Marginalization is often exacerbated for middle-class individuals because they feel as though they have done everything right.

I frame the North African second generation as "citizen outsiders," a term that Cathy Cohen (2010) uses to characterize the precarious social locations of African American youth. Cohen considers the degrees to which African American youth feel like full members of the citizenry as a way of understanding how marginalized individuals relate to the state and how that complicates the relationship among race, citizenship, and belonging. This is reminiscent of Patricia Hill Collins's (1986) notion of the "outsider-within" and Tina Campt's (2005) notion of the "other-within," which conceptualize how individuals may be simultaneously members of a society yet kept on its margins (and the simultaneous insider and outsider positions they hold). The middle-class North African second generation is both included and excluded from the citizenry—they have made it, so to speak, but only to a point, as they are continually reminded of how their citizenship is suspect and often questioned by others. This is reminiscent of W. E. B. DuBois's notion of "double consciousness," referring to how African Americans must negotiate two seemingly different and unreconciled identities—American and black, as articulated in his *Souls of Black Folk: Essays and Sketches*.[53] The North African second generation must bridge the different cultural worlds of France and the Maghreb. They have what DuBois has termed a "second-sight," a way of looking at oneself through the eyes of others.

The concept of a minority group based on identity is antithetical to the ideals of French universalism and Republicanism, which recognize individuals and not groups. There is no framework for acknowledging racial and ethnic minority groups and incorporating them within France's national community. *Citizen Outsider* grapples with this paradox—that France does not acknowledge racial and ethnic minorities yet marks those individuals as different. If these middle-class individuals feel excluded from mainstream society, their socioeconomic status is not the explanatory variable. Their racial and ethnic origin is.

FRANCE'S RACIAL PROJECT: THE CONTINUING SIGNIFICANCE OF RACE AND ETHNICITY

Asserting the significance of race and ethnicity is provocative in France, as under Republicanism, being French is supposed to trump all markers of difference. Despite the promotion of a colorblind ideology and an official masking of possible and real ethnic differences, the state has a narrow definition what of it means to be French, a definition with particular racial and ethnic underpinnings. Specifically, white supremacy structures the definition of who is French. To the extent to which race is mentioned, it is not as a social construction, but rather a physical definition of human groups, so acknowledging race propagates racism and furthering divisions among humans (Keaton 2010).

Race and ethnicity are salient in marking boundaries of inclusion and exclusion in France's "racial project." In this racial project, "racial categories are created, inhabited, transformed, and destroyed" (Omi and Winant 1994, 55). A racial project signifies differences among individuals and creates a "racial common-sense" (55), or a way of understanding populations seen as "other," which is continually made and remade (Silverstein 2008). This racial common sense is created in a seemingly colorblind society. The North African second generation is racialized as "other" (Kastoryano and Escafré-Dublet 2012; Winant 2001), and it is this process that prevents them from being fully included in France's "imagined community" (Anderson 1991). Racialization is revealed through citizenship laws, mechanisms of state control, external ascription, criminalization, spatial segregation, popular and political discourse, and daily interactions (Weiner 2012). The French context reveals how these processes of racialization can occur in a supposedly antiracial or colorblind society and without legally substantiated boundaries around racial and ethnic categories. This contrasts with the United States, where race and ethnicity, as measured in the census, have had specific, though evolving, definitions as categories dependent on the larger societal contexts (for example, the "one-drop rule" as a determination of black identity). French Republicanism merely obfuscates differences; it does not minimize or eliminate them.[54]

Even though *race* as a term exists in the French language, the National Assembly suppressed its use in legislation in 2013 (Beydoun 2013). It is this context that makes race in France both necessary and difficult to discuss. Specifically, race "signifies and symbolizes social conflicts and interests by referring to different types of human bodies" (Omi and Winant 1994, 55), which "form a distinctive stigmata of inferiority" (Keaton 2010, 106). It is a way of making meaning out of differences that are historically and socially informed. I center France's colonial history and postcolonial legacy in understanding the experiences of nonwhite individuals. As I demonstrate, North African–origin individuals are read as nonwhite through a variety of markers. "Skin color, hair, features, language varieties, and by extension family name, religion, in short, people's ways of being and knowing—have longstanding social meanings in France, underpinned and enlivened by ideologies and policies acting on them" (Keaton 2009, 108).[55] Constructing Frenchness as white, and French identity as a white one, is part of this racial project, which dates from the construction of the nation itself. French culture is portrayed as an unchanging, homogenous entity.

To clarify, I am not using ethnic origin or group in opposition to race, as I do not want to suggest that ethnic origin is not racialized in France.[56] I use ethnic origin in the Weberian sense as the subjective belief in a group's common descent, cultural, and historical experiences (Weber [1922] 2013).[57] North African–origin individuals are constructed as a separate ethnic group (as having ethnic origins in the Maghreb) and racialized as nonwhite. These processes are coconstitutive of each other.

As such, this book is in conversation with research on racial and ethnic identities, including how immigrant-origin individuals negotiate their identities in light of existing racial and ethnic hierarchies, and how individuals are shaped by their experiences of racial and ethnic marginalization in how they see themselves (see K. Hall 2004; Sharma 2010; Warikoo 2004; Waters 1999).[58] They respond to both the ethnic identities of their immigrant parents from their home country and the nation-based identities in their current environment (Chong 1998; Cornell and Hartmann 2007; Eid 2008).[59] Identity based on ethnic origin relies on an interplay between external and internal self-identification, subject to various structural constraints.[60]

Throughout this book, I demonstrate how race and ethnicity remain salient not only at an individual level but also as a macrolevel project structuring boundaries of inclusion and exclusion around full citizenship. Race and ethnicity are inextricable with nationhood and nationalism, as the construction of race and ethnicity occurs simultaneously with the construction of the nation (Brubaker 2009). As the experiences of my respondents reveal, belonging in France is circumscribed by race and ethnicity, and being included or accepted depends upon racial and ethnic status. In France, one's racial and ethnic status, or being nonwhite, is a barrier to full cultural citizenship, a framework upon which I later elaborate.

Beyond denying *race* as a term, common discourses about race and ethnicity in France say that race does not exist; that race is less significant in France than in the United States; and that France is a colorblind society (Ndiaye 2008). Understanding France's racial project requires understanding the salience of race and ethnicity in Europe more broadly. Race structures the nation-state yet is framed as existing everywhere but in Europe (Goldberg 2006). Racism is discussed solely in relation to the Far Right, not as a boundary against "those historically categorized as non-European, as being not-white" (347).[61] Within France, in place of a discourse on race and ethnicity, scholars have traditionally focused on class and socioeconomic status as the explanatory variable for social marginalization in French society (Amiraux and Simon 2006; Ndiaye 2008). This scholarly focus does not acknowledge France's history of slavery or colonial legacy, nor the structural nature of racial and ethnic relations, and rejects race and ethnicity as analytical categories in social scientific inquiry.

A few scholars have argued for increased attention to race and ethnicity in France, and how they shape daily experiences and life outcomes. In *La condition noire: Essai sur une minorité française* (The black condition: Essay on a French minority) (2008), French historian Pap Ndiaye excavates France's black population and demonstrates its paradoxical status as simultaneously visible and invisible as a minority. This visibility of a minority depends upon "the presence of phenotypical characteristics that racially or ethnically characterize those persons concerned . . . that is, people whose supposed ethnoracial membership can be deduced from their appearance" (Ndiaye 2008, 57–58). The black condition in France is one of a transnational blackness, or a product of social relations that characterizes the shared experience of being black (or at least regarded as black by others). In chapter 5, I discuss how this extends to maghrébin-origin individuals in France, who often assert identities situated and informed by blackness as it relates to black populations worldwide. Moreover, France's blindness to race is coupled with race-based assumptions that lead to a consciousness of race, and therefore antiblack racism, which masks itself in different institutions (Keaton 2010).

However, Michèle Lamont (2002), in *The Dignity of Working Men: Morality and the Boundaries of Race, Class, and Immigration*, argues that France's Republican and colorblind ideology enables not an antiblack racism but a cultural racism—one that distinguishes between individuals seen as native French and immigrant-origin individuals who are not. This cultural racism is a remnant of France's colonial history and is often directed toward immigrants from North and sub-Saharan Africa. Therefore, when individuals draw symbolic boundaries that exclude those of immigrant origin, they can claim to do so based on cultural differences, rather than on racial or ethnic ones.

Yet the focus on cultural racism in France misses how "culture" is code for race and ethnicity, historically and in the present. French culture and identity are implicitly and explicitly framed as white (Constant 2009). Culture is therefore a social and symbolic boundary (Lamont and Molnar 2002).[62] A focus on cultural distinction ignores the structural dynamics at play in the marginalization of maghrébin immigrants and subsequent generations. In addition, this focus ignores how even maghrébin-origin individuals—such as my respondents—who do not necessarily see themselves as different from their white counterparts are still treated as different.

Racial and ethnic minorities can feel as French as anyone else but still not be treated as such or accepted as French by others. Therefore, their difference is one that is assigned, and one from which they cannot escape. Focusing on culture instead of race also sustains the denial of race and ethnicity and furthers the myth of colorblindness in France (Keaton 2009; Ndiaye 2008). This resembles how ideologies of colorblindness in the United States not only perpetuate racism but also minimize its importance (Bonilla-Silva 2013). Minimizing race, and therefore racism, perpetuates the idea that race and ethnicity as statuses do not affect life chances or outcomes. This allows France to continue to ignore the consequences not only of its colonial past but the racial and ethnic dimensions of its national identity. Because of the emphasis on colorblindness in Republican ideology, marginalization based on race and ethnicity is harder to combat.

As I discuss in chapter 4, the social location of North African–origin individuals relies on the distinction between the legal and cultural dimensions of French identity—that is, between being a French citizen and being accepted as French by others. Individuals like Abdelkrim can assert that they are as French as any other French person, yet because of the boundaries around this identity, they find that this claim to French identity is not easily accepted or legitimated by others. The boundaries around the identity of native French render maghrébin-origin individuals "unassimilable" and marginalized regardless of their socioeconomic status. I argue that the boundaries structuring who is accepted as French continually exclude North African–origin individuals and remind them that they are not. As social and cultural barriers, these boundaries are racial and ethnic demarcations of belonging within France.

As culture is a euphemism for race, so too is religion—in this case, Islam. While previous research has argued that religion is the basis for the construction of symbolic boundaries between "us" and "them" (Zolberg and Woon 1999), I argue that religion is also code for racial and ethnic boundaries (Barth 1969). Therefore, race is not a mask for something else; rather, religion, culture, and other factors are masks for race. When maghrébin-origin individuals are deemed too culturally different from other French individuals, it is not because of their affiliation with Islam (which is nonetheless heterogeneous and contextual); it is because of their status as "ex-colonial citizens of color," to borrow Hall 2004's terminology for second-generation Sikhs in London. Abdelkrim and others are marginalized not because of their religious identity or practices but because of their maghrébin origins (Beaman 2016). I discuss respondents' marginalization as Muslims in chapter 3.

The maghrébin second generation can assert a French identity, yet because of the ethnicized and racialized nature of French identity, these North African–origin individuals are assigned another racial or ethnic identity: nonwhite. Even if France does not explicitly recognize distinct racial and ethnic categories, I argue that it recognizes French as a specific identity category that is not accessible to minorities of color. While race and ethnicity do not exist as something to be measured or quantified in French society, they operate in everyday life, as the ethnoracially marked experiences of my respondents reveal. As such, a consciousness of racial and ethnic differences exists simultaneously with a denial of race and ethnicity. Throughout this book, I discuss how individuals interpret and respond to these boundaries that exclude them. Furthermore, these respondents inhabit a tenuous social location, in that they fit within the confines of the social boundary of citizenship, but not within the symbolic boundaries around French identity. They are citizens but are not made to *feel* like citizens. They are not *treated* like citizens. Because of the symbolic boundaries around national identity, in this case, Frenchness, boundaries based on racial and ethnic origin serve to marginalize immigrant-origin individuals.

CULTURAL CITIZENSHIP AND RACIAL FORMATION

That immigrant-origin individuals are continuously marginalized—which is linked to ethnic-minority status—challenges what would be expected in French Republican society. The French Republican model rejects any implication of a distinction between culture and citizenship, meaning that to be a French citizen is to be French, or to be French is to be a French citizen. Comparing national boundary patterns of the United States and France, Lamont argues that citizenship serves as a salient boundary between in-groups and out-groups, or "us versus them" in France (Lamont 1995; see also Brubaker 1992 and Lamont 2000). However, I demonstrate how simply having French citizenship is not a sufficient marker of who is regarded as French and who is not, as individuals who are citizens remain excluded from mainstream society.[63]

I show that citizenship does not confer the same benefits on other populations as it does on whites, as children of immigrants, who are racial and ethnic
minorities, are marginalized to degrees similar to their immigrant parents. They
are denied cultural citizenship because of their North African origins and because
they are not white. This denial of cultural citizenship challenges a French exceptionalism regarding marking difference among citizens. What exists in France is
citizenship without societal inclusion, an "ambiguous citizenship" (Cain 2010).

My framework of cultural citizenship emphasizes how citizenship operates
for marginalized populations, who despite being formal legal citizens are nonetheless not fully included in the citizenry. Cultural citizenship focuses on what
would allow an individual to traverse the cultural-symbolic boundaries defining
a particular national community and identity and be accepted as a full member
(Beaman 2016b). Insofar as cultural citizenship is a claim, it is a claim to full
societal belonging by fellow members of one's community rather than a claim to a
specific set of rights. Being denied cultural citizenship denotes an impaired civic
status (Meer 2010). Furthermore, cultural citizenship means being fully included
in society, despite one's difference from others. When children of North African
immigrants indicate that their fellow citizens do not consider them as French as
they are, they are expressing how their fellow citizens are denying them cultural
citizenship. These are individuals born in France who insist upon their Frenchness and are still denied it. When respondents seek to be viewed as French by
others, they are ultimately making a claim for cultural citizenship—a claim to be
regarded as a legitimate member of the French mainstream or a part of French
culture.

I build upon cultural anthropologist Renato Rosaldo's formulation, based on
Latinos in the United States and used to resist dominant racialized power structures. He speaks of "the right to be different (in terms of race, ethnicity, or native
language) with respect to the norms of the dominant national community, without compromising one's right to belong. . . . [This] includes and goes beyond the
dichotomous categories of legal documents, which one either has or does not, to
encompass a range of gradations in the qualities of citizenship (Rosaldo 1994, 57).
He argues that cultural citizenship presumes a universal citizenship based on white
men, where those who are different are excluded. Latino identity has been shaped
by experiences of discrimination and efforts toward full inclusion in American
society. The denial of cultural citizenship to Latinos in the United States, as well
as to the North African second generation in France, reveals how race and ethnic
origin keep certain populations on the margins of mainstream society. Cultural
citizenship challenges the stigmatization and marginalization of different populations that are supposedly antithetical to the laws of the nation-state.[64]

Traditional conceptions of citizenship have a culturally normative dimension
that makes some legal citizens more or less accepted than others.[65] However, it

is this nonlegal dimension that often goes unacknowledged. Cultural citizenship acknowledges the relationship between culture and citizenship and considers citizenship beyond its legislative status (Bloemraad 2015; Delanty 2002; García-Sánchez 2013; Vega and van Hensbroek 2010), including how it creates both full and second-class citizens. It also allows us to unpack how citizenship is socially and culturally constructed and how race, class, and immigrant status are barriers to full societal acceptance (Ong 1996). Specifically, "citizenship is both a cultural and anti-cultural institution. . . . Citizenship positions itself as oppositional to specific cultures, even as it is constituted by quite specific cultural values" (Volpp 2007, 574). The cultural attachments associated with being of North African origin are positioned as oppositional to being French (Lamont 2002). There is only one way to be French (Volpp 2007).

Difference is seen in relation to a normative center, in which all other cultures are on the periphery. As legal scholar Leti Volpp (2000) argues, what is viewed as cultural or culturally different is often what is associated with people of color and other minorities. In this way, culture is closely linked to race and ethnicity. Once we recognize this connection, we can fully consider how culture is code for race and ethnicity, particularly in contexts where explicit discussion of race and ethnicity is not permissible. It is therefore radical to think of cultural citizenship in the French context, as it implies that citizenship status is not the only marker of difference. For marginalized groups, citizenship is more precarious (Glenn 2011). Racial and ethnic minorities are often denied cultural citizenship or full belonging in society (Bonilla-Silva and Mayorga 2011; Cohen 2010).[66]

This denial of cultural citizenship is evidence of France's racial project. By focusing on cultural citizenship as an explanatory framework for marginalization, I specify how citizenship operates as a marker of difference, through its relationship to race and ethnicity (Beaman 2015a). We cannot understand citizenship in France without acknowledging its racial divides (Silverstein 2008). Nonwhite citizens are denied cultural citizenship. Citizenship as a racialized status is fragmented, in that people who are formal citizens are informally excluded from full societal inclusion. Citizenship therefore exists as a "surveilled performance of national belonging" (25), in which whites reinforce boundaries of who really gets to belong.[67] Citizenship in this way is better understood as local, everyday practices (Brettell and Reed-Danahay 2012; Silverstein 2008).

This resembles how second- and subsequent-generation Asian and Latino immigrants in the United States are considered "perpetual foreigners" (Wu 2001), often questioned about where they are from and having to prove their "Americanness" (Zhou and Lee 2007). They are still pressured to identify based on their ethnic origins, even as they assert that they are American (Zhou and Lee 2007). Though they were born and grew up in the United States, only a *partial* assimilation is possible. They are often asked, "Where are you really from?" thereby drawing boundaries determining who an American is and reinforcing that they are not truly American (Wu 2001).

THE RESEARCH

This book is based on longitudinal ethnographic research I conducted primarily during the 2008 to 2009 academic year, including semistructured interviews in French with 45 adult children of maghrébin immigrants living in the Parisian metropolitan region beginning in fall 2008 (I discuss further details of this methodology in the methodological appendix). I was initially interested in exploring what it means to be a minority, and how minorities understand their social locations in French society. I moved to Paris in fall of 2008 for this purpose.

Recruiting interview respondents proved more difficult than I anticipated, because of my outsider status, and I used snowball sampling after contacting various organizations and associations for potential respondents. My respondent sample includes twenty-four men and twenty-one women.[68] Respondents range in age from twenty-four to forty-nine years old (the average age is thirty years old). Twenty-five of them (about 55 percent) are of Algerian origin; twelve (about 26 percent) Moroccan; and eight (17 percent) Tunisian. Three respondents are products of mixed-race relationships, meaning one parent is white and the other is maghrébin. All respondents live in the Paris metropolitan region, or Ile-de-France. Thirty-five percent of respondents live in Paris, and 65 percent live in the banlieues, mostly in the inner-ring *départements* (in France a department is a major administrative subdivision or branch of government) of Seine-Saint-Denis, Val-de-Marne, and Hauts-de-Seine. All respondents have French citizenship, and about a third of them have dual citizenship (the other being in their respective maghrébin countries of origin).[69] Most respondents' parents emigrated from the Maghreb between 1950 and 1970, primarily for economic reasons. Many of these parents have low levels of educational attainment, often not past middle school, speak little French, and communicate mostly in Arabic or Berber (Kabyle). Usually, the fathers worked in low-skilled jobs, such as construction and factory employment, while mothers were homemakers or did domestic labor.

In marking respondents' middle-class statuses, I focus on respondents' educational attainment levels and professional statuses. With regard to educational attainment, I focus on those who passed the *baccalauréat (bac)* exam and attended college (whether or not they actually graduated). In terms of employment, I focus on those who have professional types of employment—including the French socioprofessional categories of *cadre* (salaried or executive-level employment) and *professions intermédiaires*.[70] Some of these jobs include technical director, journalist, doctoral student, lawyer, banker, human resources associate, hospital director, high school teacher, insurance agent, governmental administrator, information technology consultant, public relations consultant, and television reporter. I therefore use a combination of occupation and educational attainment as indicators of the socioeconomic locations of my respondents (Weber [1922] 2013; see also Landry and Marsh 2011).

In addition to these interviews with forty-five middle-class maghrébin-origin individuals, I conducted nine months of participant observation with some respondents. I went to networking events, both professional and social, with my some of my respondents. For example, I went to a book-signing event with one of my respondents at a literary festival for maghrébin-origin authors. I also attended various *débats* (panel discussions) and lectures on relevant topics.[71] I spent time with my respondents' families and visited their workplaces. In the process of contacting various organizations and associations for respondents, I connected with the Nanterre Association, a community organization in the western banlieue of Nanterre (about ninety minutes from Paris by commuter train), and was able to supplement my interviews with participant observation there. The organization, located in an impoverished community in Nanterre, serves the local neighborhood by offering educational, cultural, and social activities, including field trips to Paris monuments, panel discussions, and after-school tutoring.

My position as an outsider, not only as a researcher but also as a native-born American and a black woman, undoubtedly shaped how my respondents perceived me. I discuss the role of my identity further in the methodological appendix. While I was an outsider in some ways, many respondents also perceived me as an insider—as we both shared the status of racial and ethnic minority (see also Khanna 2011). These perceptions of my personal biography, particularly my racial and ethnic identity, were often invoked in interactions with respondents, most often to draw symbolic boundaries with or against their own identity. As I discuss in chapter 5, these boundaries had implications for studying race and ethnicity from a different national context.

OVERVIEW OF CHAPTERS

In the next chapter, "Growing up French? Education, Upward Mobility, and Connections across Generations," I focus on my respondents' childhood experiences growing up in France with immigrant parents and how they learn to navigate the different cultural worlds of home and school. I situate growing up French as a question because respondents relate how their place within France was first questioned at an early age. This is reminiscent of the experiences of second-generation immigrants in other societies (Alba and Waters 2011; Essed 1991; Kasinitz et al. 2004; Portes et al. 2011; Waters 2000) but also complicated in the French context because racial and ethnic categories are not acknowledged as meaningful bases for identity. There are no identity "options" (Waters 2000). I also discuss how respondents navigate these different cultural worlds throughout their education and how they contributed to their upward mobility in adulthood.

In chapter 3, "Marginalization and Middle-Class Blues: Race, Islam, the Workplace, and the Public Sphere," I examine experiences and perceptions of discrimination and marginalization across different domains. I discuss how respondents frame and make sense of these experiences, and how their middle-class status shapes these meaning-making processes. Chapters 2 and 3 establish how this segment of the maghrébin second generation is marginalized because of its North African origins. Chapters 4 and 5 address the impact of this on their consciousness and identity as minorities.

In chapter 4, "French Is, French Ain't: Boundaries of French Maghrébin Identities," I unpack how individuals identify and how being French and having North African origins are implicated in their self-identities. I build upon previous examinations of ethnic identity for immigrant-origin individuals and show how respondents negotiate their identities vis-à-vis their maghrébin ethnic origin. I focus on a continuum ranging from a hyphenated and combined identity, seeing oneself as neither French nor maghrébin, to a singular identity as only maghrébin. Republicanism constrains the identity options available to this population and creates the tension between assigned versus asserted identities. I also interrogate how children of North African immigrants interpret French Republicanism as an ideology, as well as the boundaries determining what it means to be French. I revisit the concept of cultural citizenship to consider how Republicanism as ideology and in practice creates boundaries defining French as an identity that forces these individuals to occupy a liminal position in relation to mainstream society.

In chapter 5, "Boundaries of Difference: Cultural Citizenship and Transnational Blackness," I consider how this minority population invokes blackness, based on the experiences of black populations elsewhere, in making sense of their social locations. Considering how the maghrébin second generation relates to other black populations, such as African Americans, allows us to consider how notions of diaspora and transnational blackness apply not only to blacks in France but to North African–origin minorities in France as well.

Finally, in the conclusion, "Sacrificed Children of the Republic?" I review how the racial and ethnic underpinnings of French Republicanism disallow even "successful" children of immigrants to ever truly be viewed as French by others. I also discuss how cultural citizenship increasingly becomes a relevant question in multicultural and plural societies. I consider the important lessons provided by the French example in drawing conclusions about the role of difference, race, and ethnicity in the twenty-first century. I further consider the implications of this study for the future of France, particularly in light of the massacre at the offices of Charlie Hebdo and the November 2015 terrorist attacks.

I first moved to Paris to conduct this research amid the campaign and first presidential election of Barack Obama in fall 2008. As the debate of whether the United States had entered a postracial era raged on, across the Atlantic Ocean in France was an example of a society struggling with how colorblind ideologies operate in practice. The fever of Obama's presidential campaign and election spread to France (Benia 2009; Erlanger 2008), where it raised the question as to whether France could produce its own Obama. I discussed this question one afternoon with Sabri, a thirty-year-old of Tunisian origin:

> It will be hard, but we have to find our own French Barack Obama. There might be more than one. . . . But first we must help those who are still stuck in the past. Colonialism is still in the spirits of some people. Meaning when I tell you that people treat us like children, for me that's because of colonialism. Today people think children of immigrants in France are still strangers. That we are not really French. So we have to show them that they are not superior, that it's a question of equality. Once they see us as equal to them, once we have that relationship, then things will change, but now, today, that's how it is.

As I finished this book, Donald Trump was elected president of the United States and Far Right politicians have increased in popularity throughout Europe, including in France, where Marine Le Pen of the Front National (National Front) launched a presidential campaign on the claim that France is losing its identity and will soon be unrecognizable (though she made it past the first round of the election, she lost the second round, nevertheless winning 34.5 percent of the vote). If France is to move in another direction and produce a president who is an ethnic minority like Obama, if it is to fully incorporate individuals who are legacies of its colonial empire, it will have to grant all its members, including the forty-five I discuss in this book, cultural citizenship.

2

___

Growing Up French?
Education, Upward Mobility, and
Connections across Generations

Many people of color living in this country can likely relate to the onset of outsized ambition at too young an age, an ambition fueled by the sense, often confirmed by ignorance, of being a second-class citizen and needing to claw your way toward equal consideration and some semblance of respect. Many people of color, like me, remember the moment that first began to shape their ambition and what that moment felt like.

—ROXANE GAY, "THE PRICE OF BLACK AMBITION"

France views and portrays itself as a white country. My whole life, I've felt erased by the national narrative. People even keep complimenting me on how good my French is. It's deeply embedded in the national consciousness that "true" identity is one that has been here forever.

—ROKHAYA DIALLO, FRENCH JOURNALIST AND WRITER OF SENEGALESE ORIGIN

On a February morning sitting in a café near the Palais Garnier at place d'Opéra, Safia—a petite and professionally dressed thirty-two-year-old with dual Tunisian and French citizenship—described her experiences growing up in France with Tunisian immigrant parents. Safia remembered the shame and humiliation her parents experienced because of their immigrant status, lack of educational attainment, and illiteracy:

> I remember working very hard in school because I really wanted to escape my social background. I didn't want to be as poor as my parents or mistreated. Because when you don't know French perfectly well or have a certain level of education—especially when you're an immigrant—that's what happens. So I said to myself that when I grow up, it's out of the question to be treated like that. And I also worked hard because I

wanted to earn a lot of money, to help my parents, to have my parents be proud of me, so it was a bit of a social retaliation there.

Safia grew up in a middle-class neighborhood near the Musée du Louvre with her two younger brothers and younger sister, who all still live in the Parisian metropolitan area. Her parents migrated separately to France, where they then met and got married.[1] Her mother had been widowed in Tunisia and immigrated to France to "make a change in her life." Her father came to France for better employment opportunities. Despite speaking little French and communicating mostly in Arabic, they were able to make do—get around, read metro signs, and make a life in Paris. Her father worked as a cook and her mother worked as a nursery school assistant.

Growing up, Safia always had cousins and other extended relatives living with her family, particularly in the initial months after these relatives immigrated to France. In retrospect, Safia thinks it was great having these other relatives around because it helped her learn about various aspects of maghrébin culture.

Safia remembers learning she was different when she entered high school and a classmate told her she had "matte" skin. From that moment on, she understood that she would "never be completely considered as a French person." This only intensified as she grew older. As a law student, she remembers classmates calling her a dirty Arab and telling her she should return to her country. Safia remembers constantly being reminded of how she did not belong, particularly in an environment of mostly white students and faculty. "I remember crying a lot during that time," she explained.

However, she managed to be successful in her studies, earning both undergraduate and graduate degrees. Safia now works as a journalist and rents an apartment in Cergy-Pontoise, a western banlieue, with her two young children and her husband, who is a child of Algerian immigrants and works as a banker. There is much that makes her proud to be French, such as the values exemplified in the motto of "*Liberté, égalité, fraternité.*" But she hates that her "Frenchness" is still often questioned by others: "Today, when I'm with my children, people still ask me, 'What are your children's origins?' or 'Where do you come from?' That drives me crazy, because my children were born in France to French parents. And me, I was born here, my children were born here, and they still ask me that. It is so annoying to have to continually justify myself based on the color of my skin or the color of my children's skin."

Safia feels her place in France is questioned because she of her maghrébin origin. Reflecting on her status in French society, she feels that she is "French in the second degree." Despite her middle-class status and educational and professional accomplishments, she nonetheless feels like she occupies a France that continually reminds her of how her visible difference and nonwhite status excludes her from being accepted as French by others.

Like Safia, most respondents remember when they first felt different—because of their maghrébin origins—from others growing up. Yet intergenerational mobility is complex for immigrant-origin individuals. Despite her upward mobility vis-à-vis her immigrant parents, she is not treated much different from them on an everyday basis. While Safia is very accomplished in realms of education and employment, she remains marginalized. Throughout Safia's childhood, she worked hard to counter the stigmatization her parents faced, yet because she could not change the thing that really mattered—being nonwhite—she did not dramatically change her status in relation to mainstream society. She continues to be denied cultural citizenship by her fellow French citizens.

In this chapter, I discuss respondents' childhood experiences and how these experiences shaped both their upward mobility up to and including adulthood and sense of social marginalization in wider society. Respondents learn that they are not seen as French by others as children. And they are continually reminded of this difference as adults. While all my respondents grew up in France, they did not grow up *feeling* French, for they were told at a young age that they were different or treated and seen as outsiders. I therefore situate growing up French as a question because many respondents remember how their "Frenchness" was questioned starting at an early age: Do they *really* grow up French?

Moreover, children of maghrébin immigrants had to navigate two different seemingly incompatible cultural worlds—home versus school, or maghrébin versus French. I investigate the messages these individuals received from their parents and extended family regarding what it means to be French, as well as how these compare and contrast with the messages they received at school, both in their primary and university educations. Because of this distinction, children of North African immigrants had to become "cultural brokers" (Sharma 2010), bridging different cultural worlds. I also trace the influence of these messages on their later upward mobility and unpack the cultural repertoires and cultural and social capital this generation inherited from their parents. Respondents' childhood experiences set the stage for their later upward mobility and attainment of middle-class status. For children of immigrants who are also racial and ethnic minorities, the processes of identity formation are especially complicated, as these individuals must situate dual cultural worlds within a particular racial and ethnic hierarchy (Ali 2008; Waters 1999). Their experiences might be different if they were second-generation Italian or English immigrants and did not have to navigate their second-generation status while also being an ethnic minority connected to a colonial history. In France immigrant-origin individuals also must navigate this in the absence of state-sanctioned identity categories.

LEARNING OF ONE'S DIFFERENCE:
HOME VERSUS SCHOOL

As Zara describes the boundaries in her Perpignan community: "There were Français du souche and there was everyone else." Born to an Algerian immigrant mother and a Moroccan immigrant father, Zara, a twenty-eight-year-old, remembers learning she was different in her predominately white elementary school when her schoolteacher did not understand what the henna on her hands meant and made her wash it off her hands. This experience was her first denial of cultural citizenship. Growing up in Perpignan, in southern France, she had many experiences like this one, which helped her realize she was *étranger*, or foreign. She also remembers getting dirty looks and stares from other students when she did not eat pork at the school cafeteria because it was not halal.

It was early childhood moments like these that reinforced dual cultural worlds to Zara. Her way of life at home was markedly different from her life at school, and this difference was something that not everyone had to consider. In France there was and is a stigma attached to North African origins, and children of North African immigrants grow up with messages from society at large that they should be ashamed of such origins. They became conscious of the distinction between the maghrébin and French cultural worlds, and its consequences, through their parents' socialization of them.

Zara's family, including her two older brothers and one younger brother, was one of only five maghrébin-origin families in her neighborhood. Her father worked as an electrician and her mother was as a homemaker. Both parents stopped attending school just before high school. Twenty-eight years old and living in Seine-Saint-Denis, Zara works as a social worker in the nineteenth arrondissement and is actively involved in cultural, social, and political organizations related to maghrébin life in France. Her early experiences continue to resonate in her work with maghrébin-origin youth.

School is where children of maghrébin immigrants learn both Republican principles and what it means to be French, which in turn shapes how they define themselves in French society. These factors also shape the boundaries respondents draw around French as an identity, and the degree to which they claim such an identity as adults. Education is an important means of Republican integration, and school is often the first state institution that immigrant-origin individuals confront (Fernando 2014; Rojas-García 2013). It is where they are exposed to French history and the boundaries of French national identity. As Pierre Bourdieu (1984) articulated, the French educational system values the culture of the dominant class and enacts a "symbolic violence" against other individuals by delegitimizing their values and concealing the power relations inherent in doing so. This symbolic violence becomes meaningful as symbolic distinctions are translated into real social boundaries.

School is also a site where difference is learned and reinforced (Kleinman 2016). Through the homogenizing nature of its curriculum, school also reifies a national history and national cultural repertoire, one that often excludes the contributions of immigrant-origin individuals (Keaton 2006; Lamont 1992).[2] This automatically marginalizes children of immigrants and contributes to how symbolic boundaries are translated into social boundaries around French identity and citizenship. It is, therefore, no accident that controversies over wearing the hijab, or Islamic headscarf, are often situated in schools because it is framed as contrary to French national identity and French schools are Republican institutions (Fernando 2014; Judge 2004; Raveaud 2008).

Because education is relatively centralized in France, schools are crucial sites for producing French citizens and instilling Republican principles (Bowen 2008; Chabal 2015; Keaton 2006; Maier 2004).[3] As their parents were not educated in the French Republican system, children of North African immigrants often receive the most significant messages about what it means to be French from their school. Schools are also sites of otherness for this population, since it is where children of North African immigrants first feel inferior to and different from their white classmates (Noiriel 1996). Their early educational experiences therefore influence how they understand their social location. Martinique-born philsopher and writer Frantz Fanon (1967) discuses how in his homeland (an overseas département—a major administrative subdivision or branch of government in France) schoolchildren were told to look down on their native creole language in favor of French, which helped create a separation between the worlds of home and school. Similarly, in Spain schoolteachers exclude immigrant children from Spanish cultural citizenship, which in turn shapes immigrant-origin children's notions of national belonging (García-Sánchez 2013). This is not unlike how the American educational system reifies a particular American ethos and historical narrative, which marginalizes those individuals seen as outside this dominant narrative.

The North African second generation experienced a dual education—one in French schools and another at home. School thus serves two identity-related functions for this population—it defines what it means to be French and distances them from this definition. Members of this group must then work through how to reconcile these two educations, which have different implications for their identities. School mainstreams individuals by socializing them in the norms and values of mainstream society (Carter 2005; Maier 2004). Yet there is a limit to the degree to which school mainstreams the North African second generation. They are socialized in these norms and principles of mainstream society but kept apart from it. School helps establish cultural citizenship and then reinforces its denial.

Sabri's experience is an example of this phenomenon. Growing up with four siblings in one of the only immigrant-origin families in Amiens, a town in northern France, he was reminded of his difference at an early age:

> I realized when I was around eight or nine or ten years old, that we were different from other people; the other children recognized that, meaning that they'd tell us, "You're Arab; go back where you came from; you're not from here," and other insults. There were not many immigrants, maybe three or four families. . . . Everyone else was white. We quickly understood the image that they had of us. For that reason, we

understood we were different from others. . . . We felt different and not completely French, and that remains today.

Sabri would tell his parents about incidents in which he was insulted. However, although they were upset, they could not do anything because they experienced the same discrimination. These experiences were clearly traumatizing for Sabri. Though thirty years old and an eight-year resident of the Parisian metropolitan region (he lives in Porte de Saint-Ouen, a banlieue north of Paris) when we met, he is still reminded that his maghrébin origin marks him as different—in a society that supposedly does not mark racial and ethnic differences.

The experiences of the North African second generation bring to mind Fanon's realization that, as a nonwhite, he was therefore different. In *Black Skin, White Masks,* he recalls how, when in France a white boy identified him as black to his mother: "For the first time, I knew who I was. For the first time, I felt as if I had been simultaneously exploded in the gaze, in the violent gaze of the other, and at the same time recomposed as another." Like Fanon, who was labeled black, Sabri was labeled other, something outside the norm, nonwhite, not French. They are "forever foreigners" (Lowe 1996) within France, the country of their birth. Yet despite their later successes, particularly compared to their immigrant parents, the North African second generation is unable to escape this assigned otherness. This is a difference that is imposed on them at a young age, not one they themselves choose.

CULTURAL CAPITAL AND CONNECTIONS
ACROSS GENERATIONS

I will now discuss the influence of their immigrant parents on respondents, including the messages they received about being maghrébin and French and how this shaped their later experiences, and how they understand those experiences. Although respondents received somewhat differing messages from their immigrant parents, they all experienced marginalization by their white counterparts. As school provided one message regarding what it means to be French and how immigrant-origin individuals are outside this definition, home provided a contrary narrative helping to situate them as racial and ethnic minorities within France. Often, respondents discussed how their parents (and other relatives) provided them cultural tools and frameworks to make sense of their social locations. Cultural capital, meaning "skills individuals inherit that can be translated into different forms of value as people move through different institutions" (Lareau 2015, 4), is transmitted through one's family. For children of North African immigrants, this cultural knowledge involves navigating being maghrébin in France and preparing them for the obstacles they will face, which become particularly acute as they move through spaces where there are few other racial and ethnic minorities. Such cultural capital allows them to make sense of their maghrébin backgrounds, which are continually and simultaneously marked and denied in France—denied in the sense of being viewed as part of French culture and history and marked in the sense that maghrébin-origin individuals are never seen as French.

For example, Safia learned both directly and indirectly from her parents the difficulties of being an immigrant in France. This fueled her in part to improve her social status, through work and educational attainment. Oubii feels that he learned what it means to be a Tunisian from his parents; it's "what they gave [him]." But beyond teaching him about being Tunisian, they related how to be a Tunisian-origin individual in France and reinforced the connection between his life in France and his parents' and extended family's lives in Tunisia. He learned how his life in France is an extension of his family's life in Tunisia. "That is where the clash comes in, meaning the meeting of the two, how to find an equilibrium between Western society and maghrébin culture, how to synthesize it all. Some people can do it, some cannot. As for me, I do not say that I've figured it out; I am always trying to find a compromise, it is a continual negotiation," he explained. Developing his own identity as he has grown up has involved reconciling his Tunisian origins with his existence as a French person.

One mechanism for transmitting cultural capital from the first generation to the second was trips to the Maghreb, often to visit relatives during the summer. For example, Diana, a twenty-four-year-old of Algerian origin, has traveled to Algeria at least once a year since she was a child. She often spent the summers with her seven older siblings in a small village, which she describes as very traditional, where most of her extended family lives.

When I return there, I have the impression of being closer and closer to my origins, to the rest of my family. . . . My grandparents are buried there, and I just find that so important, to not forget where I came from, where my parents came from, to really see their path, to where they are today. They have really lived through some things, they were born in these small villages, and they ended up, for my father, destined to be farmers taking care of the land, my mother taking care of her children. . . . They evolved with the times, transmitting all their culture, all their values, which were developed in a context that is totally different, that had nothing to do with France.

When I press Diana on what exactly she feels she learned from her parents, she explains:

Well, the language for one—that's very important in terms of culture. Also, the food. I know that sounds silly, but as an adult, I know how to make all the dishes I ate as a child, the ones that are really typical from the region where my parents grew up, that people of the same origins as me eat. I learned how to make these dishes from my parents, and I really liked that. . . . As for the story of what drove us from Algeria, my parents have told me about that time. It was difficult for them to talk about at first, because they lived through the Algerian War of Independence, and that was really difficult for them. It's true that they have lots of awful memories, of losing members of their families, their parents, et cetera, who were part of the Algerian resistance. . . . And it was a really difficult period—they didn't have easy access to food. Really, their story is the story of Algeria. We don't feel it much anymore. But since I was born—I really wasn't that old—I have understood better the change or the shift, the history even. Because it's true that we read books and learned it a little, but living it through people who lived it is important to have a sense of this war, and what stemmed from it, so even at a cultural level I find that it's very important to transmit a culture, the culture of your country to your children.

Diana conveys how her existence in France stems from its colonial relationship with Algeria. This is a history that is both intertwined with and separate from her everyday life in France. Her Algerian origins have direct implications for her social status in France, including the otherness assigned to her. Her parents recreated their culture within France, namely, through the Arabic language and a particular cuisine. But part of their connection to their Algerian culture requires acknowledging that colonial relationship and its psychological and material consequences for Algerian immigrants and their descendants. Diana recognizes the intense struggle of her parents, even while she faces the difficulties of being a maghrébin-origin individual in France. As an adult, she can feel connected to Algeria, at least in part through her regular travel there, while also recognizing how different her life would have been if her parents had not immigrated to France. Because of her own experiences growing up as well as her knowledge of her parents' history, Diana dislikes how immigrants and their descendants are referenced in France.[4] She feels that most immigrants are very respectful of French law, and that their descendants are just as French as anyone else. They do not have to integrate, since the French culture is the one into which they were born and in which they grew up. It is their culture, too.

Other respondents also referenced childhood travel to the Maghreb as helping situate their lives in France and fulfilling an important cultural function. Hicham, a twenty-nine-year-old of Moroccan origin, visited Morocco every summer during his childhood with his parents and four younger brothers. Now, as an adult, he goes whenever he can. He says, "It allows me to rediscover my origins, language, customs, family. It's just not the same unless you go there." He anticipates doing the same thing for his children. Semi, a thirty-six-year-old of Tunisian origin who lives in the twentieth arrondissement, spent much of his childhood, sometimes entire years, living in Tunisia. His parents wanted him to have that experience so that he "could discover his origins, history," he explained. "Many second-generation immigrants in France are not in a good situation; many of them do not know where they are from." Semi thinks it has been easier for him to live in France because of his experiences in Tunisia. He has a better sense of his culture and origins than other children of North African immigrants and feels he is more grounded then they are.

Similarly, Soria, a thirty-four-year-old of Algerian origin who lives in a condo in the fifteenth arrondissement and has worked as a human resources director for the past decade, grew to appreciate her Algerian origins because of, in no small part, an extended trip she took to Algeria when she was a teenager: "One of the best moments of my life, the most life changing, was when I spent four months in Algeria. It allowed me to gain what I had been missing, notably in relationship to my identity. When I returned, I started speaking Arabic more, because before, when I spoke to my parents, I spoke in French, and now ever since then I've always spoken Arabic with my parents."

Her travel to Algeria allowed her to capture something previously unavailable to her had she never visited. However, her Algerian connection is not without its complications. Soria does not travel there as often now because she is not as close to her family there, and also because security concerns make her increasingly anxious about possible terrorist attacks in Algeria. Her attachment to Algeria has become less about the place and the need to physically be there and more about how Algeria represents a connection to her immigrant parents, to French colonial history, and to Algerian culture. The Arabic language plays a role in strengthening connections across generations in maghrébin-origin households. It is not uncommon for children of North African immigrants to return to studying (or speaking) Arabic later in their lives, as it remains the "highest-status vehicle for religious knowledge," though the language itself is gradually declining in maghrébin-origin Muslim households (Bowen 2004b, 48; see also Cesari 2002).

Samir, a twenty-nine-year-old of Algerian origin pursuing a doctorate in political science, remembers growing up in Tours and feeling uncomfortable owing to his visibility as a member of one of the only Algerian families in his town. He felt his teachers did not understand him and thought he was different and strange. Samir also vividly remembers tensions with white neighbors. He valued his frequent travels to Algeria to see his family and believes they counteracted his experiences growing up in Tours. He explained to me how Algeria is the site of his "culture of remembrance," as opposed to his present culture, which is in France.

As these representative examples suggest, the connection between the middle-class North African second generation and parents of maghrébin origin, developed through, for example, summer vacations and stories related to them by relatives, is a tool that helps them make sense of the marginalization they face in France. For many respondents, travel to their parents' maghrébin country of origin further reinforced their difference and illuminated their denial of cultural citizenship within France.

Beyond travel to the Maghreb, children of North African immigrants recalled specific messages their parents gave them about growing up in two different cultural worlds. Mohamed, a thirty-year-old of Algerian origin, remembers how his parents reinforced that home was France. He grew up in Avignon, near Marseille, in the south of France, with his four brothers and two sisters. His father was a factory worker and his mother a domestic worker. His father had originally come to France to work for a few years and then returned to Algeria. However, he found he was uncomfortable there. He returned to France in the mid-1960s with his wife and had seven children there, Mohamed being the youngest. What he learned from his parents was contrary to what he learned at school: he was taught at an early age that he was different from whites. Growing up, the mixed messages were challenging for Mohamed. As an adult, he sees his French and maghrébin status as a richness. He locates himself in the liminal space between what his parents taught him about being of maghrébin origin in France and what he learned at school; that is, he is simultaneously maghrébin and French.

These connections between the first and second generation are both symbolic and real. Cultural capital allows individuals to be able to navigate a diverse number of situations. What children of North African immigrants learned, both explicitly and implicitly, from their parents reflects the complications inherent in being both descendants of immigrants as well as racial and ethnic minorities. Their schooling imparted certain messages to these children, and their parents helped them interpret and confront them through their own cultural capital. Despite their education in a French Republican school, respondents quickly learned that they were not a part of the French Republic. Though they tried, their parents were ill-equipped to help them navigate this dual status. As first-generation immigrants, they themselves were never assumed to be part of the French mainstream. And yet neither are their children.

HIGHER EDUCATION

That children of immigrants felt different from others was also reinforced by their university education. All respondents have a university education above the baccalaureate level.[5] Higher education facilitates their upward mobility into a middle-class status yet erects barriers to their full societal inclusion.

I noted earlier how Abdelkrim's sense of having been marked as different was heightened when he began his university studies in Tours. "We [he and the other students] don't have the same lives," he explained. "The more you advance in your education, the harder it is to find people like you." The quest for compatibility is not limited to maghrébin-origin individuals in France but also applies to racial and ethnic minorities around the world, whether they are African Americans in predominately white colleges and universities or immigrant-origin individuals in a predominately white town or neighborhood in some other corner of the globe. French higher education does not systematically address its lack of ethnoracial diversity.[6] This can create added complications for individuals like Abdelkrim, who may have had similar and like-minded friends growing up but have difficulty making connections in a university setting. This has implications for the development of one's identity and the perception of one's status in society at large, as research on racial and ethnic diversity in higher education and the workplace attests (Feagin 1991; Tatum 1997).

By most accounts, Mourad, a thirty-year-old of Algerian origin, is very successful. He will soon earn his doctorate from the Institut d'études politiques de Paris, better known as Sciences Po, and also works as a freelance writer. He lives in an apartment in the seventh arrondissement, a neighborhood near the Eiffel Tower, which he described to me as "very rich and very white." Mourad is very close to his parents. His father immigrated to France in the 1960s for factory work; his mother migrated about ten years later, caring for Mourad and his five brothers and one sister. His parents are not educated, which he explains was common in Algeria at the time of the Algerian War of Independence. Mourad remembers being marked as different at a young age, including being called an Arab as well as ethnic slurs by his classmates. Yet he managed to complete his studies in political science and sociology and earn a master's degree studying immigration in the Arab world. He is the recipient of a prestigious fellowship funding his doctoral research on the French military.

Still, Mourad acknowledges how hard it has been to accomplish all of this and cites the various barriers he has faced along the way because he is not white. He explains that coming from a modest and maghrébin-origin background, it is not easy to succeed:

> It's difficult, difficult, because, for example, to complete your studies you are obliged to have a side job. . . . I'm a student at Sciences Po. It's a prestigious university in France. Because my parents cannot afford to give me money, I must have a side job. That means that I have less time to complete my studies, so that adds a lot of pressure. . . . It's difficult to come from a modest background, whether you're of immigrant origin or not, because in France there are a lot of barriers. . . . I think that in French society, to climb it, you need to go through the *grandes écoles* [prestigious, university-level colleges that require entrance examinations], and in France these schools remain very, very white and bourgeois. Actually, the university is democratized in France; there are many minorities in the regular universities, Paris 8, Paris 1, and Paris 2.[7] But ... it's not because you have a diploma from a university like this in France that you are going to experience social mobility, because what's happened is that a lot of people have these kinds of degrees, and so the value of that diploma is lowered. That means that if there are five hundred people who have a master's, there are not a lot of jobs that require a master's, so there are a lot of people who are going to be left out. Myself, I know people who have a bachelor's, who have a master's, who

have jobs that don't have anything to do with [their degrees or topic of studies], who work at McDonald's, places like that. So there are people from modest backgrounds who are at universities, it's true. However, the *grandes écoles,* they remain as before. With the exception of Sciences Po, which has been making small steps in the past four to five years, the other *grandes écoles*—Polytechnique, Ponts et chaussées, ES-SEC, HEC—remain [mostly white and bourgeois].[8] . . . In France, if you really want to move up, to advance socially, it's necessary to go through the *grandes écoles.*

Mourad recognizes the education necessary for upward mobility. Approximately one-fourth of respondents attended or attend these schools.[9]

When he finishes his doctorate, he hopes to become a university professor, though he realizes how many more obstacles exist at that stage. Mourad has confronted the same obstacles throughout his educational trajectory. He frames his experiences of higher education in France simultaneously as linked to his ethnic origin and working-class background. He is not just working-class and upwardly mobile, but also maghrébin. A focus on just socioeconomic status or class would omit the salience of race and ethnicity for determining his life path.

Despite his successes, Mourad fully realizes the barriers that all maghrébin-origin individuals face—regardless of socioeconomic status. He recounted to me how he and his other North African–origin friends are regularly stopped by the police, who check their identification (the French version of stop and frisk).[10] He has also been followed in department stores by salespeople and been denied entry to nightclubs regardless of how he is dressed.

While higher education is a means to upward social mobility, it is not without its complications. Members of the maghrébin second generation are also first-generation university students. Their higher education again reminds respondents of their difference from the mainstream. And it also reveals how the denial of cultural citizenship continues for these individuals well into adulthood.

NAVIGATING TWO WORLDS:
BETWIXT AND BETWEEN

The 2004 French film *Le grand voyage (The Great Journey)* by director Ismaël Ferroukhi, who was born in Morocco before moving to France as a young child, beautifully illustrates the complicated connections between maghrébin immigrants and their children. Réda, the teenage son of Moroccan immigrants, accompanies his father on a pilgrimage to Mecca from southern France. His father insists on communicating in Arabic, while the son speaks French. Their tense interactions across eight different countries reveal how children of maghrébin immigrants live in dual worlds—in their parents' traditional culture and the Westernized French culture in which they have grown up.

In France the denial of cultural citizenship through an assigned otherness begins in childhood and is reiterated throughout primary, secondary, and higher education. Children of North African immigrants must navigate two cultural worlds—French and maghrébin. This reflects the cultural citizenship they have been denied, which positions their maghrébin origins as non-French. Those cultural worlds were often in conflict or positioned against each other. This dynamic is true for other minority populations in different contexts as well, including Latino and African American students in the United States who must straddle multiple cultural worlds or invoke multiple cultural repertoires—the dominant culture versus the culture of their minority group (Carter 2005). However, the maghrébin second generation does this in a context where, ideologically speaking, they should not have to. Per French Republican ideology, they are as culturally French as any other French person, so long as they adhere to the values of the Republic. In this context, navigating two cultural worlds—and never being firmly in one or the other—reveals the degree of their marginalization, or distance from mainstream society. They move and interact in the dominant cultural world but remain outside of it. In this context, the North African second generation is never allowed to see itself as whole or integrated; rather, French culture and North African culture are placed in opposition to each other.

Moreover, their attachment to dual cultural worlds or, as Samir puts it, their "belonging to two universes," is something their white peers do not face. However, Mohamed grew to see this as beneficial. "Growing up, I didn't really understand it," he explained. "But now I see it as more of a positive thing. . . . It has added to the richness of my life." Mohamed's ability to reframe his narrative has helped him be successful as a technical director for his company. Because he is middle-class, he can access multiple codes to navigate different kinds of spaces. His and his peers' middle-class status forces them into the role of cultural broker (Warikoo 2011), as they must bridge the differences between French and maghrébin cultures, as well as the differences between the cultural worlds of the middle-class and the working class.

I opened this chapter by situating growing up French as a question, and I want to return to it now. As my respondents' experiences reveal, they grew up in France, but they did not necessarily grow up French. That matters, because it reveals the limitations of the Republican model for incorporating or including nonwhite individuals. It also underlines how France, historically, has not acknowledged race and ethnicity as salient. The North African second generation learned about their difference from mainstream society at an early age. Their Frenchness, or their place within the Republic, has been questioned by others since they were young. The denial of their cultural citizenship involves the continual questioning and denial of their belonging in France. And this begins in childhood, when they learn of their visibility as racial and ethnic minorities. Most individuals did not grow up believing that they were legitimate members of the Republic. Essentially, they were socialized into what they are not—that is, not French. They continue to navigate this dual status and opposition between French and maghrébin in other spheres, including Islam, the workplace, place, and the public sphere, as part of being middle-class.

3

Marginalization and
Middle-Class Blues

Race, Islam, the Workplace, and the Public Sphere

It dawned upon me with a certain suddenness that I was different from the others; or like, mayhap, in heart and life and longing, but shut out from their world by a vast veil.

—W. E. B. DUBOIS, *THE SOULS OF BLACK FOLK*

"Here I am, a black man who has done all the things I was supposed to do,"
he said, and proceeded to tick off precisely what he done: gone to Harvard,
labored for years to make his mark in an elite law firm, married a highly mo-
tivated woman who herself had an advanced degree and a lucrative career.
He and his wife were in the process of raising three exemplary children. He
had surmounted every hurdle life had thrown in this way. Yet he was far from
fulfilled. "Blacks who have made it up the ladder have had to put up with a
lot more crap" than have those who had given up along the way. But these
successful people, he mused, were the very ones likely to be especially sensitive
to the "crap" they encountered.

—ELLIS COSE, *THE RAGE OF A PRIVILEGED CLASS*

The middle-class North African second generation are cultural brokers (Warikoo 2011) in two senses—between white and maghrébin cultural worlds and between the cultural worlds of their immigrant parents and other working-class North African–origin individuals, and the middle-class world they occupy at work and school. They are cultural brokers in terms of race and ethnicity and in terms of their socioeconomic status. Their educational and professional successes in adulthood only exacerbate their feelings of occupying multiple worlds. Their middle-class status only heightens the difficulty and frustration of not being fully accepted as French by others. Their upward mobility and middle-class status launches them into a world different than their immigrant parents', but having arrived there, what happens next?

In this chapter, I explore how individuals navigate these dualisms by demonstrating how middle-class, North African–origin individuals access different codes in different spaces. I also discuss their experiences of being marked as different across the different domains of Islam, the workplace, place of residence, and the public sphere. Those are all domains where their denial of cultural citizenship is evident. The North African second generation is marginalized owing to its North African names, identification with Islam, and residential locations—all of which are proxies for race and ethnic origin (Silberman 2011). I further illustrate the pervasiveness of the racism they experience, which has implications for the relationship between marginalized individuals or minorities and the state. Despite Republican ideology emphasizing how all citizens are the same in their relation to the state, middle-class North African–origin individuals are still not treated as full and equal citizens.

Second-generation immigrants in other societies occupy a liminal status between the country where they were born and raised and their parents' home country—never feeling as if they belong in one or the other, or in both (Eid 2008; Imoagene 2012; Kasinitz et al. 2004; PRC 2013; Portes and Rumbaut 2001; Portes et al. 2011; and Zhou and Lee 2007). For second-generation immigrants who manage to be upwardly mobile, there is another dimension to navigate as cultural broker—their dual minority and middle-class status (Warikoo 2011). It exacerbates their feeling of being between two worlds, as they are not only between French and North African, but also between working-class and middle-class. As with middle-class populations more generally (Frazier 1957; Lacy 2007; Pattillo-McCoy 1999; Vallejo 2012), middle-class children of North African immigrants move through different symbolic and real spaces, their interactions not limited to other maghrébin- or immigrant-origin individuals. This is a product of their upward mobility; their working-class roots did provide them with the same cultural and social capital as their white counterparts. They are second-generation immigrants, yet first-generation middle-class individuals. They can study at Sciences Po, for example, but they may not fit in or feel as comfortable as their white classmates. They may hold a leadership position at work, but they may not feel they are regarded as competent or knowledgeable as their white counterparts in comparable positions. This is a problem, not only for France, which espouses a particular model of identity politics, but also for all minorities in plural and diverse societies.

UPWARD MOBILITY, BECOMING MIDDLE-CLASS, AND THE GLASS CEILING

Consider Farid, a thirty-two-year-old with dual Algerian and French citizenship, whom I met at a café near the new Bibliothèque François Mitterrand building.

I had connected with him through an immigrant-related organization. He lives in the southwestern banlieue of Melun with his wife and two young children and works for the Ministère de la ville, de la jeunesse et des sports (Ministry of the City, Youth, and Sports, since renamed). At a very young age, his parents told him, "You are not French. We live in France, but you are Algerian." They imparted to him their love and appreciation of Algeria, which took priority over any attachment to France, and their connection to Algerian culture—which he and his wife intend to pass on to his young children. His parents shared with him the family history and educated him in Muslim and Algerian cultural traditions, including music, common expressions, and speaking Arabic. "I do not feel an emptiness in this regard," Farid explains, "meaning. culturally, I believe that I have an Algerian heritage. I am connected to a family. I am connected to a region in Algeria."

This might be interpreted as a failure of children of North African immigrants to assimilate into French society and adopt its norms and values, and as a preference for retaining an attachment to former French colonies in the Maghreb. However, Farid's story is more complex.

Looking back, Farid feels that he adopted an Algerian identity rather than a French one because he grew up in Rouen, in the northwestern part of France, near Normandy, in a predominately Muslim and maghrébin neighborhood, which was labeled a *zone d'éducation prioritaire* (educational priority zone, or ZEP) by the French government. He rarely interacted with whites growing up. Many of his neighbors also took Arabic courses on the weekend, and many of his classmates and friends fasted during Ramadan. His father was a factory worker and his mother, twenty-five years younger than his father, was a housewife. His father came to France when he was twenty-three years old to work, and then returned to Algeria to meet his wife, who would later join him in France.

Because neither of his parents was educated or literate, they always stressed the importance of him doing well in school. Farid credits his parents for his educational and occupational success; none of his childhood friends managed to graduate from college and hold a professional job, as he did. He remembers that his mother signed him up for a library card when he was young, though she herself could not read. Farid later studied at the University of Rouen, where he met his wife, a child of Algerian immigrants, and then earned a graduate degree from the University of Bordeaux. "It was just something I understood at an early age," he said, when explaining the importance of education. "I just really wanted to make my parents proud." His four older siblings have the same education level. Friends from his old neighborhood (also of North African origin) are less educated. Those who are consistently employed mostly have menial or working-class jobs, and some have had trouble with the law. "I think about that a lot, why I was the only one of them to finish high school studies, go to college," he explained. "I think it's attributable to the motivation of my parents." His parents served as role models, in that they struggled when they first immigrated to France because they were uneducated and did not speak French but "were able to adapt, to move forward," he explained proudly.

The nature of social segregation in French society made it difficult for Farid to identify as a French person. The French state, through its policies and practices, has created and fostered his isolation and separation from mainstream society, a sense shared by other children of maghrébin immigrants. This difference was thrust upon him, not one he coveted.

If Farid does not necessarily see himself as part of the French mainstream, he nonetheless has moved up the ladder and is successful. He enjoys his job, but it presents its challenges, particularly in terms of advancing in the department hierarchy. But, he says, "it is always important for me to remember that I have it a lot better than my parents." This is an example of the dualism Farid and others experience. They recognize their continuing difficulties as mediated by their maghrébin origins, but they also consider them relative to those experienced by their immigrant parents and economically disadvantaged.[1]

Farid is a minority within a minority group. As such, he experiences ambivalence about his social position. Farid recognizes the advantages of his educational accomplishments and professional status, yet he is not far removed from his immigrant parents and his childhood friends from his neighborhood.

Middle-class North African–origin individuals are distinct from their white counterparts in France, as they do not experience the full advantages of middle-class status. Like second-generation Mexican Americans and other middle-class racial and ethnic minority populations, second-generation maghrébin immigrants can achieve upward mobility through education, yet face a "glass-ceiling mobility" (Rojas-García 2013) or an insurmountable barrier to being viewed as truly French. They are "qualified, yet excluded" (Rojas-García 2013). Though educated in the society where they were raised, they are not permitted to truly fit in.

I was struck by this when I began conducting fieldwork in Paris. Following the 2005 uprisings in France's banlieues,[2] many news reports focused on the impoverished and unemployed segment of the second-generation population and how their lower socioeconomic status had kept them outside the French mainstream.[3] These individuals were seen to have turned their backs on France, rejecting its norms and practices. It was they who were the problem, not France. They cultivated an oppositional identity and did not see themselves as French. Marginalization in France was based on class or socioeconomic status, not race and ethnicity. The issue was that this population did not work hard enough to make it in French society (Beaman 2015b). For members of the second generation who were educated and employed, marginalization was not an issue.

Yet maghrébin-origin individuals themselves know differently. The upwardly mobile are not viewed differently than their economically disadvantaged or disenfranchised counterparts. Individuals like Farid still do not feel as though they fit in or are included. Their success is not a panacea for the racism and discrimination they face. And their marginalization exists across multiple domains, including the workplace, residential location, and religious life.

Ndiaye's (2008) minority paradox, the theory of the simultaneous visibility and invisibility of France's black population, also applies in this middle-class minority population; their visibility is heightened by their presence in predominately white spaces (including elite universities and professional and executive-level offices), but they are invisible because their presence is ignored in mainstream society. The discrimination and marginalization they experience is more evidence of how race and ethnicity are constitutive of French identity.

North African–origin individuals have an ambiguous status vis-à-vis being middle-class in part because of their proximity to their working-class counterparts–often individuals in their own families or neighborhoods. For example, Hamama, a thirty-five-year-old of Algerian origin who works as a hospital director and studied at Sciences Po, has been more successful than her three younger brothers, who live in Lille in northern France, where she also grew up. One brother has been unemployed for about three years and another one works a bus driver. Hamama therefore realizes that her own material circumstances could have been widely different. "People see me differently once they learn that I am educated, that I went to Sciences Po," she explains. She started an activist organization denouncing discrimination and working to help banlieue residents and maghrébin-origin individuals who are trying to get ahead but lack the opportunities to do so. Individuals who have made it feel they cannot forget those who have not.

Many respondents are heavily involved in maghrébin-related professional organizations, which seek to provide opportunities for their working-class counterparts (as well as networking opportunities for fellow professionals). As the African American middle-class maintains connections to other African Americans to maintain their racial and ethnic identity even while seeking full incorporation into the American mainstream (Lacy 2004, Pattillo-McCoy 1999), so too do North African–origin individuals use professional and social networks to maintain and foster ties with other middle-class maghrébin-origin individuals. However, maghrébin-origin individuals must make these ties amid institutional contexts that do not recognize their ethnic identity as legitimate. There is no legally established maghrébin-French or North African–French identity. They are supposed to just be or act French, yet they are not treated as such. These networks allow them to cope with their position at the bottom of the ethnoracial hierarchy, despite their middle-class achievements.

Part of being middle-class and maghrébin is moving in multiple spaces, inter-acting with maghrébin individuals and whites. Assimilation is not an appropriate framework for understanding the experiences of this population. That they were born and have spent their entire lives in France allows them structural assimila-tion, yet they are not culturally assimilated (Lacy 2007), for they are not regarded as part of French culture. This is not a group that desires separation from non–immigrant origin individuals or whites; rather, its members become adept at strategically moving through in two different cultural worlds. Respondents often attend schools where other students do not resemble them, or they work in spaces where they are one of few immigrant-origin individuals.

My focus on the stigmatization and marginalization on middle-class maghrébin-origin individuals because of their race and ethnic origin challenges Loïc Wacquant's conclusions about the nature of assimilation and ethnic identity in France. He argues that this demographic has adopted "the mainstream cultural and behavioral patterns of the French" and has failed to form a distinct maghrébin community or assert any "ethnic specificity" (Wacquant 2007, 194), and thus has successfully assimilated. According to Wacquant, the second-generation immi-grant population demonstrates how race and ethnic origin are insignificant for French daily life and how France is more successful at integrating its immigrants and their descendants than is the United States. He says that even if African Americans and North African–origin individuals in France have similar lived experiences, the explanations for each are markedly different. He favors socio-economic explanations for marginality in France, versus a race-based explanation for marginality in the United States. However, in addition to neglecting an inter-sectional analysis focusing on race and socioeconomic status, Wacquant neglects how, though children of maghrébin immigrants may be socialized or assimilated along traditional lines (for example, by education or language), they nonetheless feel excluded from full participation in mainstream French society. Their racial and ethnic status do not allow them to identify as French, or have that identity accepted by others. He places the onus of this nonassimilation and noninclusion on the North African second generation rather than on French society at large: it is its members who are responsible for claiming their place within it. This dis-course, of course, holds true for racial and ethnic minorities elsewhere: African American and Latinos, for example, are held responsible for discrimination or mistreatment they experience.[4] By contrast, Wacquant and others believe that if maghrébin-origin individuals assert their French identity, they will be accepted as such. However, his theory does not acknowledge that even individuals who do everything right are still stigmatized and excluded. Socioeconomic factors are not the sole explanation for societal exclusion. Race and ethnicity play significant roles, regardless of class and socioeconomic status. More attention, therefore, must be paid to the everyday manifestations of France's racial project.

DIFFERENCE ACROSS DOMAINS:
OCCUPYING MULTIPLE WORLDS

I. Islam

The continual marginalization of this middle-class population is also due to the intersection of race and religion—here, Islam—in French society. Children of Muslim immigrants in Europe "grow up in a world in which Islam is a chronic object of discussion and debate, a world that is thick with self-conscious and explicit discussions about Islam" (Brubaker 2013, 4). The denial of cultural citizenship extends to this religious context. Maghrébin-origin individuals are associated with Islam, and they owe their marginalization in part to that.[5]

Much research on Muslims in France is based on the assumption that their religious identity, practices and beliefs are homogenous (Brubaker 2013; Lamont 2002).[6] I am not interested in Islam in terms of its tenets (see Bowen 2009 for more on this), but rather in the degree of their religious-based marginalization and their individual religiosity, or degree of religious commitment (Voas and Fleischmann 2012), and how this shapes their status in and marginalization from mainstream society.[7] This parallels Cadge and Ecklund's (2007) "lived religion perspective," which examines religion's importance outside religious organizations, in social institutions such as families, workplaces, and schools.

Second-generation Muslim immigrants construct and negotiate a religious identity, but they do this in the context of a religion that is stigmatized in society at large. Second generation–immigrant religious participation has been found to depend more on the salience of religious identity than ethnic national identity (Voas and Fleischmann 2012). France complicates this, as religion stands in for race and ethnicity as a marker of difference because race and ethnicity are not officially acknowledged. When North-African origin individuals are considered too culturally different from the French mainstream, their Muslim identity is often referenced because of the nation's Islamophobia (Bleich 2006, 2009; Voas and Fleischmann 2012). This is even though respondents say their religious participation and religiosity do not hinder them from feeling French or asserting a French identity (Beaman 2016; Maxwell and Bleich 2014). Rather, they frame their religious practices in a way that corresponds to the tenets of French Republicanism—they frame their religiosity a personal and private matter.[8]

Islamophobia, then, is not just about Islam; it is also about ethnoracial exclusion. Religion stands in for racial and ethnic difference in a society that refuses to grapple head-on with these differences. Islamophobia is a form of racism—it sees certain individuals as too culturally different to ever be fully accepted as part of the mainstream. The connection between Islamophobia and racial and ethnic marginalization was perhaps most recently seen in the wake of the massacre in the offices of the satirical magazine *Charlie Hebdo*, in January 2015 and the resulting international rally cry of "*Je suis Charlie.*" Samir explained to me in a conversation a few months after the attacks:

> It was so weird. . . . After the attacks, I got a text message from a friend from high school, a white guy, asking me what I thought about the attacks, if I condemned them. It doesn't make any sense. Of course, I condemn the attacks. . . . I mean, it's not as if we ever ask Catholics and Christians to condemn the attacks that other Christians commit. . . . This is a republic. I'm part of a republic. I'm an individual in relation to the republic. When I pay my rent each month, I'm just paying for myself, not for anyone else or any group.

The experience of Samir, who migrated to France from Algeria when he was two years old, reflects the collective punishment (Hajjat 2015; Hajjat and Mohammed 2013) that many North African–origin individuals experienced in the wake of the attacks. Such remarks—to him and to his cohort—serve as a constant reminder to children of maghrébin immigrants (and other French Muslims) of their marginal status in French society, and reflects that their Muslim identity is secondary to the Muslim label constructed for them by others.

About 80 percent of my respondents identify as either practicing or cultural Muslims. For many of them, Islam serves as a symbolic marker of maghrébin culture, just as Christian symbols and rituals are part of African Americans' cultural toolkit, which they invoke in certain contexts to make sense of their marginalization (Pattillo-McCoy 1998). *Musulmans pratiquants* (practicing Muslims) among my respondents engage in practices such as *salat* (ritual prayer); observing Ramadan; abstaining from alcohol and cigarettes; following halal food regulations; attending mosque; observing Muslim holidays; and wearing the hijab. About 68 percent of respondents self-identified this way. Zara, a twenty-eight-year-old of Moroccan origin who works as a social worker, is a devout Muslim who considers being maghrébin and French as constitutive elements of her identity. For her, being a Muslim means "respecting Islamic principles, the five pillars—faith, fasting, praying, making donations, and making the pilgrimage. I do all these, except the pilgrimage, which I haven't done yet. *Insha'Allah* [God willing], I will have an opportunity to make it." Although her parents raised her as Muslim, Zara did not really take the religion that seriously until she was about fifteen years old. It was not until she was twenty years old that she started to say the daily prayers.

Some of my respondents say they are *Musulmans croyants*—believers who do not practice the religion but who nonetheless profess cultural ties to it. They participate in only a few rituals, such as observing Eid al-Fitr, the holiday that celebrates the end of the fasting period and of Ramadan. About 13 percent of respondents self-identified this way. For those individuals, their Muslim status is more of a cultural claim than a religious one (also see Bowen 2004a; Venel 2004). They essentially see themselves as less Muslim than other French Muslims. Nadia, a twenty-four-year-old of Algerian origin and graduate student studying human resources and communications, explains this distinction: "I tend to say I am a cultural Muslim, which means that in terms of culture I am Muslim, because I was raised that way, though my father was not. . . . Algerian culture is anchored in the Muslim religion, so . . . the education I received had a religious foundation."

Nadia does not remember being particularly interested in Algerian or maghrébin culture until she was a teenager. She increasingly felt a need for an attachment to her culture, sought out connections with other maghrébin youth online, and began to learn more. She owes her identity as a cultural Muslim in part relates to this social network of like-minded Muslim friends. Those Muslim friends characterize themselves similarly in terms of their religious identity and religiosity. Like most respondents, Diana believes religion should remain a private matter, per French Republican ideology.

That respondents' Muslim identity and practices contributed to their marginalization underscores how religion is another space where this population is marked as different. It is important to note how this marginalization is often based on others' perception of their religious identity and practices, not the actual practices themselves.

Harmellia, a twenty-one-year-old college student of Moroccan origin, was raised in a public-housing complex in Nanterre, a banlieue west of Paris, with other maghrébin-origin individuals. Her phenotypical features do not immediately convey North African origin—she has pale skin and long blonde hair. She remembers her early marginalization because she was Muslim: "When I was young, I did not eat pork. . . . But when I tried to explain that to my schoolteacher, she did not believe me. They forced me to eat it." Her teacher's ignorance and stereotypical views of maghrébin-origin individuals' appearance resulted in a refusal to believe her.

Mourad also characterizes himself as a practicing Muslim who observes Ramadan but does not eat pork and does not say the ritual prayers. He says, "If a Muslim wanted to become French, he had to renounce his religion. He had to say, 'Voilà, I want to be French, so I'm abandoning Islam.' That's how it was before. And I think in the minds of many French people today, you can still find this mindset, this idea that it's difficult to be French and Muslim at the same time. Either we are French and not Muslim, or we are Muslim and therefore cannot be French."

Mourad positions his religious identity as one barrier that keeps him from being fully accepted as French by others. He vividly remembers how his Muslim identity was used against him when he tried to rent an apartment. He had called a landlord to schedule an appointment to see it. When he arrived, the landlord asked him if he was Muslim. Mourad did not completely understand why he asked this question and responded that he was, indeed, Muslim. He later felt uncomfortable and did not pursue the rental.[9] This experience was one of many in which he was treated differently because of his ethnoreligious identity. Of note is how Mourad was set apart for merely identifying as Muslim, not for his practices. Here we have yet another example of how difficult it is for the middle-class maghrébin second generation to escape the difference assigned to it.

Nasar, a thirty-two-year-old Parisian of Algerian origin, often has similar experiences of feeling different based on his religious identity. He feels most challenged in this regard at his workplace, an organization related to French soccer:

> At my job, there about ten Arabs, five of whom drink alcohol, do not observe Ramadan, who love to go out, go to clubs, hang out, smoke . . . and there are five others who do not go out. Me, I do not drink, I do not smoke, I do not really go to clubs and all that. But it's to me that they say, "You are extremist," yet they love the others. . . . But with an Arab like me, it's different. . . . If tomorrow you give in and follow what the French do, what they are, that's great. Then they'll say, "Nasar is a great guy, he drinks, he can drink two barrels of beer."

Nasar's coworkers see him as different because he practices the tenets of his Muslim faith. Unlike some of his coworkers, he refuses to perform a Muslim identity that the French more easily accept, one that Nasar considers inauthentic. He is unwilling to sacrifice his religious identity.

Hicham, a twenty-nine-year-old of Moroccan origin, feels that although he agrees with the Republican tenets of keeping religious practices in the private sphere, he is repeatedly reminded of his Muslim status and North African origin:

> I know they always mock me in terms of halal, what you can eat. Saturday, I went to a conference . . . and there was a buffet with different sliced meats that I could not eat. I didn't say anything. It didn't bother me at all. I ate salad. And people said to me, "You don't eat the sliced meat?" And I said, "No, it's not halal". And one guy said, "But this isn't a Muslim celebration." I didn't understand . . . why they would say that to me, especially when I never asked them anything. I didn't say anything, I didn't ask why there weren't other options. . . . I consider it my choice to eat halal, something others should respect. There were people there who were vegetarian, who eat neither meat nor fish, but I'm not going to ask them why they don't. . . . I respect their decision. I'm not going to tell them, "Well, this isn't a vegetarian meal." It's things like this that we encounter more and more.

Hicham was particularly bothered by others' reactions to his avoidance of nonhalal meat because he feels that he does not force his religious practices on anyone else. His Muslim faith represents a racial and ethnic otherness to his colleagues that they would not apply to a vegetarian. He is continually reminded how he is a practicing Muslim and therefore not considered French. This despite his nonmaghrébin-like appearance—he has fairer skin than many of his counterparts, which has sometimes protected him from discrimination.

While religion is a site of difference for this population, respondents nevertheless claim a French identity by how they frame their religion. By relegating their religious practices to the private sphere, they assert their place in France and consider themselves as French as anyone else.

II. Workplace

The exclusion of Muslim respondents extends into the workplace. For example, Farid remarked how, when there are meals or events at his office, it never comes to mind to his coworkers that Muslims generally do not eat pork. Though he has mentioned to them that he is Muslim, it is rarely taken into account. Though they have achieved professional success and have middle-class jobs, respondents feel that, compared to their white colleagues, they are regularly treated poorly.

The workplace is yet another context in which the middle-class North African second generation is denied cultural citizenship on the basis of its racial and ethnic origin. All my respondents are stably employed in professional or similar types of jobs: they are lawyers, journalists, teachers, bankers, social workers, and entrepreneurs. But to better understand the social locations and positions of immigrant-origin individuals, it is crucial to address not only underemployed and unemployed individuals, but also those who are stably employed. About 15 percent of second-generation maghrébin immigrant men and 23 percent of second-generation maghrébin immigrant women hold salaried or professional jobs (Lombardo and Pujol 2011). Although this is a minority of the North African second generation, it is not a negligible segment, especially when considering the successes and failures of France's assimilationist framework. Existing theories on assimilation among descendants of immigrants (Alba and Nee 2003; Zhou 1997), which emphasize upward mobility across generations as a key barometer of societal inclusion, are not applicable to middle-class children of maghrébin immigrants. While economic disadvantage plagues most of the North African second generation—and the North African–origin population more generally—even individuals who do not face such difficulties are reminded that their maghrébin origins are an inextricable barrier to full societal inclusion. Again, this is reminiscent of the marginalization black middle-class professionals face in the United States (Cose 1994). As long as the framework for understanding integration into mainstream society relies upon upward occupational mobility across generations, it is incomplete. The upward mobility of the North African second generation occurs in tandem with subtle and not so subtle mistreatment and discrimination when they enter predominately white institutions.

Being othered in the sphere of employment manifests in two ways—when seeking employment and, if hired, subsequent treatment in the workplace. The road to the current professional and employment status of the North African second generation was a long one. This corresponds with existing research, which shows how proxies for race and ethnicity, including name, skin color, or residential location, led to discrimination in hiring practices (Silberman 2011). For example, Hicham, who lives with his family in the western banlieue of Poissy, feels that his Tunisian origin has directly shaped his experiences on the job market: "As soon as we make an effort, we find a wall in front of us. . . . As for me, I had a lot of trouble finding my first job after I finished school. It took one and a half years to find my first job, but my classmates who were named François, Édouard, Frédéric. It took them six months or four months to find a job, but for me it took one and a half years." Hicham's name thus betrays his maghrébin origins.

Lila, a twenty-five-year-old high school teacher in the banlieue of Drancy, remembers having trouble finding a job as well: "I remember realizing when I was very young and looking for a job for the summer . . . that all my friends with blond hair and blue eyes named Émile were able to find jobs and I was not. . . . It's more the leverage we don't have, the power we don't have, or sometimes last names or appearances that don't please employers."

The markers of differences, including physical appearance and names, serve as proxies for being nonwhite and an ethnic minority to employers. Because the hiring process for teachers is different than for other occupations (requiring a certification exam, for example), Lila's job search was less colored by discrimination. Yet she says, "I have felt obligated . . . to show that I was more capable than others." Other respondents say they felt they had to work twice as hard to prove themselves as worthy as their coworkers, which mirrors their experiences as university students. This dynamic is echoed by racial and ethnic minorities in predominately white workplaces in the United States (Cose 1994; Deitch et al. 2003; Feagin 1991; Harvey Wingfield 2011, 2013; Neckerman et al. 1999; Skrenty 2014; Van Laer and Janssens 2011).

Though Hicham eventually obtained a professional-level job at a bank, the process was more challenging and complicated for him because of his ethnic origins. He was laid off during the economic crisis. Since he did not actually like his job, he saw the layoff as an opportunity to do something that would really fulfill him. He has since started an organization assisting the physically disabled (such as his younger brother) and began perfecting his English-language skills. Yet Hicham is quick to note that only maghrébin workers were laid off with him; white coworkers who began work after him were not. Hicham saw that he was more disposable in the eyes of his company than his white colleagues. He remembers a colleague suggesting he change his name to one more traditionally French, like Pierre or Jacques, to fit in.

Ahmed, a twenty-nine-year-old practicing Muslim who has dual citizenship, has also faced difficulties at his work as a technical director for his company owing to his Algerian origins. He feels somewhat protected from more overt discrimination because of his educational background (he has a *bac* plus 5, or the equivalent of undergraduate and advanced degrees). Ahmed feels that the "two different educations" (the maghrébin one at home and the French one at school) of his youth provided a rich experience, though he did not always

FIGURE 1. Nanterre, a western banlieue of Paris. Photo by author.

see it this way. However, as a maghrébin-origin employee, he feels he must work harder than his white colleagues and "cannot make any mistakes." Other maghrébin employees at his company feel the same way and say they are treated differently than their white coworkers. "A Maghrébin making a presentation will have no credibility if he makes a mistake," Ahmed says. He adds that he is made to feel different in more subtle ways at work. For example, he says, "In my conversations with coworkers, sometimes people say 'you people,' and it's like, who is 'you'?" The language of his colleagues thus "others" different people or groups. Sitting in a café outside his office, he described the glass ceiling maghrébin-origin employees confront, which impedes upward occupational mobility. Though Ahmed has substantial responsibilities as part of his job, including managing other employees, he believes that, however hard he works, he cannot advance significantly in his company's hierarchy. "No one wants to see an Arab at the top," he said. Middle-class status and occupational accomplishments are not sufficient barriers to marginalization based on race. Their successes do not challenge the existing ethnoracial hierarchy. Though they have made it on a socioeconomic level, middle-class children of maghrébin-origin immigrants are not accepted by others.

III. Place and Residential Location

Place, or one's residential and spatial environment, is another domain where we can examine the relationship among race and ethnicity, marginalization, and citizenship and explore the denial of cultural citizenship to racial and ethnic minorities. Put simply, "place is space filled up by people, practices, objects, and representations" (Gieryn 2000, 465). The meanings individuals attach to place are implicated in how they see themselves (Cuba and Hummon 1993; Gieryn 2000). Place also marks and sustains difference and hierarchy (Gieryn 2000). Regardless of whether children of North African immigrants live in banlieues or in Paris proper, place is one lens through which we can understand this population's perceptions of and responses to marginalization; it offers a spatial dimension to the denial of cultural citizenship. Like the patterns of Muslim religiosity among respondents, respondents' attachments to where they live do not negate their assertion of a French identity or feeling French. For many of these respondents, especially those who live in banlieues in the Seine-Saint-Denis département, where the proportion of immigrant-origin individuals is dramatically higher than in Paris proper, there is both a physical and social separation.

We can see how this manifests in France by considering the banlieues and the associated stigma of living in them (Balibar 2007; Oberti 2007; Préteceille 2008; Silverstein 2008; Simon 1998). I specifically situate the banlieue as a site of racial and ethnic otherness and marginalization, regardless of these communities' heterogeneity and where children of North African immigrants live. In a context where race and ethnicity are not acknowledged, place or residential location becomes more salient as a marker for one's racial and ethnic status (Silverstein 2008; Tissot 2008). If the assumption is that banlieue residents are of North African and sub-Saharan African origin, then by identifying someone as living in a banlieue, the implication is that he or she is of North African or sub-Saharan African origin.[10] So someone's ethnic origin can be referenced or identified without explicitly doing so, and place euphemistically stands in for race and ethnic origin (Calvès 2004).[11] Residential location is a proxy for ethnic origin, and this creates obstacles to employment for banlieue residents. Audits comparing identical CVs of individuals living in banlieues with those from other areas confirm this: employers preferred workers who do not live in banlieues typically associated with racial and ethnic minorities (ENAR 2014). Though France is not characterized by the same degree of racial and ethnic residential segregation found in the United States (Wacquant 2007), and residential integration within France increases from one generation to the next (Shon 2010),[12] there remains persistent concentration of minorities in banlieue communities (Shon 2010) that results in their stigmatization (Dikeç 2007; Silverstein 2008; Tissot 2007).

North African–origin individuals are often associated with the banlieues even if they do not live there (Amara 2006; Bouamama 2009; Hargreaves 2007; Silverstein 2008; Stovall 2003). This association of people of color with the banlieues is further evidence of France's racial project, though ethnic-related segregation is antithetical to Republican ideology: the banlieues are stigmatized and considered undesirable places to live. France's colorblind ideology veils the marginalization of individuals because of their ethnic origin.

Banlieues, regardless of the variation in socioeconomic status and ethnic background one finds there, are framed as synonymous with disadvantage and "otherness" (Hargreaves 1996); they evoke "the image of housing projects, with young people hanging around wearing baseball caps and sweat suits, smoking joints, perhaps standing beside a burning car. Banlieues have become the symbol of a bleak urban environment, deviant youth, and segregated minorities" (Tissot 2008, 1). The term *banlieue* has also become a catchall for *quartiers sensibles* (at-risk or vulnerable neighborhoods); *quartiers difficiles* (problem or underprivileged neighborhoods); *zones d'éducation prioritaire* (educational priority zones, or ZEPs); *zones urbaines sensibles* (sensitive urban zones, or ZUSs); *zones à urbaniser en priorité* (priority urban zones, or ZUPs); and *quartiers populaires* (working-class neighborhoods) (Dikeç 2007; Hargreaves 1996; Tissot 2008). They are flattened to characterizations of mass unemployment; the predominance of *cités* (high-rise public housing complexes) the absence of two-parent family structure; a deskilled workforce; a high percentage of residents on public assistance; low levels of educational attainment; and physical compactness (Avenel 2007; Balibar 2007; Dikeç 2007; Kokoreff 2003; Lapeyronnie 2008; LePoutre 1997; Maurin 2004; Rey 1996; Silverstein 2008; Stébé 2007; Tissot 2007; Wacquant 2007).

Within the French academy, scholars tend to emphasize the socioeconomic segregation of banlieues (Oberti 2007; Simon 1998; Wacquant 2007) over their ethnoracial segregation (Lapeyronnie 2008; Tissot 2008). Furthermore, marginalization is considered place-specific, so that banlieue residents are marginalized and Parisians are not, further separating them from mainstream society. Wacquant (2007) questions the marginalization of the middle-class segment of the North African second generation. He argues that banlieue residents can pass in larger society if they do not exhibit markers of living in a banlieue (including one's demeanor or speech patterns) (Wacquant 2007). But his argument ignores the connotation between the banlieues and racial and ethnic minorities who cannot overcome the association and be fully accepted as French.

Immigrants from the Maghreb originally settled in the banlieues of major cities (Tribalat 2004b). Immigrant-origin individuals who reside in the banlieues represent multiple ethnic origins, including Algerian, Tunisian, and Moroccan, as well as sub-Saharan African (Shon 2010; Simon 1997). Most of my respondents, about 65 percent, live in the banlieues, primarily in the inner-ring départements of Seine-Saint-Denis, Val-de-Marne, and Hauts-de-Seine (the rest live in Paris proper). Many respondents who are residents of the banlieues nonetheless work, attend school, or regularly socialize in Paris and travel back and forth by metro, bus, and tram.

This cross-boundary movement appears to be a privilege of the middle-class segment of the North African second generation, for working-class individuals I encountered spend more time in their neighborhoods or banlieue communities and are less likely to spend time in Paris. While doing my fieldwork at the Nanterre Association, I realized that though Nanterre is only ninety minutes by commuter train or a twenty-minute drive from Paris by car, it is more isolated from Paris than that spatial distance suggests. One time, when I was typing on my laptop in the main room of the Nanterre Association in between sessions teaching English, a maghrébin mother from the neighborhood approached and greeted me. We spoke briefly. The wallpaper on my computer screen was a photo I had recently taken of the Jardin des Tuileries, near the Musée du Louvre. She asked whether the photo was of Chicago (since I lived there before I moved to Paris) or somewhere else in the United States. I was struck that she did not immediately recognize a popular Parisian landmark next to a world-famous museum. On another occasion, several children were taking a field trip to a photography exhibit at the Galerie nationale du Jeu de Paume, near the Place de la Concorde, one Wednesday afternoon in spring 2009. Since school is only a half day on Wednesdays, the Nanterre Association often organizes excursions for those afternoons. An older Algerian man who lives nearby and does occasional janitorial work for the organization explained to me that he was excited about going on the field trip because he had not been to Paris in about nine years, despite living in Nanterre. Another time, when I went on a field trip to the Arc de Triomphe with some of the students, many of them were unfamiliar with it, though it is a major Parisian landmark and not far from Nanterre. Experiences such as this reinforced the separation of Paris and this banlieue community and demonstrated that for its residents, the distance between them is mediated by socioeconomic status.

The residential communities, past and present, of my respondents, how they came to live there, and how location has determined their place in French society warrants examination. For racial and ethnic minorities, interactions with whites outside their ethnic enclave are often characterized by heightened discrimination and prejudice (Eid 2008). This is true for Abdelkrim. He grew up in a HLM complex in a predominately immigrant neighborhood in central France. It was only later, when he attended a school where there were fewer immigrant origin individuals, outside of his neighborhood, that he felt out of place. In this new environment, his difference from others became more tangible to him, causing him to reconceptualize his identity. He now lives in the Malakoff banlieue, just south of Paris, which he describes as better than most banlieues. He prefers living there because the residents seem more authentic than Parisians and he feels more comfortable and welcome. As with his childhood HLM complex, Malakoff is a place where he does not stand out as much.

Though he works and spends a lot of time in Paris, Hicham is closely attached to the banlieue where he lives. He has spent most of his life living in a *cité* in Poissy, a western banlieue about fifteen miles from the center of Paris. His family settled in Poissy because the French car company Peugeot employed his father at a factory there. He describes his neighborhood as special because it is part of an urban renewal program. Hicham fought against the demolition of his public housing complex, which he feels was motivated by racist perceptions of immigrant-origin residents:

> We had a mayor who wanted to destroy the neighborhood, because . . . you have a lot of people of foreign, maghrébin, African origin, and he wanted to eradicate the population. . . . That's what he said: "I no longer want any of you in this neighborhood or in this town." This is a racist person. . . . We had a meeting where he came to present plans for renewal, and at the end he said, "If I had known, I would have brought a translator with me to explain this to you." . . . But we understand French very well. And then he said, "I'm going to ask you to leave the room because we are going to have to ask the cleaning staff to disinfect." He believes that we are germs. He kept saying such violent things.
>
> Author: And what did the residents say?
> Hicham: They revolted. We revolted and we formed a collective. That was in 2005. We fought against him for four years. . . . The apartments, their exterior, everything has deteriorated. Come see. . . . Everything is degraded—the living conditions, there are rats. We had everything. . . . We had the odors from the sewer . . . the smell of piled-up trash, rising almost to the second floor. . . . Oh, yeah, the trashcans—they wouldn't come to empty them. . . . We had no hot water during winter, no heat.
>
> Author: But isn't this illegal?
> Hicham: Yes, it's illegal, and we complained . . . but the government was slow to do anything. . . . They had posted a sign stating that [the *cité*] was going to be demolished. We hired a lawyer and fought to delay demolition until the mayoral election. . . . Now there's a new mayor. He's launched a new plan. The residents are involved in it. We're staying in the neighborhood.[13]

Hicham emphasizes the social cohesion of his neighborhood, despite its problems. "It's like a family here. . . . There's a solidarity. Everyone knows each other. Sure, the living conditions are a bit difficult, but now they're improving. It's getting better." He sees living in his Poissy *cité* as part of who he is, and he hopes to be a role model for others in his community. He attributes the difficulties he has faced in finding a job to being maghrébin. He understands why the frustration of minority youth, led, for example, to the 2005 uprisings. Contrary to what Wacquant (2007) would argue, Hicham could not "pass" in larger French society. His name connotes not only that he lives in one of Paris's beleaguered banlieues, but also his maghrébin ethnic origin, considered inferior to white "native French" identity.

Nadir, a thirty-six-year-old of Algerian origin who works as a journalist for a major television news outlet, is similarly passionate about his *banlieue* and eager to refute its negative depictions in the media. Nadir lives in a Seine-Saint-Denis *cité* near the Stade de France soccer facility, one of the sites of the November 2015 terrorist attacks. Seine-Saint-Denis is directly north of Paris, and generally considered one of Paris's most troubled banlieues (Ichou and Oberti 2014; Kepel et al. 2011; Kiwan 2009; Truong 2015). He has lived there his entire life, save for eight years when he lived in Australia. Nadir describes this community as a typical French *cité*, with lots of immigrant families of modest or poor backgrounds. One day, when I was taking the tram with him from a café to his apartment so he could give me a copy of his memoir, he pointed out the window at all the nonwhite individuals on the street and asked me, rhetorically, how these people could ever see themselves as part of France.

Nadir is well aware of the perceptions others have of banlieue residents and feels it is important to challenge this stigma and set a good example for others in his community. Sitting in his office at the television station, one evening, he explained: "I feel more and more the fact that I live in Seine-Saint-Denis, because it is the poorest département in France, the département of the excluded, the département no one cares about, that we are really just left there." This, of course, influences how he sees himself, not just in France but also in the world:

> That's why I feel solidarity . . . with the blacks who suffer in our country, solidarity with those in Gaza. I feel a solidarity with all who suffer . . . because I lived the same suffering myself when I was a kid. We didn't have money to buy things. We were constantly stopped by the police for no reason, and because we didn't have a lot of opportunities we had the same [kinds of] jobs. And as you can clearly see, there are only whites [in my office]. All the people are white. I am the only one [who's not]. To be honest, it is difficult for me to be proud of my country because today, me, I am doing well, but if there is one person [from the neighborhood] who is doing well, there are still forty others who are not.

Nadir's consciousness as a minority (Meer 2010) is situated both vis-à-vis place and race and ethnic origin and connects him to other minority populations. He distinguishes himself from other residents who have no real attachment to their *cité* and move away as soon as they can, once they have the financial resources to do so. "If everyone who succeeded left the neighborhood," he explains, "only those who could not leave would live there, and that is what creates problems. Then you have a *real* ghetto." Nadir and Hicham are individuals who, though middle-class, continue to live in banlieue communities to which they are attached. This attachment helps them cope with their experiences in predominately white spaces.

Within Paris city limits, the link between place and residence and the marginalization of respondents is also apparent. Mohamed, a thirty-year-old insurance agent of Algerian origin, moved to Paris in 1998 for work and lives in a *quartier populaire* (working-class neighborhood) in the thirteenth arrondissement, near the Porte d'Italie. He explains how his neighborhood is full of people who look like him. "There are many blacks and Arabs, and I like that . . . because I feel like I'm in a familiar element," he explains. Mohamed prefers to live among fellow minorities, rather than in a more bourgeois or middle-class neighborhood with more white residents. As one of the few nonwhites at the insurance office where he works, it is a comfort to make his home among people to whom he can relate. Mohamed's residential environment helps counter the marginalization experiences at his predominately white workplace. He operates within a French code while at work but operates within a maghrébin code at home and in his neighborhood.

Reda, a thirty-two-year-old human resources consultant of Algerian origin, has lived in both Paris and the banlieues. He grew up in in a *quartier populaire* in Meaux, a banlieue in the Seine-et-Marne département near Disneyland Paris and lives in the ninth arrondissement, which he describes as nice and bourgeois. He does not recall feeling different in any way growing up, since he was surrounded by other racial and ethnic minorities. It was only when he moved to Paris that he felt excluded, partly because of his childhood in the banlieues, or ghettos, as he refers to them. He sees himself as "socially marked" because of his connection to the *banlieues*. Reda sees himself as occupying two different worlds—French and Maghrébin—because of he grew up in a predominately Maghrébin environment and currently lives in a predominately white environment.

Nasar has a strong connection to where he lives or has lived. He grew up in Marseille, second to Paris in the number of immigrant-origin residents, and connects his early years in a predominately immigrant environment with his understanding of being an ethnic minority today. He is quick to identify himself as *marsellais*, someone from Marseille; in fact, his coworkers identify him as such. Nasar has fewer issues with his identity than his counterparts, he says, because of his early environment. He did not feel like an outsider growing up in Marseille. Only after moving to Paris for work in 1998 did he first feel like one. The experience of maghrébin friends who grew up in other cities like Paris, Lille, Strasbourg, or in smaller towns did not mirror his own. In Marseille, he says, one was more likely to draw attention for being white than as a racial and ethnic minority:[14]

I remember the newspaper *Le Monde* did a study related to the children of immigrants, and when people were asked, "What are you?" 98 percent of them said *marseillais*. Whether they were children of immigrants or not, they said *marseillais*. I should say that in Marseille there are many emigrants. It is the first French port [from the Mediterranean Sea]. It was the point of entry from the colonies. People here claim to be *marseillais* first of all, so it's for this reason that I see these differences [between Marseilles and other cities]. I don't care if people see me as French or not. As long as I am *marseillais*, I'm fine.

Nasar's insistence on the stark differences between his city of birth and the rest of France provides a coping method of sorts when he confronts challenges as a racial and ethnic minority living in Paris. Should others not recognize him as French, he can assert his *marseillais* identity.

Many respondents have also experienced overt discrimination when searching for housing. Mourad, whom I introduced in the previous section, attempted to rent an apartment and the landlord asked whether he was Muslim. When asked how long his parents had lived in France, Mourad answered thirty years, to which the landlord responded, "Only thirty?" Mourad was not shocked by this exchange. Rather, he says, this is common among his maghrébin peers: "It's simple, really. You're looking for a place, you see an ad, you call, and you don't say you're of Algerian or maghrébin origin. They say, 'Yes, OK, come by and check it out.' And then the day you come . . . [the unit is no longer available]. Or if on the phone you give your name—for example, 'My name is Mohammed' or something like that—then it's 'Oh, I'm sorry, the apartment was just rented by someone else.' It happens all the time."[15]

Safia, a thirty-two-year-old journalist with dual Tunisian and French citizenship, relates a similar story:

> It took my husband and I six months to find housing, and still it was a friend of a friend who rented us his apartment, who was the landlord. But our application file was never taken seriously [by other landlords], though my husband works in finance and I also work. We make enough money. I remember they were asking for three times the rent, and with my salary alone we had enough money. So we had a lot, and they didn't want us. They kept telling us, "We just rented to another couple. It happened quickly." It was always this, or "We changed our mind, we have to do some repairs, so we're not going to rent it." It was always something. And once, an older woman told me very clearly when we checked out an apartment, "Yes, why not?" And when we called again to schedule another viewing of the apartment, she said, "No, you understand, there was a French couple who came, so we rented it to them. It's just easier." And me, I vividly remember feeling disgusted, and I said to her, "But Madame, we are French also." But they were white French. . . . And my husband, it was at that moment . . . he told me, "You see, we have to leave France. We'll never be recognized as normal people, because we both have jobs, but we could find an apartment only through a friend."

Married with two young children, Safia and her husband, a banker and of Algerian origin, rent an apartment in Cergy-Pontoise, a western banlieue They want to buy a house but are already worried that it will be difficult—and not for financial reasons.

The couple demonstrate the paradox of the upward social mobility of children of North African immigrants. Despite their educational and professional successes, they cannot live anywhere even if they can afford it, a difficulty that Safia attributes to being nonwhite or of maghrébin origin. Her experiences of living in France are like those of her immigrant parents, although their material circumstances differ. This affects how Safia locates herself in mainstream society. Her experiences of exclusion place her on its margins. Individuals like Safia are continually denied cultural citizenship across multiple domains, including place and residential location, though her educational attainment and occupational status would seemingly permit integration into mainstream society.

IV. Public Sphere

In addition to other sites of exclusion, the middle-class segment of the maghrébin second generation is denied cultural citizenship in the public sphere. Ahmed experiences this denial when walking through Paris or taking public transportation: "If I'm walking in a bourgeois Parisian neighborhood and an old French lady sees me, she'll cross the street to walk on the other side. . . . I think it's going to take several more generations for people to not see differences like this, for someone to see a black person or an Arab walk by on the street and not even notice it."

This is reminiscent of what Lacy (2007) identifies as "public identities," referring to the ways that black middle-class individuals negotiate racial discrimination in the marketplace, the workplace, and as they engage in other activities in public. The marginalization of racial and ethnic minorities in public space is not unique to France, as research on racial and ethnic minorities in the United States has shown (Anderson 2015; Jackson 2001). What is different about the French context is that racial and ethnic minorities were never segregated from whites by denial of access to public accommodations, as were black Americans and other minorities (Feagin 1991). Still, racial and ethnic minorities in France are devalued and discriminated against in public space in both subtle and explicit ways: their association with low-wage work means they face excessive surveillance when shopping. Race and ethnic origin mark Ahmed and others as outsiders in French society.

When Safia is out for a walk with her young children, she says that people often ask her, "What are your children's origins?" or "Where do you come from?" These questions imply she and her children are not French and not legitimate members of the French Republic. Despite the state's renunciation of racial and ethnic categories, she is a "perpetual foreigner" (Wu 2001).

IMPLICATIONS FOR EXPRESSING DIFFERENCE

At the end of one conversation I had with Hicham, he sighed and said:

> They don't want me. They tell me to integrate. Me, I don't want to integrate. I am French. I don't need to integrate. I was born in France, I respect the laws of the Republic. . . . But they still tell us, "No, you're not French. You'll never be French."

They tell us that because our parents have foreign origins, we automatically do too. . . . We're sometimes obligated to hide our differences, as if we're ashamed of them. But I've arrived at an age when I tell myself, "It's my difference. I am not looking to put it out front, but I don't want people to tell me to hide it."

That is the dilemma of Hicham and many immigrant-origin individuals and racial and ethnic minorities in both France and other plural societies: whatever they do, whatever they accomplish, they are not accepted as full citizens. Salim, a thirty-five-year-old of Moroccan origin and self-described hip-hop journalist, concurs. In his living room in Ivry-sur-Seine, a banlieue south of Paris, he tells me, "In France we have to hide our differences." But how? Salim explains that before he even speaks, people often assume he was born outside of France. Salim often travels to the United States for his work, and he says he was struck that Americans openly wearing hijabs and other religious attire were not, as he saw it, stigmatized for it. He is happy to say that he is French, but in France he does not feel it's true. To him, the French Republican model is hypocritical. Salim grew up in Paris, and he and his family went to Morocco once a year to visit relatives. But he states clearly that "Morocco is not my country." When in Morocco, he was perceived as a foreigner. And in France, he is perceived as a foreigner.

At the end of my interview with Djamila in her office, in the eighth arrondissement, near the Gare Saint-Lazare, the forty-nine-year-old of Algerian origin sighed and said:

I think we see racism more and more these days in France. When I was younger . . . it all seemed normal. . . . I didn't experience it as much as other people. But I do remember hearing "Go back to your country." People thought that. But you know, my country, it's here, so how do you want me to return to [it]? But today [I hear it] even more. . . . I had thought that as I grew older, that would change, that it would subside, that it would fade. We would no longer mark differences or distinguish between people. And I see that we do differentiate. . . . We do it more and more. And I regret that, I find it sad.

Author: Differences like what?

Djamila: For example, there's discrimination. It's not necessary to pretend otherwise. . . . For someone named Rachid Ben Machin, it is difficult to find an internship. . . . It's not only a question of a foreign-sounding name, because there's also a territorial racism. If you live in [the Seine-Saint-Denis département], it's the same thing. . . . You can run into difficulties just because of where you live. We see that every day. . . . But I also believe it's because France has not addressed certain problems in its past. It hasn't always acknowledged its past.

Djamila says, "France belongs to everyone who lives here." She recognizes, however, that this is more theory than practice, as there are barriers to full societal inclusion for maghrébin-origin individuals, even those who are "successful." Djamila feels French. She affirms it as her identity before acknowledging her

Algerian origin. She considers herself as French as any other French person, even if she is made to feel separate and apart from the French nation.

Djamila grew up in the twentieth arrondissement and continues to live there with her partner. She has worked hard to get to her current executive-level position in a membership-based social development association. Yet her success has not shielded her from the same prejudices and mistreatment experienced by her less economically successful North African–origin counterparts. Djamila remains troubled by how immigrant-origin individuals are still considered different, treated as foreigners. The North African second generation grew up in a France that communicated to them—and still communicates to them—that not only are they different, but that they should be ashamed of their difference. They were not and are not considered French, yet many nevertheless assert their French identity.

In the several domains discussed above, my respondents, are repeatedly denied cultural citizenship. They feel their exclusion acutely. Though citizens on paper, they remain outsiders in the society into which they were born. And they acknowledge this status takes a toll over the course of their lives.

4

French Is, French Ain't

Boundaries of French and Maghrébin Identities

I went back to England and I became what I'd been named. I had been hailed as an immigrant. I had discovered who I was. I started to tell myself the story of my migration. Then Black erupted and people said, 'Well, you're from the Caribbean, in the midst of this, identifying myself with what's going on, the Black population in England. You're Black.

—STUART HALL, "OLD AND NEW IDENTITIES, OLD AND NEW
ETHNICITIES"

France is not a race. It is not a religion. It is values!

—BRUNO LEMAIRE, FORMER FRENCH MINISTER OF FOOD, AGRICULTURE,
AND FISHING

Mourad, a thirty-year-old of Algerian origin, moved to Paris in the early 2000s for his doctoral studies in sociology at Sciences Po. He grew up in Tours, near the center of France. He lives alone in the seventh arrondissement, a bourgeois neighborhood not too far from the Eiffel Tower. Neither of his parents went to college, so it will be a significant accomplishment for him to get an education at one of the world's best universities.

When I first met with him at the university café in the Saint-Germain-des-Prés neighborhood, he described what it means to be French:

> There's the theory and there's the practice. . . . There was a French philosopher named Renan who said that every day you have to want to be French.[1] You accept living together. It's a community of the future. . . . For me, being French is a desire, a desire to live together despite our origins. That is the theory, but in practice being French when you are of immigrant origin . . . of Swiss or Swedish or British origin, there isn't a problem. You're viewed as French, and no one talks about integration. However, if you're of maghrébin origin, that's different. There are barriers. And in the eyes of others, you see that you are not always considered French.

66

Though Mourad acknowledges that he is a French citizen, there is a difference between citizenship and the degree to which he personally can identify as French, and have that identity accepted by others. All nonwhite immigrant-origin individuals find themselves in the same position; their white counterparts, despite their immigrant origins, identify as French citizens and are accepted as such. We spoke further about the degree to which Mourad feels he can successfully assert a French identity: "Yes, I feel French, I want to be French, but what's certain is that in the eyes of others, we are not always seen as French. That's the hardest part. . . . If I say yes, I am French, I am French. But I cannot get into a nightclub. If I submit my CV [to apply for employment], I get no response. I'm discriminated [against in] housing. [They tell me] I'm not French."

His otherness is thus assigned. France tells him he is not French and denies him cultural citizenship because of his maghrébin origins. He and others like him do not feel they fit within the boundaries that define a French person, and they find it difficult to negotiate a status that is both maghrébin-origin and French. White citizens clearly have no such difficulty. The invocation of ethnic origin by Mourad and other members of the second generation reflects the boundaries they draw around French and maghrébin identities, as well as the influence of French Republicanism on boundary-making processes.

I discuss below the dual identity of the middle-class North African second generation, which is at once both French and maghrébin. I examine how its members define what it means to be French, and how their perceptions of French identity, and the boundaries around it, are shaped by their own experiences of racial and ethnic marginalization. I examine their insider-outsider status and the salience of their maghrébin origins in their self-identification. Most respondents claim a French identity, but they vary in the degree to which they assert their North African origins. Identity is relational and therefore influenced by how others regard one's claims to it. The rejection of such claims is tantamount to exclusion from the mainstream.

I further unpack the cultural complexity of French identity and its racial and ethnic nature. What does it mean to be French? Can one become French? How can one signify or perform "Frenchness" to others? Because others question whether they belong in France, members of the middle-class North African second generation employ various strategies to assert and justify their French identity. Individuals will point out that, having been educated in France and having spent their entire lives there, they are no different than other citizens. Or they will demonstrate their acceptance of French Republican ideology, even if Republicanism in practice places them on the margins of French society, whatever their accomplishments and despite their middle-class status. For all that, the North African second generation sees itself as part of France's racial and ethnic hierarchy.

FIGURE 2. Covers of two French newsmagazines, *L'Express* and *Le Point*, with features about what it means to be French, at a Parisian newsstand in 2015. Photo by author.

French Republicanism determines how individuals are identified—as French or foreigner. French citizenship or having been born in France do not ensure one's acceptance as French. Children of Maghrébin immigrants formulate their identity in accordance with French Republicanism, yet in their interaction with whites, they experience discrimination and marginalization. Their white counterparts use race and ethnicity to reassert the symbolic boundaries separating insiders and outsiders. American identity is imbued with racial and ethnic meaning, complicating the efforts of racial and ethnic minorities to effectively assert it as their own (without adding a prefix, as in "African American"). Yet in France it is no different. Ethnic categories are not codified by law, and it remains difficult for racial and ethnic minorities to effectively assert a French identity. National ideologies constrain identity options. In the United States, the census defines racial and ethnic categories, whereas in France, Republican ideology does not allow the census to measure race and ethnicity. In a society that does not acknowledge multiculturalism, "doing race/ethnicity" is a negotiation of the private rather than the public sphere (Khanna 2011).

Though identity politics in France and the United States differ, children of immigrants in both countries are pressured to identify according to their ethnic origins rather than base identification on nationality. They are still under an "immigrant shadow" that frames second and subsequent immigrant generations (Zhou and Lee 2007). The title of this chapter is a nod to Marlon Riggs's 1994 documentary, *Black Is . . . Black Ain't*, an examination of the diverse notions of what it means to be a black American.[2] In referring to this title, I highlight how all individuals operate within boundaries of different identities, whatever the heterogeneity within the North African second generation. Demographically speaking, France is quite diverse,[3] but the definition of who is accepted as French is quite narrow.

DEFINING FRENCH IDENTITY AND MARKING ITS BOUNDARIES

About 67 percent of respondents reference French Republican values, including those exemplified in the French motto *Liberté, égalité, fraternité*, when they define what it means to be French. Many respondents were well versed in the tenets of the Republican model and quick to invoke them. Mourad and other middle-class children of North African immigrants distinguish between cultural and legal dimensions when defining French identity, for they are included in the first and excluded in the second. Which is to say that the social locations of many children of maghrébin immigrants are tenuous. When individuals invoke the cultural dimensions of French identity, they reference values, customs, traditions, and practices, as well as the racial and ethnic underpinnings of each of these. Other common definitions include speaking French perfectly, sharing a common destiny and history, and having spent most one's life in France. As Linda, who is of Algerian origin, points out, being French "is not just a plastic card. . . . It's not just being born in France. . . . It's about values and a spirit, a culture, not just the legal things." "Frenchness" thus is not equated with citizenship but involves "cultural markers of birth, ancestry, and accent as well as residence" (McCrone and Bechhofer 2010, 921). These cultural markers are sustained by race, ethnicity, and religious distinctions. French identity is defined by whiteness and the exclusion of immigrant-origin individuals tied to its colonial empire.

Nadir, a thirty-six-year-old Algerian-origin journalist who lives in Seine-Saint-Denis, is one of many respondents who invoke race and ethnicity as marking whether someone is French. "Many people think being French, it's being white, eating pork, going to mass every Sunday morning, being Catholic and so on," he explains. "But . . . for me, being French is simply working in this country, paying taxes. It's just living here." By framing being French in this way—that is, focusing on the legal or technical definition—Nadir actively resists and challenges the racialized nature of French identity, where being white means being French.

Zara, though she acknowledges feelings of difference, believes that participation in everyday life in France qualifies her as French: "Being French is being a citizen, meaning behaving in a citizenlike manner . . . and having the power to decide what happens, via the vote, for example. Being French is having a voice in France, being heard in France, because unfortunately, even with French residence, you are not necessarily treated as if you [are]." Although Zara is marginalized as a "visible minority" (Ndiaye 2008), she nonetheless sees being French as a core, inescapable element of her identity. She does not believe her North African origins should disqualify her in this regard. Rather than defining herself in opposition to French identity, she embraces it.

One winter evening I met Mohamed, a thirty-year-old insurance agent and aspiring journalist of Algerian origin, at the metro stop near the Opéra Bastille. We walked to a nearby café, and en route he asked whether I liked living in Paris and about my overall perceptions of Paris as an African American. He was really fascinated by and curious about my experiences. We sat in the crowded café, sipping glasses of vin chaud (mulled wine), and dressed in a suit, Mohamed, a tall, statuesque man with almond eyes and dark brown, slicked-back hair told me: "For me, being French means to believe in the ideals of France, meaning loving France and all its freedoms, the France of the Enlightenment, the France of equality, the France of universal values. She has values that transcend differences . . . that pierce through [them]. You can be black or white or gray, but . . . you share those values. You can be Muslim, Christian, whatever you want."

In emphasizing values that supersede individual differences, Mohamed draws boundaries around being French that include him, and claims a privilege associated with being French. He sees it as an advantage to live in a democratic and occidental society. As he said in a later conversation: "[Former French president François] Mitterrand once said, 'We are all from the country of our childhood.' To me, that means I spent my childhood here, I didn't spend it elsewhere, and there is no one who can take that from me."

As he grew up, Mohamed's parents continually told him that his home was here in France. Because his parents emphasized this, he feels like he has fewer issues with his identity as an adult than other children of North African immigrants. Mohamed grew up in France, just like any other French person, and therefore this is something that is a part of him. Despite the stigma associated with having maghrébin origins, he still feels fortunate to be French, and to have been raised in France. He sees his dual French and maghrébin status as a richness—both constitute his identity—and believes France's values are what set it apart from other societies.

Aurélien, a thirty-two-year old of Algerian origin who works as a human resources consultant, associates being French with Republican principles of the 1789 *Déclaration des droits de l'homme et du citoyen (Declaration of the Rights of Man and of the Citizen)*. "It's great French men, great authors, Rimbaud, Hugo," says Aurélien, who lives with his wife and baby daughter in Paris. "It is an image and a country in which *Liberté, égalité, fraternité*, would not be vain words." He sees himself as embodying both French and maghrébin cultures, yet coming from a *quartier populaire* in the banlieue of Meaux, he feels marked as different by whites.

Yet as Aurélien, Abdelkrim, and others reference principles of French Republicanism in how they define French identity, they simultaneously critique how such principles are implemented in French society. They do not reject Republicanism as an ideology; rather, they feel it does not apply to them. Because they support French Republicanism, many respondents are fearful about *communautarisme* (communitarianism) in France, or the idea that different groups would interact only with each other and not with people of different identities. Many respondents drew a parallel to American identity politics and multiculturalism. Linda, a twenty-one-year-old medical student of Algerian origin, says, "It's a problem for both [whites and nonwhites], people sticking to people like themselves." She was once in a relationship with a white man and believes that they broke up in part because of the racist views of her ex-boyfriend's family. She remembers his father's obsession with Islam and her Algerian origins. Yet this painful experience demonstrates, Linda says, that "you cannot live in France without interacting with others who are different."

Similarly, Salim, a thirty-five-year-old of Moroccan origin who lives in Ivry-sur-Seine, a banlieue south of Paris, recognizes the good and bad parts of French Republicanism. Under the French Republican model, he says, "We are all the same," but he also finds its implementation hypocritical. Respondents thus critique French society—and often, their own circumstances—within the confines of French Republicanism, but do not establish or seek an alternative framework.

FEELING FRENCH: CLAIMING A PLACE IN FRENCH REPUBLICAN SOCIETY

While racial and ethnic minorities are continually told, both implicitly and explicitly, that they are different from or do not share the values of their white counterparts, they nonetheless reference these same values when defining what it means to be French and see being French as part of their identities. This resembles how marginalized individuals in the United States identify with and relate to the mythologies of being American, such as the American dream, despite their own experiences of racial and ethnic marginalization (Waters 2000; Young 2006).

About 18 percent of respondents consider themselves exclusively French. They privilege their French over their maghrébin ethnic origins in how they view themselves. They acknowledge that they are treated differently from their white counterparts, yet they respond by asserting how they are just as French as any other French person. That is, they follow the Republican model by asserting an identity based on citizenship. They do not believe that their North African origins negate their being French, even if others deny their claims to French identity because of their racial and ethnic status.

Karim, a thirty-five-year-old of Algerian origin, works in Levallois-Perret, a banlieue northwest of Paris, near the seventeenth arrondissement. He was born and raised there and clearly distinguishes between the discourse by which French identity is defined and the reality of who can legitimately lay claim to it. He struggles to do so, for he has repeatedly been told that he does not meet the definition of a French person: "To be French, you must forget yourself a little bit, adopt the behaviors that are imposed on us. There is a path to follow to become French . . . but as a French person of Algerian origin . . . when I'm in France, I don't feel *French* French. . . . France has to accept all French people as they are, and not as they wish they were."

Sitting in a café in Levallois-Perret, Karim becomes increasingly animated:

The French really don't accept us, they tolerate us, that's all. But I have a million more reasons to be here than [then–French president] Nicolas Sarkozy. . . . In the last few centuries, there wasn't a shared history between France and Hungary,[4] right? But between France and Algeria, I mean, we used to be a French colony. . . . But even if I don't want [to be French] . . . even if I say no, it's not true [that I'm not French]. It's a part of me. . . . If not, I wouldn't be here. . . . [I've] said I wasn't French. But I am French, whether they want it or not. . . . That means . . . we're really here. But that's why I say that it would be good if the French [reached out to] us, gave us opportunities. Why can't I, Karim, Algerian—I'm educated, I went to a French school, I'm not dumber than anyone else—how come, when I apply for a job, they pick a French person and not me? The day that changes, we can say France has evolved, but for now, it's not the case, and we are very far away from that.

Despite the colonial relationship between Algeria and France, and though he is a result of that relationship, Karim is treated as not French. He regularly confronts racism, marginalization, and exclusion. Though the French identity he claims inevitably intersects with race and ethnicity, Karim still wants to assert it, even when others refute that assertion. Rather than developing an oppositional identity, he instead asserts his French status and his place in society, even if he is not always proud to identify as French and others do not acknowledge that identification.

Soumeya, a forty-nine-year-old divorcée of Algerian origin who has spent her entire life in Paris, is one example:

I never pose that question to myself. People ask me all the time what my origins are. So I say I'm Parisian, I'm French. And then they ask me, "But what are your *origins?*" Because you have a name that sounds different, strange. . . . I don't claim an Algerian identity. I'm French. I see myself as French. . . . Some people say, "I'm French of maghrébin origin," but . . . it's stupid to say you're French of this or that origin. . . . We're all humans. . . . No one ever asks someone named Sylvie Dupont what her origins are, even though she [has] them. . . . When people talk to me about Algeria, I always shock them, even my own mother, because I say my country is France. It will always be France.

Soumeya believes she is French because she was born and raised in France. This is the only relevant criterion. She rejects any relationship to her parents' country of origin, and she does not understand why other descendants of immigrants would insist on one. Like Soumeya, many respondents grew up in families that did not emphasize their connections to the Maghreb and, as a result, have a weaker relationship with their parents and with their parents' country of origin.

Soumeya is unwilling to deny her "Frenchness" and considers herself no less French than a white person, even in the face of her differential treatment by others as a North African–origin individual. She maintains that those who question her French identity or refuse to accept it are in the wrong. She believes in French Republican ideology but attributes racism and discrimination to the failure to implement it. For all that, Soumeya can imagine a France without racism where all citizens are equal.

Other respondents claim French identity in the absence of strong ties to any other. Sonia is a single thirty-year-old of Algerian origin, has a doctorate in economics, and owns a home in the northern banlieue of Le Bourget. "Being French is something so deeply inside of me that I cannot separate it out," she says. Sonia's privileging of a French identity stems from her life experiences. Though she has spent her entire life in the Seine-Saint-Denis département, she does not feel particularly attached to where she lives. Nor is she affiliated with any religion. Sonia felt different growing up in Le Bourget—not from whites, but from other maghrébin individuals. Her parents were literate and fluent in French, which set her family apart from other maghrébin families. As a child, she had more educational opportunities and always excelled academically, which contributed to her sense of difference. Now she has had a successful career working for an association that advocates for rural workers. She has not been to Algeria since she was sixteen years old. "I know it sounds bad, but I don't feel any affinity for Algeria," she says. "I have no desire to go back. It doesn't mean anything to me." These sentiments may be partially explained by her estrangement from both her parents and her four older siblings. She has not spoken to them in years.

Nacira, a twenty-five-year-old biology teacher at a high school of Algerian origin, connects her claim to French identity with her experiences as a student and teacher. The older she gets, the more she accepts herself as French: "For me, [being French] is really bound to where you did your studies, and I realize that the references that I have are references linked to the French Republic. When I think, I think in French. When I dream, I dream in French. Even if the French system has its faults, it also has its advantages. . . . For me, being French is bound to the education you get in this country. . . . When I teach, I teach how a French teacher teaches, with the same tools, the same resources, etc."

Nacira references the ontological nature of French identity, which exists from birth and cannot be denied. Her French identity does not, however, preclude a critique of how French Republicanism is practiced, particularly of the inequalities she sees between schools in bourgeois areas of Paris and those in the Seine-Saint-Denis département where she teaches.[5]

Yacine is a thirty-three-year-old of Algerian origin and the divorced father of a seven-year-old daughter. An IT freelancer, he lives in the western banlieue of Asnières-sur-Seine. He, too, links his French citizenship to his educational experience. As a child, he attended what he refers to as a "Republican school." His socialization there as a French person ties him to his compatriots: "I had the same scholarly training as most French people, so I think we are the same group, in theory. Yes, we each have our own paths, but me, I consider myself as French as anyone else." Though Yacine grew up as one of the only maghrébin-origin individuals in his community, he never identified as anything else but French. He thus invokes his educational trajectory to insert himself within the boundaries of a French identity. But he acknowledges an anti-maghrébin racism that is particularly acute when it comes to employment opportunities in mid- and upper-level positions, and feels he has been treated differently because of his North African origins.

Loubna, a twenty-seven-year-old of Moroccan origin, laid claim to a French identity when she realized how much her life in France had shaped her. "If I had grown up in Morocco, I would be completely different [as would] my ways of thinking. . . . So, yes, I would say I am French," to the point that she distances her-self from her Moroccan counterparts. Diana, a twenty-four-year-old of Algerian origin who lives south of Paris with her parents, identifies as French above all else, though her values may differ because of her ethnic origin. "I was born here," she says. "I grew up here. I speak French. I have Algerian origins, but I definitely feel French before I feel Algerian. When I speak, I'll speak in French. I can sort of speak Arabic, but not well."

FEELING MAGHRÉBIN: INVOKING ETHNIC ORIGINS

These citizen outsiders invoke their maghrébin origins as part of their iden-tity in different ways. The distinction between assigned and asserted identities complicates identity-formation processes for the middle-class French second generation. The racial and ethnic hierarchy in France means that that nonwhite individuals are not considered French. A claim to French identity by children of North African immigrants is not accepted. They are denied cultural citizenship and their rightful place as French citizens. In short, the North African second generation has no ethnic options (Waters 1990); it cannot dictate the salience of its ethnic origin to the perception of other citizens. For its members, that salience is critical to how they see and understand themselves in French society and how their North African origins intersect with their French status in defin-ing their identity.

Many children of North African immigrants get their first lesson in what it means to be French when they begin school in predominately white neighbor-hoods. They learn at an early age that they are not French, a continually lesson reinforced when they reach adulthood. Their differing responses to discrimination and marginalization determine how they invoke their ethnic origins, how they define their identity, and how they position themselves in French society.

The invocation of ethnic origins by the middle-class maghrébin second gen-eration is contextual and varies. Neither this generation nor its middle-class segment is monolithic. That is, there is a continuum and no prescriptive cat-egories. Most individuals identify in a way that acknowledges their French and maghrébin status, highlighting the space between the categories of French and other. This includes adopting a hyphenated and combined identity, viewing one-self as neither French nor maghrébin, or viewing oneself as only maghrébin.[6] Their relationship to parents and country of origin, as well as to childhood and educational and work experiences, influences how respondents invoke their North African origins.

Inevitably, these contribute to consciousness of one's ethnic minority status in France, as do interaction with and the mutual influence of ethnic community members, culture, and the state.[7] This phenomenon is also seen in the emergence of a Muslim consciousness in the United Kingdom, which challenges existing notions of assimilation and informs identity-related claims-making among British Muslims (Meer 2010), and of DuBois's ([1903] 1994) notion of a minority double consciousness, or the "second-sight" African Americans possess.

HYPHENATED AND COMBINED IDENTITY—FRENCH AND MAGHRÉBIN

Many respondents see being French and having North African origins as coconstitutive elements of their identity. Noura, a thirty-seven-year-old single mother of Algerian origin who works as a nurse's assistant, says: "To be French is to have French citizenship. I don't know if I feel completely French. It's complicated. When people ask me what I am, I say I am French of Algerian origin." Her Algerian origins play the greater role in her daily experiences. Noura is more comfortable with her hyphenated identity in the *quartier populaire* of the nineteenth arrondissement where she lives, than she was when she lived in Deux-Sèvres, a département in western France. Noura describes her current neighborhood as having a "Brooklyn element" to it because there are so many immigrant-origin residents. She identifies as French of Algerian origin because she acknowledges that being technically French—having French citizenship—does not mean others will accept her as French. France, through macrolevel structures and microlevel interactions, "others" people like her.

When Noura's young children experience racism or discrimination, she finds it difficult to explain to them that others do not regard them as French. She told me that her eight-year-old son's teacher is racist, holding the boy's darker skin color against him. Her seven-year-old daughter is spared such racism because her lighter skin allows her to pass as white. To Noura, this is one of many examples that demonstrate the salience of race and ethnicity in how individuals are treated in France.

Of the individuals in this study, about 44 percent have adopted a hyphenated or combined identity like Noura. Respondents identify as French of maghrébin origin, French of Tunisian origin, French of Algerian origin, and French of Moroccan origin. Those constructions mirror the strategy of Asian Americans and African Americans in the United States, whose American identity is contingent upon acknowledging their racial or ethnic origins. But it should be noted that the French part of the hyphenated identity always precedes the maghrébin origin, such as Français d'origine marocaine (French person of Moroccan origin) or Français d'origine maghrébine (French person of maghrébin origin). That in effect foregrounds French identity, obstructing the full fusion of French and maghrébin. In a country that does not acknowledge ethnic origins in identity construction, some members of the French North African second generation turns to a hybrid identity, or ethnic hybridity (Jiménez 2010), that incorporates both.

When Linda, a twenty-one-year-old medical student who lives with her parents in the western banlieue of Rueil-Malmaison, visits her Algerian relatives every few years, she is made aware of how French she is. "My life," she says, "would be completely different if my name were Fatima." Linda identifies as French of Algerian origin, but her name and features do not immediately convey her North African origin. She tells the story of a patient who had to go to another hospital for tests. When he returned, he told her that his stay there was unpleasant, as his roommate was Algerian. Besides being offended, she found it ironic that her patient did not realize that Linda herself was of North African origin.

She grew up in a mainly white neighborhood, and her parents wanted her to fit in with the other children. So she celebrated Christmas, though she was and remains a practicing Muslim.[8] As an adult, Linda is ambivalent about her position. She is successful and will soon become a doctor. She plans to move to Paris and share an apartment with a friend. But, she says, "I sometimes feel guilty that I have made it when so many others like me have not."

Some respondents say they occupy separate French and maghrébin cultural worlds simultaneously. Diana, a twenty-four-year-old graduate student in communications with dual Algerian and French citizenship, grew up in Orsay, a predominately white banlieue south of Paris and a more economically advantaged banlieue than most.[9] She lives there with her parents in an HLM complex supported by the factory where her father, now retired, used to work. "I used to feel closer to the French mentality than to the maghrébin mentality," she says. "And I think that's an effect of living in Orsay. . . . There just aren't many foreigners there. There are many French people. It's a really nice neighborhood with a high standard of living."

As a child, Diana does not remember being particularly interested in Algerian or maghrébin culture. But when she entered her teen years, she set out to learn more about it, sought out connections with other maghrébin youth online, and developed a deeper attachment to her origins. Diana is now well versed in her French and maghrébin identity and appreciates how both elements made her who she is: "There are parts of the maghrébin culture that I value, for example, the strong family ties and large families. . . . But there are also parts of French and Western culture that I value, such as gender parity and feminism."

She now has as many white friends as maghrébin but acknowledges the differing perspectives of the two. Diana considers her parents as modern as those of her white friends' parents and more modern than the parents of her maghrébin friends. She feels comfortable dating white men and would not hesitate to marry one (two of her sisters married whites). However, she knows that some maghrébin friends do not understand why she would date someone who is of different origin. Though her parents would be happy if she did marry a maghrébin man, they do not insist on it. "They would have stayed in Algeria if [marrying an Algerian man] were a requirement," she says.

Diana affirms the French and maghrébin elements of her identity in a context in which North African–origin individuals are defined as nonwhite, and therefore not French, and at the bottom of the racial and ethnic hierarchy. Her lighter skin and name mask her North African origins, which has allowed her to evade, to a degree, the discrimination experienced by her maghrébin-origin friends. One of them had considerable difficulty finding a job after finishing engineering school. Diana does not anticipate the same fate once she completes her studies: her résumé does not betray her origins. Though Diana recognizes the prevalence of racism in French society, she has been confronted it less than others like her because she is not as visible as an ethnic and racial minority.

A combined French and maghrébin identity may also be viewed as the simultaneous possession of two separate cultures. Hicham, a twenty-nine-year-old with dual Moroccan and French citizenship who lives in a public housing high-rise building with his parents and three of his brothers in Poissy, puts it this way: "There is a real gap between us, people of immigrant origin, and those who are of pure French origin, . . . and we can understand them because we have this double culture. At home we were raised in a maghrébin way and at school we are educated in the ways of the French Republic."

As discussed in chapter 3, Hicham and others know how to operate in two worlds. This is comparable to the bridging of different cultural worlds by African Americans through code-switching and behavior-switching (Jackson 2001; Pattillo-McCoy 1999). Here, respondents access different codes in different spheres (home, school, and work) and cultural worlds.

As Hicham grew up, his parents emphasized the importance of the family's ties to maghrébin culture through annual summer trips to Morocco. They also cultivated in him a love and appreciation for French laïque (secular) society, underlining the freedoms it affords, freedoms not available in the Maghreb. Hicham sees the value in being fluent in multiple codes but is nonetheless repeatedly reminded of his difference from others, such as when he was fired from his bank job and his white coworkers were not. Hicham reluctantly accepts the limitations of having to navigate two worlds. His lighter complexion makes it sometimes easier for him to pass as white in public spaces, but his name gives him away as maghrébin.

Soria, a thirty-four-year-old Muslim of Algerian origin, owns a condo in the fifteenth arrondissement and has worked as a human resources director since 2000. She grew to appreciate how maghrébin and French cultures are equally implicated in her sense of self. After an extended trip she took to Algeria at the age of sixteen, she began to assert elements of her Algerian culture. As an adult, she has been involved in many cultural organizations and activist causes concerning maghrébin-origin individuals and immigrants in France. She has organized group travel to the Maghreb for an association and participated in demonstrations in solidarity with Palestine. Soria makes it a point to assert the maghrébin and Algerian component of her identity, partly to refute misconceptions associated with maghrébin-origin individuals. She rarely introduces herself as French; rather, she claims she is an "Arabe de France":

> Soria: When I introduce myself like that, it's not a rejection [of French culture]. Not at all. But it's obvious I'm French. I grew up here. When people who aren't French, especially Arabs, ask me, I always tell them, "My culture is also French, it's true. I have a double culture, but I express myself in French. Even if I speak Arabic, the language I express myself the best in is French." And if I travel abroad tomorrow, it will be the French element . . .
> Author: So you feel you'll be perceived more as a French person than as an Algerian?
> Soria: Yes, exactly, even if I feel intensely Algerian as well.

Soria's attachment to being maghrébin does not negate her attachment to being French and living in France.[10] For these individuals, the one does not negate the other and vice versa.

NEITHER FRENCH NOR MAGHRÉBIN

One winter afternoon, I met Termoul in a café in Les 3 Fontaines, a large shopping mall in Cergy-Préfecture. Twenty-eight years old and possessing dual citizenship, he lives in in the northwestern banlieue of Pontoise with his wife and two young children and works in a bank in Paris. He speaks of alienation. "[Second-generation North African immigrants] don't have an identity," he told me. "No one thinks we're French in France, and no one thinks we're Arab in Algeria." Travel to Algeria influenced his view of himself as neither French nor maghrébin, but rather an occupant of some space between the two. He visits his in-laws and extended family there annually and wants his children to learn Arabic in their "native environment," but he nonetheless feels like a foreigner there. And also in France.

About 20 percent of respondents see themselves as neither North African nor French. While gender is not a significant determining factor in any of the other identity configurations, more men than women described themselves in this way. Their sense of otherness leaves them between two cultures.

Or, as Ahmed, a twenty-nine-year-old practicing Muslim with dual Algerian and French citizenship, puts it, "We are sitting between two chairs." He adds: "I am a manager at my company. I drive an expensive car. I go to a club . . . but cannot get in, and then I return to reality. You are never 100 percent either way. Maybe I am asking for too much, wanting to be both 100 percent Algerian and 100 percent French. But I can't choose between them. I want to combine the best parts of both into something great, but . . . I still feel different."

Ahmed cannot reconcile his North African and French components. He has attained middle-class status, but despite his success, he feels he does not fit into French society. At the same time, he does not necessarily relate to other Algerian-origin individuals, particularly those who are working-class. Ahmed remains close to his parents and six older sisters, and lives in Nanterre so he can be near them. He has traveled to Algeria to visit his relatives every year since he was a child. One of his sisters has spent most of her life in Algeria with her godparents, and Ahmed believes her sense of self is very different as a result. But Ahmed himself feels he is labeled as "other" in the two cultural worlds he occupies.

Ahmed poses a contrast to Diana, whom I discussed earlier and who identifies with both French and maghrébin cultures, revealing a heterogeneity in how children of immigrants invoke their North African origins. He is well educated, successful, and actively involved in maghrébin organizations, and has close familial relationships and several maghrébin-origin friends and acquaintances. But like Hicham and Abdelkrim, Ahmed had two different and opposing educations as a child—one at home and one at school. And his adult experience in the workplace was one of differential treatment. In contrast to Diana, who claims a combined French and maghrébin identity, Ahmed feels he has none.

Like Ahmed, Mona, who is thirty-four years old and also of Algerian origin, straddles two different cultural worlds. Dual French and Algerian citizenship (she was born in Algeria and immigrated to France when two years old) has made her feel neither French nor Algerian. "It's just a fact," she says. "You're not really one or the other." She views the two as in opposition to each other. Mona grew up in a middle-class neighborhood in the seventeenth arrondissement of Paris but lives in the banlieue of Épinay-sur-Seine, in the Seine-Saint-Denis département, where it is less expensive. A business manager who works in Paris, she is involved with the same maghrébin networking and business association as Ahmed.

Sofiane, a twenty-six-year-old with dual French and Algerian citizenship, lives with his wife in a *cité* in the impoverished banlieue of La Courneuve. Of his neither French nor maghrébin status he says:

> For me, being French is many things. . . . I'm French. I'm also Algerian because I have double nationality. But being French means being included in French society . . . living in this society, being responsible, representing your country, doing everything you can do so that your country does well. For me, that's what being French is. . . . It's everyone having the same rights, which is not yet the case here, because when you live in Neuilly-sur-Seine [an upper-class banlieue] or in La Courneuve, it's not the same thing. . . . I don't really have an identity, as I was born to parents who are foreigners. When I go to Algeria, they say I'm a foreigner. When I'm in France, they say I'm the son of immigrants, which really means I'm neither French nor Algerian. I'm between the two.

Here, Sofiane claims French identity by referencing the Republican model, which acknowledges his citizenship. But only to a degree, for he does not feel included in

French society, and he attributes that to the failure of France to practice Republican principles. Sofiane feels he has no identity. He travels to Algeria annually, owns two houses there, and enjoys its different way of life. Still, he feels like a foreigner there. His treatment in France is comparable. As a resident of a much-maligned *cité*, he feels marginalized. Residents of La Courneuve face exclusion from French society. "France is one of the most diverse countries in the world, but it has a big problem with racism," he says. "France has a bad history with immigrants. They are happy to use them when they need them but just discard them afterword."

Ahmed, Mona, and Sofiane are thus constantly reminded of their difference. Others do not consider them French, denying their cultural citizenship. And they cannot claim an identity based solely on their Maghrebin-origin status. They draw strict boundaries around what it means to be French and what it means to be Maghrébin, yet they do not fit within them. Unable to define themselves as French *or* maghrébin, without any sense of belonging, they are people without identities.

ONLY MAGHRÉBIN

About 5 percent of respondents identify solely as maghrébin, even if they have French citizenship and have spent their entire lives in France. Hamama, a thirty-five-year-old practicing Muslim of Algerian origin, told me, "Just because I was born in France does not make me French. I am not like my parents who immigrated here, who chose to come here. I did not choose where I was born, where I grew up." Though she does not reject French society, she has no affinity for it. Fortunately for her, that claim to a singular maghrébin identity has not been a hindrance. Hamama studies health policy at Sciences Po and works as a hospital director in the western banlieue of Plaisir. Not identifying as French does not inhibit her ability to succeed in French society. Her success is self-evident.

Farid, a thirty-two-year-old with dual Algerian citizenship who lives in the southwestern banlieue of Melun with his wife and two young children, also completely rejects a French identity. When he was very young, Farid's parents would tell him, "You're not French. We live in France, but you're Algerian. There's no difference between your family here and your family in Algeria." Clearly, Farid got the message: "It is impossible, impossible for me to say that I'm French." His parents instilled in him a love and appreciation for Algeria, which takes precedence over any attachment to French society.

BECOMING FRENCH?
THE CONTINUING SIGNIFICANCE OF RACE AND ETHNICITY

The example of former French president Nicolas Sarkozy offers a different perspective on the intersection of national and ethnic-origin identities. Born in France to a Hungarian immigrant father and French mother, Sarkozy's immigrant origin posed no barrier to his presidential campaign or ascension to the French presidency. He had become French and was never considered anything else. Such success is almost unimaginable for an individual of Algerian, Moroccan, or Tunisian origin. He or she would not be considered a legitimate member of the French Republic.

Farid is a thirty-two-year-old of Algerian origin who lives in the southwestern banlieue of Melun with his wife and two young children. He feels that, were Sarkozy to acknowledge his immigrant origins, it would benefit all immigrants and perhaps widen the definition of French identity. Sabri recalled how Sarkozy once likened himself to Obama in an interview, on the grounds that both were second-generation immigrants, though Sabri noted that "the son of a white immigrant is not the son of a black immigrant. It's not the same thing."

In this chapter, I have painted the portrait of a group of individuals who for the most part see themselves as French but are continually told they are not. I have highlighted how the middle-class French North African second generation learns of and interprets its difference and responds to its marginalization, a phenomenon first experienced in childhood. In France, North African–origin individuals and other visible minorities are racialized. They occupy the bottom of France's ethnoracial hierarchy. Such is France's continual racial project, in which distinctions among citizens based on visible and socially meaningful differences are reinforced.

There exists in France a fear that identity-based groups will desire self-segregation and separation from others, yet as I have shown, individuals of maghrébin origin, viewed by others as different, still wish to be considered French. Their attachment to their maghrébin origins do not negate their attachment to French society. The social separation they experience is not one of desire, but of circumstance. Many middle-class maghrébin-origin individuals are racialized as nonwhite but still see themselves as French. But ethnic origins remain salient, and they are denied a French identity.

Contrasting citizenship and nationhood in Germany and France, Brubaker (1992) states that France has a territorially inclusive principle, or civic notion of citizenship, while Germany's is based on ethnicity. In theory, French identity is accessible to any citizen. But racial and ethnic minorities, particularly those connected to former French colonies, find that identity out of reach. The experience of this population proves that the symbolic boundaries around French identity are not malleable. Respondents may assert their French identity, and they and they may say they are French when questioned about their background, but that is the extent of their agency. There is a distinction between the identities they assert and the identities they are assigned.

By focusing on second-generation individuals who are racial and ethnic minorities, I show that citizenship does not confer the same benefits on other populations as it does on whites. Like their immigrant parents before them, children of immigrants experience marginalization. They are denied cultural citizenship and excluded from the imagined community of France, yet members of the North African second generation are faithful to the French Republican model and do not cultivate an oppositional consciousness or identity. Rather, they seek to reconcile how they see themselves and how others see them. Even as they wrestle with what being French means and attempt to determine their place as an ethnic minority in French society, they still wish to claim French identity and be accepted as such by others. In the meantime, they inhabit a marginal social location. The distinction between their assigned versus asserted identities allows these individuals to continue to identify as French—but with a caveat.

5
_____

Boundaries of Difference

Cultural Citizenship and Transnational Blackness

"Dirty nigger!" Or simply, "Look, a Negro!"
—FRANTZ FANON, *BLACK SKIN, WHITE MASKS*

One sometimes has the strange impression of upsetting others by being black in a country that thinks of itself as white.
—RAMA YADE, *NOIRS DE FRANCE*[1]

Of Antillean origin, he has lived in Bordeaux for many years, so he's a European. But he is black; so he is a Negro. There is a conflict. He does not understand his own race, and whites do not understand him.
—FRANTZ FANON, *BLACK SKIN, WHITE MASKS*

After a long discussion in a Starbucks with Nasar, a thirty-two-year-old of Algerian origin who works for the French Soccer Federation, he asked me some of the same questions I had posed to him. How do I see my identity? I said I identify as black American or African American. "But what does that actually mean to you?" he asked. "Why not just say you're American?" I answered that, for me, being African American implies a link to the African diaspora, especially the forced migration of West Africans to the United States for enslavement.

"But what if I put you in the same room with a white American, a white person from Tanzania, and a black person from Tanzania," he challenged. "Who do you think you'd have the most in common with?" Before I could respond, he answered for me: "You'd have the most in common with the white American, not anyone in Tanzania or anywhere else in Africa. That is because you are American."

As Nasar points out even if I am not always treated as an American or as American as any other American, I would still have the most in common with white Americans because we share a national identity. In the same discussion,

84

Nasar acknowledges that he has been treated differently from others because he is not white and is a racial and ethnic minority, but it does not make him less French. He does not negate being French, even if that identity can be difficult to assert, for he is denied cultural citizenship. He is not ashamed of his Algerian origins, and in his mind, they do not make him less French than others. Even if French identity has racial and ethnic underpinnings, Nasar and his counterparts, though marked as different and treated differently because of their race and ethnic origin, still identify as French. Nasar sees me in the same light. He knows I am a racial and ethnic minority in the United States, but that doesn't make me any less an American.

While my conversation with Nasar, including his hypothetical scenario, was a bit jarring, it was also illustrative of how the middle-class maghrébin second generation thinks about the relationship between nation-based identity and racial and ethnic identity, and more specifically the relationship between race and the nation. For Nasar, his lower rank in a racial and ethnic hierarchy does not negate his attachment to his nation-based identity.

In this chapter, I discuss the varied ways respondents marshal blackness, including a transnational blackness connecting them to black populations elsewhere, and the experiences of racial and ethnic minorities in other societies, to understand, and sometimes challenge, the racial and ethnic hierarchy of which they are a part. Most of these individuals see their interests and experiences as aligned with black populations, even if they do not want a French reclamation of an American or other model of identity politics.

Beyond demonstrating how race functions as a basis for the marginalization of and denial of cultural citizenship to the North African second generation, I argue that the connections made by French racial and ethnic minorities with other racial and ethnic minority populations worldwide, including black Americans and Palestinians, are part of France's racial project. Such ties allow respondents to make sense of their social locations. In a society that does not recognize racial and ethnic difference, identification with others contributes to the consciousness of their ethnic minority status. It is also a "diasporic consciousness" (Smith 2014), in that they see themselves as sharing the struggles against racial and ethnic inequalities that other populations confront. Such connections are especially valuable to respondents in a nation where there is no accepted and legitimate language for discussing race and ethnicity in society, a nation that purports colorblindness yet exhibits racial and ethnic consciousness (Keaton 2010). In the absence of such language, respondents look to other societies, including the United States, to understand the racism and exclusion they face.

Blackness operates as a socially constructed vessel of otherness. Respondents develop a consciousness of what it means to be subsumed in this vessel, and use it to make sense of their position on the margins of French society. That consciousness connects them to black and other minority populations across the globe.

I argue that the conception of blackness they invoke builds upon French historian Pap Ndiaye's (2008) notion of "transnational blackness" and Tommie Shelby's (2002) notion of "thin blackness." For members of the maghrébin second generation, the diaspora and transnational blackness apply to them as well.

SHARED EXPERIENCES, SHARED OPPRESSIONS

Abdelkrim, a journalist of Algerian origin, believes his own experience parallels that of Malcolm X, whose autobiography he has read (X and Haley 1965). He is inspired by accounts of Dr. Martin Luther King Jr. and the Black Panthers and how they responded to racial oppression. Even as a young student, he wanted to be a journalist. He remembers a white teacher who told him as an adolescent that he would never be good enough to realize this aspiration. It is one of his earliest memories of being treated differently because of his maghrébin origin.

"Maybe it wasn't false at the time," Abdelkrim says. "Maybe I didn't have the grades that would have allowed me to follow that path. . . . But it reminds me of the day of when Malcolm X said to his teacher that he wanted to be a lawyer and his teacher responded that "you are a negro and you will never be anything but a carpenter." Here, Abdelkrim accesses the framework of another marginalized population—African Americans—to make sense of his own experiences and position in an ethnoracial hierarchy. It brings to mind another respondent, Nadir, who in chapter 3 expresses his solidarity with blacks and Palestinians because of his experience in Seine-Saint-Denis and as the only nonwhite person in his office.

But the connections he makes to black Americans are not just historical. "The media here always encourages negative portrayals of blacks and Maghrébins," he says. "It's the same thing the media does to blacks in the United States." He gestures in my direction, assuming I immediately understood the reference. When he and I discuss the 2005 banlieue uprisings, he again draws a parallel between maghrébin-origin individuals and black Americans and other racial and ethnic minorities: "The problems of the police in the banlieues are like the problems between the police and blacks, African Americans. . . . These uprisings involved all of France, because we share a common destiny . . . being a minority, being a child of an immigrant . . . [and they are] just like uprisings throughout the world." Abdelkrim and other children of North African immigrants make sense of being a racial and ethnic minority in France by viewing their experiences in a broader context.

Respondents closely followed the 2008 presidential campaign in the United States and wondered what Barack Obama's election might mean for them. In October 2008, there was a *débat* (panel discussion) entitled "Barack Obama: Un modèle pour les minorités dites visibles en France?" (Barack Obama: A model for so-called visible minorities in France?) at the Nanterre Association. Many in attendance were of North African and sub-Saharan African origin. Mamadou, a thirty-six-year-old of Algerian origin and association director, was enthusiastic about the new president: "We are all really excited about Obama. It's such a good symbol for minorities here, especially because his father is African." The general sentiment of that evening's *débat* was that Obama's election would be a positive and encouraging symbol to minorities in France and throughout the world, and that it would also serve to change perceptions of African-origin individuals everywhere. Almost every time I visited the Nanterre Association that fall, Mamadou or someone else would ask me about Obama. What did I think of him? What did I know about him? Was I going to vote for him? Did I think he could win? As an African American from Chicago, I was expected to respond positively and say I was happy he was running for president and hopeful that he would win. The prospect of the first black president often led to discussions about such a prospect in France and what would have to change to make that a reality. If it could happen in the United States, could it happen here in France? Many saw the civil rights movement in the United States as leading to Obama's election and wondered if France needed its own civil rights movement to produce its version of Obama.

In January 2009, I watched the president's inauguration on a television at the Nanterre Association. Several of the children could barely focus on their homework—much to Mamadou's chagrin—because they were so captivated by watching him being sworn in, with his wife, Michelle, by his side. At one point, Mamadou said, somewhat jokingly, "Obama is more my president than Sarkozy!" Clearly, he identified far more with the black American president than with his own. Obama's story resonates not just because of his African-born father, but also because of his life story and upward mobility: he grew up with a single mother and was elected to the highest post in American government. His extraordinary move up the social ladder was really striking to many interlocutors.

At one point, Hafid, another director at the Nanterre Association, who is thirty-six years old and also of Algerian origin, told me, "While it'd be great to have [a black president] in France, it's much easier . . . in the United States. . . . There are more possibilities for blacks there." Though my respondents share with their American counterparts a history of racial oppression and hope to follow their lead and overcome it, like them, they are not necessarily sanguine about the prospect of a minority president in France.

ARE MAGHRÉBIN-ORIGIN INDIVIDUALS BLACK? DIASPORIC CONNECTIONS AND TRANSNATIONAL BLACKNESS

This was a question often posed to me, either literally or rhetorically, when I discussed my research with others.[2] It is useful, therefore, to consider the meaning of *black* and *blackness* in France and Europe more generally.

In *Black Skin, White Masks*, Frantz Fanon (1967), the Martinique-born psycho-analyst who would later support the Algerian Revolution through his involvement in the National Liberation Front, writes about French colonialism's codification of different statuses for whites and nonwhites: colonizing whites are superior; colonized blacks are inferior. Fanon details how his blackness and skin color are more important to others than any other facet of his identity. He is not viewed by whites as a doctor but as a black man who is a doctor. His visible otherness always comes first. Blackness, he writes, is "overdetermined from without." And "France is a racist country, for the myth of the bad nigger is part of the collective uncon-sciousness" (92). To be seen as black—as a "Negro"—contrasts with being French, or even European. This is an opposition with which the North African second generation is all too familiar.

Moreover, blackness functions as a "social uniform," setting individuals racialized as black apart from others or from mainstream society. The assign-ment of racialized identity experienced by maghrébin-origin individuals in France connects them to black populations elsewhere. Historian Tyler Stovall (2009) points to the convergence of black lives in the United States and France. Fanon himself makes this connection: "In America, Negroes are segregated. In South America, Negroes are whipped in the streets, and Negro strikers are cut down by machine-guns. In West Africa, the Negro is an animal" (1967, p. 113). Blackness is defined as otherness, outside the norm, an identity forced upon or assigned to individuals rather than chosen. Even if maghrébin-origin individuals do not identify as black, they nonetheless reflect a consciousness situated in and informed by blackness. This is a blackness defined as a vessel of otherness or of not belonging, or having a rightful place, in mainstream society. Blackness has historically been framed as a permanent otherness and inferiority in Western society (Wright 2004).

Children of North African immigrants in France are engaged in a transnational project allowing them to connect to the past and present realities of black popu-lations worldwide, including black Americans. This is an important distinction between identifying *as* black and identifying *with* the black American experience or experiences of other black populations. In her ethnography of second-gener-ation South Asian Americans, Sharma (2010) discusses the diasporic sensibility of these "desis," which reflects a "racialized consciousness that emphasizes com-monality formed in the negotiation of difference among people of color" (3–4). Minority and marginalized populations may thus feel a sustained and genuine connection to blackness through, among other commonalities, similar expe-riences of inequality, without self-identifying as black. In the case of the North African second generation, this connection to blackness is an expression of their position at the bottom of the ethnoracial hierarchy in French society. "Othered," marginalized, and excluded because of their racial and ethnic status, and without a language or discourse to discuss it, they look elsewhere to make sense of their lives: "With their national belonging perpetually in question, blacks in Europe often seek out diasporic resources that originate in other parts of the black world" (Brown 2009, 13).

Sharma's (2010) theory of "making race," and the global race consciousness of her respondents, is also instructive here, for it conceptualizes how individuals reject and incorporate the language of other racial and ethnic groups.[3] Children of North African immigrants grow up as racial and ethnic minorities in a society that does not recognize that status. As a result, in effect they "make race" through their experiences of racialization. The consciousness thus gained allows them to connect to black populations and other racial and ethnic minorities.

North African–origin individuals' self-identification *as* black is less relevant than the assignment of blackness to them as a category, one forcing them to continually justify themselves as legitimate members of society. Fanon writes of this as well: "The European has a fixed concept of the Negro, and there is nothing more exasperating than to be asked: 'How long have you been in France? You speak French so well' " (1967, 35). Blacks in France are not considered *of* France. "French" identity is positioned as nonracial, but they—and members of the North African generation—are considered neither as white nor French. Most respondents understand being a racial and ethnic minority in France through an understanding of, or reckoning with, blackness. This connection is particularly valuable in a context that does not recognize minorities based on race and ethnicity. Such blackness "continues to constitute not just a historical but also a contemporary otherness" (Smith 2006, 423).

The question of what blackness means to the maghrébin second generation is situated in a larger discourse concerning black France, black Europe, and black Paris (Boittin 2012; Boittin and Stovall 2010; Germain 2016; Stovall 1996, 2003, 2006; Thomas 2007). Such a question has emerged in recent decades in conversation with existing notions of the African diaspora. As such, black Europe is based upon colonialism and postwar migrations, whereas for African Americans, the emphasis is on the Middle Passage (Wright 2006).

Yet existing notions of black France or black Europe (Hine et al. 2009) have failed to focus on North African–origin individuals, who though they may not present phenotypically as black or self-identify as black, nonetheless reference blackness in making sense of their social locations.[4] In view of the transnational connections made by the North African second generation, I argue for using a more expansive definition of blackness, one that encompasses individuals racialized as black or other and subject to oppression or marginalization. As Keaton (2010) puts it, blacks in France constitute a "community-in-formation," as blackness in France has "transformed common oppression into shared outlook and shared ways of being" (2010, 116). That is, a politics of identity has developed in spite of Republican ideology because of the marginalization and racism experienced by blacks in France.

In *La condition noire: Essai sur une minorité française*, Pap Ndiaye (2008) conversely argues that there is no strong black community in France, but that a transnational blackness connects sub-Saharan blacks to black populations elsewhere. Rather than an essentialist notion of blackness or who is black, this transnational blackness is a product of social relations and interactions. Shelby's (2002) conception of "thin" versus "thick" blackness is also useful for considering the transnational connections the North African second generation makes with black populations outside of France. Thin blackness is a "vague and socially imposed category of difference based on certain visible, inherited physical characteristics" (2002, 239), such as having darker skin in the case of the United States. Thick blackness has a narrower social meaning and comprises racialist, ethnic, cultural, and kinship aspects. Shelby argues for a black solidarity that does not privilege black identity, but rather is based upon the shared experience of oppression and the commitment to resist it. I argue that Ndiaye's transnational blackness and Shelby's thin blackness also extend to maghrébin-origin individuals who, in the absence of discourse about race and blackness in France, invoke notions of blackness from other societies. Blacks in France must continually assert their Frenchness, as it is often the first thing that is questioned by others. Maghrébin-origin individuals, of course, must do the same.

Though respondents make transnational connections with black Americans and other black populations, they still consider themselves French. Abdelkrim's identification with Malcolm X is a case in point. But in a nation that excludes him from mainstream society, he nevertheless feels closer to marginalized populations around the globe. The same can be said of the enthusiasm generated by Barack Obama's narrative among French racial and ethnic minorities in France. Outsiders recognize those who are like them. Children of maghrébin immigrants develop a sense of blackness, or a black consciousness, which reaches beyond national borders.

Nasar, like Abdelkrim, defines himself as French. He found it difficult to understand my identification as an African American, privileging my connection to the African diaspora above my ties to nationality. Karim asserted he was more French than former president Sarkozy, stating that, as a child of Algerian immigrants and a product of French colonial history, he has closer ties to France than the Hungarian-immigrant politician. To see himself as anything but French would be absurd.[5]

Elisa Joy White (2012) describes the African diaspora as the shared experiences of individuals who are racialized as black. Like their black counterparts, my respondents have been marginalized, and their nation-state identities are considered illegitimate. This is not to reify an essentialism regarding black identity.

Instead, I position children of maghrébin immigrants as part of a diasporic project connecting them to other populations positioned on the margins of society. Blackness in this context refers to a vessel of otherness, a container of those not included in the definition of French. By connecting to other racialized populations, they construct a sense of solidarity and community.

Moreover, even though a French identity is supposedly open to all citizens, the experiences of the North African second generation reveal that it is a racialized identity unavailable to many. This has implications for considering the relationship among race, ethnicity, and nation for other black diasporic populations. In *There Ain't No Black in the Union Jack*, Paul Gilroy (1981) argues that "British" and "black" have been historically positioned in opposition to each other and that "Britishness" itself is defined by race and ethnicity, an argument to which the North African second generation can relate. Colonialism in the Maghreb, and the silence with which its brutality is met in present-day French society, unites children of North African immigrants despite distinctions among the former French colonies of Tunisia, Algeria, and Morocco and mirrors the centering effect of the transatlantic slave trade or the Black Atlantic for black populations in the diaspora, as articulated by Gilroy." The shared connections formed by children of maghrébin immigrants are a direct response to their experiences of exclusion from mainstream society. Resisting a distinction between black and British opens up the category of black or blackness and rejects an essentialist formation. Diasporic connections reveal how individuals imagine race and ethnicity beyond the boundaries of their nation-state (Edwards 2003. Diasporic connections are practiced and repracticed as the middle-class North African second generation uses languages and discourses from other contexts to make sense of their own social locations. The way in which respondents interacted with me and made assumptions about my life in the United States was further exemplification of this.

To answer the question of whether maghrébin-origin individuals are black requires broadening the definition of that term to encompass shared experiences of otherness and exclusion from the nation-state. Their connection to black populations is a product of their exclusion from national belonging. As British and black are perceived as in opposition to each other, so, too, are French and black. When kept out of state projects determining who belongs in the nation, they are forced to connect to populations with shared experiences elsewhere (Brown 2009).[6] In turn, these diasporic and transnational connections help them make sense of their present circumstances.

Differential treatment experienced by respondents because of their North African origins force them to come to grips with the salience of their racial and ethnic status. And they make sense of their marginalization by connecting with others who themselves are subject to it, such as Abdelkrim's identification with Bruce Lee or with Malcolm X. Ndiaye's (2008) theory of transnational blackness in France applies to the North African second generation, which is engaged in a transnational project of its own. Both populations share experiences of stigma and discrimination.

RACE MATTERS, BLACKNESS MATTERS

Children of North African immigrants assert a French identity, but because of the ethnicized and racialized nature of French identity, they are viewed only as North African or maghrébin. France does not explicitly recognize distinct racial and ethnic categories, but French identity is a category inaccessible to minorities of color. If, on the face of it, race and ethnicity are not measured or quantified in French society, they nevertheless operate in everyday life, as the ethnoracially marked experiences of respondents reveal. Consciousness of race exists simultaneously with a denial of race and ethnicity. At the bottom of a racial and ethnic hierarchy, children of North African immigrants feel a connection to black populations worldwide. African American culture and identity resonate with these individuals and provide a way to make sense of their own marginalized social locations. But whatever their identification with other racial and ethnic minorities, they see themselves as French.

Clearly, transnational blackness applies not only to blacks in France but to North African–origin minorities there as well. While maghrébin–origin individuals are generally excluded from our notions of the African diaspora, they nonetheless make diasporic connections. In a context where Republican ideology does not acknowledge their own racialization, middle-class North African–origin individuals invoke the experiences and vocabulary of other racialized minority populations to identify and frame their own experience. The connections they make reveal the portability of blackness.

Conclusion

Sacrificed Children of the Republic?

Heard about the guy who fell off a skyscraper? On his way down past each floor, he kept trying to reassure himself: "So far, so good. . . . So far, so good. . . . So far, so good." How you fall doesn't matter. It's how you land.

—FROM *LA HAINE*, A FILM BY MATHIEU KASSOVITZ

"Rwanda has nothing to do with race, so I'm told. Discrimination against Koreans in Japan has nothing to do with race, so I'm told. The very long struggle of the Irish in Great Britain is not about race, so I'm told. Maybe. But when is racism ever about race, pure and simple; when is religious persecution ever simply about religion; when is patriotism ever about defending the nation-state; when is misogyny nothing more than an uncontrollable and inexplicable hatred of women; when is tribalism ever merely one tribe fighting another tribe because, well, they're another tribe? The question, therefore, is not whether race matters but how it matters. How does it shape, sustain, and define systems of domination? How has it functioned in different times and places?"

—ROBIN KELLEY, "RACE AND RACISM: A SYMPOSIUM"

In 2009, in a radio debate on national identity, Nadine Morano, a Les Républicains party politician, said: "We're not putting young Muslims on trial. I respect their situation. What I want for them is to feel French because they are French. I want them to love France when they live here, to find work, and to not speak in slang. They shouldn't put their caps on back to front" (Leveque et al. 2009).

Recent events in France show that Muslims, and maghrébin-origin individuals more generally, are on trial.

On January 7, 2015, the brothers Saïd and Chérif Kouachi massacred twelve people in the eleventh arrondissement offices of the weekly satirical magazine *Charlie Hebdo*. Hundreds of thousands gathered at the Place de la République that evening for a spontaneous demonstration. President François Hollande declared the following day, January 8,[1] a national day of mourning. On January 9, Amedy Coulibaly took hostages in a Hyper Cacher kosher supermarket near Porte de Vincennes and killed four people. The Kouachi brothers, born in Paris to Algerian immigrant parents, and Coulibaly, born in the southeastern banlieue of Juvisy-sur-Orge to Malian immigrants, had ties to Islamic extremism.

In the aftermath of the killings, attention focused on the slain cartoonists and the columnists, and the rallying cry *"Je suis Charlie"* sprang up. A different cry soon appeared, in recognition of another victim of the attacks: Ahmed Merabet. Merabet, a Muslim police officer of Algerian origin, was killed while trying to pursue the Kouachi brothers. But the cry of *"Je suis Ahmed"* was far less common. Instead, French Muslims were subjected to "collective punishment" (Hajjat 2015), and many, among them my respondents, were asked to denounce violence they had nothing to do with. In the wake of the massacre at *Charlie Hebdo* headquarters, France witnessed more than 128 anti-Muslim attacks. Several supporters of the massacre were arrested as "apologists for terrorism," including the comedian M'Bala M'Bala, known professionally as Dieudonné, who joked on Facebook, "I feel like Charlie Coulibaly."[2]

Later that year, in November, another series of coordinated terrorist acts, also linked to Islam extremism, occurred at several sites in the Parisian metropolitan region, including the Stade de France, in Seine-Saint-Denis; the Bataclan theater in the eleventh arrondissement; and La Belle Équipe and several restaurants and cafés near the Canal Saint-Martin. Among the more than 130 people killed, there were several maghrébin-origin individuals. Following the attacks, President Hollande proposed stripping dual citizens convicted of terrorism of their French citizenship (a proposal withdrawn several months later amid opposition). Hollande declared a state of emergency that lasted several months, allowing police to conduct raids without warrants, among other measures.[3] Heightened Islamophobia ensued.

On July 14, Bastille Day, 2016, Mohamed Lahouaiej Bouhlel, a thirty-one-year-old born in Tunisia who moved to France in 2005, drove a truck through a crowd gathered to watch the fireworks in Nice, in southern France, killing eighty-four people and injuring more than three hundred. The Islamic State claimed responsibility for the attack, and the French government declared it a terrorist incident. The incident raised additional concern about whether Muslims could be successfully incorporated into French society.[4]

The summer of 2016 also saw the controversial ban on the burkini, the full-body swimsuit covering everything except for the face, worn by some Muslim women. Several French towns banned it, and photos of Muslim women on beaches who were fined and forced to remove their suits flooded the news and social media. Then-Prime Minister Manuel Valls referred to the burkini as a form of enslavement. The ban in the French Rivera town of Villeneuve-Loubet was overturned as a violation of civil liberties. Yet opposition to the burkini—on the argument that its presence challenges French values—remains.[5]

These events illustrate the implications of the denial of cultural citizenship to racial and ethnic minorities in French society and are only a sampling of many similar incidents. They sparked concerns about the presence of Muslims in France and their perceived incompatibility with Western society, but the role of race and ethnicity as markers of difference was rarely mentioned. Islamophobia is not just about Islam, it is also about racism. Even North African--origin individuals who do not identify as practicing Muslims nonetheless feel marginalized because of their North African origins, because they are nonwhite. They are treated as though they are not French, even if they identify as such. Even though France espouses a colorblind Republican ideology, race and ethnicity are very much present in the lives of non-white minorities.

I chose the title *Citizen Outsider* because the middle-class North African second generation qualifies as both. Its members are simultaneously part of French society and separate from it. They cannot fully belong to it because of their maghrébin origins and their connection to France's colonial history. Contemporary France cannot see them as having French origins, only North African ones. If France continues to ignore the experiences of those on the margins of society, violent incidents like those I describe above will continue to occur. She ignores her minorities at her own peril.

I have been fascinated with and curious about the politics of identity, race, and ethnicity in France for well over a decade, beginning with my first trip to Paris. I originally sought to understand what it is like to be an ethnic minority in France, and how it contrasts with the experiences of ethnic minorities in the United States. As I planned the dissertation research that later served as the basis for this book, many people—both French and American—told me, or perhaps warned me, that race and racism were dramatically different in the two countries. In France differences between children of maghrébin-origin immigrants and whites are based on religion (Islam versus Christianity), socioeconomic status, and culture. As the adage goes, "Some people just don't want to be French."

I originally thought France would be dramatically different from the United States—based in part on the history of black American expatriates there. Yet, as I have demonstrated, the experience of minorities in France is not as different as one might expect—not only of how immigrants and their descendants fare but also in how people of different races and ethnic origins are treated. France, like the United States and other pluralistic societies, is a work in progress. As the experiences of these respondents reveal, race and racism are central to their lives. And they take precedence over citizenship and socioeconomic status.

In this book, I have shown that ethnic minorities in France, even as citizens, remain on the margins of mainstream society, which underlines the salience of

FIGURE 3. Place de la République. Photo by author.

race and ethnicity. The marginalization of children of North African immigrants persists despite their trajectories of mobility and attainment of middle-class status. They are denied cultural citizenship because they are maghrébin, or nonwhite. The implicit and explicit racial and ethnic boundaries that define French identity keep the North African second generation from successfully asserting it. Its members remain vulnerable in a society that refuses to acknowledge them as French.

WHAT DOES THE NORTH AFRICAN SECOND GENERATION WANT, AND WHY DOES IT MATTER?

I have discussed respondents' experiences growing up in France with immigrant parents, and the dual cultural worlds children of maghrébin immigrants have had to navigate between France and the Maghreb. Respondents' place within French society was questioned at an early age, implicitly and explicitly. Explicitly, children of North African immigrants were told to "return to their country" or called ethnic slurs by neighbors and students. Implicitly, children of maghrébin immigrants were socialized through the French educational system and other state institutions that they were not a part of the definition of a French person. This is an example of how, from a young age, the North African second generation is denied cultural citizenship because they are of maghrébin origin. In chapter 3, I discussed how this denial of cultural citizenship continues into adulthood for respondents, including in the workplace, religion, place and residential environment, and the public sphere. Even after this generation attains a middle-class status, they cannot escape being treated differently because of their racial and ethnic status. I also discussed the implications for how the North African second generation is expected to hide its difference, even when it cannot. After discussing how respondents are denied cultural citizenship and marginalized because they are non-white, I then discussed the impact of this on how the North African second generation self-identifies in chapter 4. Most respondents configure their identities in some way that references both being French and maghrébin. Yet they are only seen as maghrébin by others and not as French. Finally, in chapter 5, I discussed how respondents connect with black populations worldwide, including black Americans, and understand blackness more generally as they make sense of their social locations and experiences of marginalization.

Children of maghrébin immigrants are rejected *despite* belonging to France. They are staunch defenders of the Republican model but feel in their case it is not implemented correctly. They want all French citizens to be treated the same. They do not assert an oppositional identity or consciousness. They accept, rather than reject, France.

Safia, a thirty-two-year-old with dual Tunisian and French citizenship, describes this view:

France confuses assimilation and integration, and that's a shame. Assimilation involves erasing. I don't want to erase my origins. I don't want to forget that my parents immigrated here from Tunisia, that I have a Muslim sensibility, that I have family that lives in Tunisia. Assimilation, it means that to be French I have to eat pork and drink alcohol. . . . But integration is understanding that I'm French regardless of those differences. And I would like people to stop asking me about my origins when they meet me for the first time. It's not the only thing that defines me. I'm reduced to my social origins, my ethnic origins. And that's the problem.

The maghrébin second generation wants to be viewed as French as any of their compatriots. Its members wish to belong in France and to be accepted as French. Its understanding of what it means to be of maghrébin origin and French is shaped by whites who deny its members their place in mainstream society. This informs the boundaries they draw around both maghrébin and French as identities. They wish to be recognized as part of the French Republic (Keaton 2010). The North African second generation desires "more integration" and "strongly supports the French model while they are perceived as threatening core Republican values" (d'Appollonia 2009, 283). They do not voluntarily reject Frenchness; Frenchness rejects them. The difference ascribed to immigrant-origin individuals is often framed as one of culture, religion, residential location, or citizenship status. But these are code words for race and ethnicity, as they know from their everyday interactions and interactions with social institutions.

THE CONTINUING SIGNIFICANCE OF RACE AND ETHNICITY

The year 2015 marked the tenth anniversary of the uprisings that spread through banlieues throughout France, following the deaths of two ethnic minority youths who were fleeing the police that fall.[6] One respondent, Mourad, described to me the sentiment of many banlieue residents at the time: "You don't see me as a French person. OK, we're not French, so we're Muslim, Algerian, Moroccan, Tunisian. I'll wear a jacket with the Algerian flag on the back. . . . That transforms into aggression. That's what the riots in November 2005 were all about."

When I asked other respondents about the uprisings, they said pretty much the same thing. The frustrations of this often-ignored segment of the French population made the uprisings inevitable. The American media bemoaned the failure of France's Republican model to integrate its immigrants and minorities or fully address its colonial legacy. It brought attention to the "other France," the one not typically seen in tourism brochures and films about France accessible to American audiences. Within France, much of the media commentary subsequent to the uprisings characterized the individuals involved as unwilling to integrate into mainstream society, and rejecting its norms and values. On a French nightly news program, then–minister of the interior Nicolas Sarkozy insisted that the individuals involved in protests must learn to adapt to France. The implication, of course, was that they were too different to assimilate into the society in which they were born and raised and that change must come from them, not the state or French society. Protestors challenged this dominant narrative and began carrying signs stating, "*Nous sommes tous les racailles*" (We're all scum), reclaiming a pejorative term Sarkozy had used against them and demanding that France see them as French.

Many respondents said that uprisings of this sort would likely happen again, for they felt that little had changed. Ten years after their occurrence, the police officers involved in the deaths of Zyed Benna and Bouna Traoré were acquitted of all charges.[7] A Human Rights Watch (2012) report found that the majority of North African–origin and sub-Saharan-origin individuals said identity checks by the police were a major problem. They are six to eight times more likely than whites to undergo "pat-downs" (see also OSI 2009). The framing of immigrant-origin individuals as rejecting France does not fully explain the occurrence of the uprisings. Even when maghrébin-origin individuals do everything right, such as acquiring university degrees and working in a professional capacity, they are still excluded from mainstream society. If French society rejects racial and ethnic framing as a means to understand events like the 2005 banlieue uprisings, ethnic minorities know differently.

The experience of Zara, a twenty-eight-year-old of Moroccan origin, again demonstrates how the onus of integration falls on racial and ethnic minorities. Her Algerian aunt had been in an abusive relationship with a white man. Zara had told her repeatedly that he was not good for her, that something was wrong with him, and that she should leave him. But her aunt did not listen and Zara eventually lost touch with her. One day her aunt called her, crying, and asked Zara to help her and come pick her up because she did not feel well. Zara did and her aunt came to live with her. Her aunt told her how they had been arguing a lot. One morning, her aunt went downstairs to use a telephone booth, and soon afterward Zara heard her aunt shouting. Her abusive boyfriend had figured out where Zara lived. Wearing a nightgown, Zara ran outside to find the boyfriend shoving her aunt into his car. "I tried to stop it, but I didn't succeed," she explained. "He drove away with her."

Zara then went to the local police station to file a report against him. The officer said that the police would go to the boyfriend's house and bring him in. Though Zara asked the police to contact her after this took place, she heard nothing from them. She returned to the station later that day and learned that her aunt was in custody. The police had removed her aunt from the boyfriend's house and then took her with them. Zara started to complain to the officer, but he told her that the boyfriend had said it was Zara who was racist toward whites like him. "It's important that you integrate," the officer told her.

The roles of Zara and the boyfriend had suddenly reversed. It was she who had become the problem; it was the boyfriend who complained. And it was Zara who needed to change. She remembers thinking that, had she been white, she would have been treated differently and the police officer probably would have taken her complaint seriously. In frustration, Zara said there was nothing she could do. A colorblind, Republican institution of the state had failed her.

In theory, the Republican model does not recognize race and ethnicity, does not want to reify differences that those terms imply.[8] What is clear, however, is that the model is not working if a segment of France's population is marked as different and treated differently because it is nonwhite.

The French model for identity politics differs from that in the United States and many other societies.[9] France essentially attempts to erase race and ethnicity from social life; by refusing to acknowledge such categories, they are deprived of meaning. The colorblind Republican model holds that race, ethnicity, and other distinctions related to identity produce identity politics, making race and ethnicity salient where they otherwise would not be. But as the experiences of these citizen outsiders show, individuals are still racialized even without state-sanctioned identity categories. The distinction between public and private spheres does not change this, for the differences drawn exist in both.

Boundaries around identity in France dictate who does and does not belong in French society. The North African second generation, and its middle-class segment, is repeatedly told it does not belong. In response to this marginalization, the second generation has formed a distinct community, and a distinct identity politics related to ethnic origins. Ironically, *communautarisme*, which is feared in France (Chabal 2015), has been recreated by the exclusion of children of maghrébin-origin immigrants and their desire to connect with others who share similar experiences.

Members of the North African second generation see themselves as racialized or ethnicized subjects. Their difference, or otherness, is an ascribed one and not an oppositional choice of their own. Race and ethnicity establish and reinforce their second-class citizenship and deny them cultural citizenship.

CULTURAL CITIZENSHIP IN FRANCE AND BEYOND

France's framework for addressing diversity and multiculturalism is assimilationist. Nonwhites are expected to assimilate into the mainstream; differences should be relegated to the private sphere. But the nation's colonial history and its unacknowledged racial and ethnic foundations deny a segment of its citizens the real and symbolic benefits that come with being part of the French nation. It is instructive to compare the French example with how other pluralistic societies deal with cultural, religious, and ethnic diversity. As Stephen Castles (1997) has noted, like

France, the United Kingdom and the Netherlands have adopted an assimilation-ist model, the United States and Canada have opted for a pluralist model, and Germany practices differential exclusion. It comes as no surprise, then, that recent research has shown how newly immigrated women in London and Amsterdam feel like second-class citizens (Ghorashi and Vieten 2012). Citizenship is a marker of difference for these immigrants, as it for my respondents. For marginalized populations, it remains a continual negotiation, not something conferred on them by law.

Maghrébin-origin individuals are depicted as uniquely responsible for their own plight: They are said to not try hard enough to fit in, even if their socioeco-nomic status and professional attainments are the equal of whites. Rather than reject their societies, however, Maghrebin-origin individuals in France and other marginalized populations around the world are, instead, claiming their rightful places *within* their societies. As citizens, they see themselves as deserving of rights and privileges meant for all. We must imagine a citizenship and societal belonging in which racial, ethnic, cultural, and religious difference do not stand in the way of full societal inclusion. This is how we address the denial of cultural citizenship. By failing to accommodate differences in the public sphere, France loses out on a true and cohesive national community. France's emphasis on monoculturalism and universalism do not allow for this. And theories of immigrant integration and assimilation fail to capture the experiences of immigrant-origin racial and ethnic minorities.

The denial of cultural citizenship exists beyond France, as demonstrated by the Brexit vote, attributed in part to xenophobic sentiment; by the heightened Islamo-phobia and rise of the Far Right in European societies such as the Netherlands and Germany; and by the debate over how to respond to the Syrian refugee crisis in the European Union. In the United States, we can see the denial of cultural citizenship to African Americans, who even though they are legal citizens, are subject to disparate treatment, as evidenced by "stop and frisk" procedures and the phenomenon of "driving while black," among other examples. Or the case of Muslim Americans and immigrants who face heightened suspicion and Islamo-phobia, including Executive Order 13769 signed by President Donald Trump in January 2017 banning immigrants from various Muslim majority countries such as Iran, Syria, and Iraq. Our idea of who belongs in a given nation and who is seen as a full member of society is undergirded or circumscribed by race and ethnicity. This point is clear when we consider Ahmed Merabet, the Muslim and Algerian-origin police officer who was one of the victims of the massacre at the *Charlie Hebdo* editorial offices. He was just as French as the other victims. He had a stable middle-class job. He was a Muslim who fought to defend the French motto of *Lib-erté, égalité, et fraternité* yet is rarely mentioned in the news reports of the events. And while the cry of *"Je suis Ahmed"* was virtually ignored, *"Je suis Charlie"* was quickly adopted as an affirmation of French values. When we consider the lack of attention paid to the plight of the North African second generation and other racial and ethnic minorities, it is not hard to understand why.

That the struggle for full cultural citizenship is a global struggle is evident most recently in the death of Adama Traoré, a twenty-four-year-old black construction worker, who died under unusual circumstances after being arrested in the banlieue of Beaumont-sur-Oise, north of Paris.[10] He was arrested for interfering in the arrest of his brother. The police first claimed that he had died of a heart attack and then later said he had a severe infection. His family asked for a second autopsy because they say he had no health problems prior to his death. Since his death, there have been demonstrations demanding justice for Adama Traoré, including one protest outside the local police station, which was met with tear gas from the police. Part of the mobilization around justice for Traoré has been connected to struggles for black liberation in other societies, including the United States. The incidents of state-sponsored violence against black Americans are being closely followed by racial and ethnic minorities in France, who also seek to affirm their rightful place in society and challenge racial and ethnic marginalization. During my recent visits to France, I remain fascinated by the transnational connections racial and ethnic minorities are making—despite differences in their societies. Within Paris and its banlieues, there have even been demonstrations in honor of Mike Brown, Freddie Gray, and other black American victims of state-sponsored violence.

In titling this chapter "Sacrificed Children of the Republic,"[11] I also want to consider what is at stake by denying cultural citizenship to racial and ethnic minorities. I return to Safia, whom I caught up with during a trip to Paris in 2015. She has achieved even more success as a journalist—now working as an editor in addition. As we met in her office in the fifteenth arrondissement, she recounted a recent disturbing incident. One day she traveled to Marseille (in the south of France) by train for some work-related meetings. She had no luggage with her since she was not spending the night and was carrying a satchel containing the items she needs for work. When Safia's train arrived at the Gare de Lyon at the end of the day, she was stopped leaving the train by a plainclothes police officer. He demanded to see what was inside her bag. She told me, *"Il m'a tutoyée,"* that is, he addressed her by using the informal, or familiar, pronoun *tu* (you) rather than the formal *vous*, not merely a breach of etiquette but, in France, a clear sign of disrespect. Safia was offended by his use of the *tu* form, and also because he did not immediately identify himself as a police officer. He demanded to see her identification and asked her why she was carrying only a satchel. "Are you smuggling drugs?" he asked. "Are you a prostitute, working for someone?" Humiliated, Safia answered that she was a journalist and had gone to Marseille for meetings. She showed him her *carte d'identité* and other identification issued by the publication for which she works.

"The craziest thing," she told me, as her eyes welled up with tears, "was that the train was packed with people, white people. There were a ton of white people. And I was the one who was stopped. No one said a thing. The other passengers just stared at me." Safia is pursuing legal means to address this incident, which as she explained, she has seen happen to too many racial and ethnic minorities in France. "You just can't let these things go by," she said. "How can people not think this is wrong?" Though in many ways Safia, like other immigrants and their descendants, has done the things that should allow her to fit in—she has worked hard, attained an education, and holds a stable, middle-class job—what's clear is that these are not enough. She does not belong in France—because she is not white.

METHODOLOGICAL APPENDIX

Another Outsider
Doing Race from/in Another Place

Just as my respondents were citizen outsiders, I, too, as a non-French American citizen doing research in France, was an outsider. Yet in some ways my identity as a black woman created an insider connection with respondents because they also perceived me as a racial and ethnic minority. I outline my methodology in what follows and discuss how respondents simultaneously viewed me as an insider and outsider. In line with the direction of previous work on the relationship between ethnographer and the "researched," I consider the different boundaries I encountered in my fieldwork and how they relate to aspects of my identity, as well as the implications for the boundaries separating insiders and outsiders and for the study of race and difference when one falls within them or outside them. Throughout my ethnographic research, my position as an outsider, as well as my personal identity, undoubtedly shaped how my respondents perceived me. I further consider the implications of this intersubjectivity for my research (Burawoy 1998) and for studying race from another national context. My own race and identity were directly implicated in conducting this research. I argue that this further reveal how race operates and manifests itself within French society.

THE RESEARCH: ENTERING THE FIELD, FINDING PEOPLE, AND
NEGOTIATING ACCESS

I became interested in race, ethnicity, and identity in France for both personal and scholarly reasons. My own experiences as an African American living in Paris with a French family as an undergraduate in a study abroad program piqued my curiosity. My identity as an American citizen sometimes affected how I was treated as a black person in public spaces like restaurants, shops, or the subway. And other times, my visibility as a black person led to differential treatment not experienced by other American visitors. Sometimes people stared at me, particularly in the bourgeois *quartiers* of the seventh and sixteenth

105

arrondissements. In the immigrant-concentrated *quartiers* of the eighteenth or nineteenth arrondissements or the banlieues of Seine-Saint-Denis or Nanterre, this was less common. My sociological imagination was beginning to develop and these questions remained in the back of my mind as I pursued my doctoral studies at Northwestern University. As I read the work of other sociologists on identity and difference in France (including Lamont 2002 and Wacquant 2007), I became interested in better understanding the experiences of the North African second generation: individuals who have been shaped by their parents' migration from former French colonies, though not immigrants themselves and born and raised in France. I wanted to understand the nature of minority identity in a society that does not recognize minorities based on identity categories and how this might intersect with marginalization from mainstream society. I moved to Paris in the fall of 2008 to study this topic.

I began recruiting potential participants by contacting over one hundred organizations and associations (in person, as well as via mail, telephone, and email) in Paris and its banlieues and placing calls for participants on Internet forums and websites that cater to immigrant populations. I stated that I was a doctoral student in sociology interested in the experiences and identities of the North African second generation and sought potential contacts who might be able to provide information. I had an idea of the questions I would ask, but I was purposely broad in my call for potential participants because I wanted to appeal to as many as possible. To participate, individuals had to be born in France, be over eighteen years of age, live in the Parisian metropolitan region, and have at least one parent from the Maghreb.[1]

Recruiting potential participants proved more challenging than anticipated. Many people said no. I believe this was because French Republican ideology makes the discussion of race and ethnicity—along with racial and ethnic identity—sensitive or taboo. Although I did not explicitly introduce race as a topic unless individuals themselves brought it up, I recognize that my visible identity as a black person perhaps made race and ethnicity more salient in our interactions than they might otherwise have been. In addition, on a practical level, it was sometimes difficult to identify potential respondents, because statistics in France are not collected based on race or ethnic origin. For example, there was no census data I could use to determine which neighborhoods were predominately maghrébin.

Because I am American, potential respondents were sometimes suspicious about why a non-French person, particularly an American and non-European, would be interested in studying them. What did I already know? What misconceptions did I have? This seemed particularly acute following the 2005 uprisings that swept banlieues throughout France. Several people told me that they were sick of the media asking immigrant-origin individuals questions about their experiences and the reasons for the uprisings and then distorting them to the public. Others also told me that Americans had many misconceptions about race and discrimination in French society and about life in France. Their hesitation to talk to me was understandable.

The difficulties of obtaining a large respondent sample resulted in my use of snowball sampling (Small 2009). As an outsider—neither maghrébin nor French—this method was crucial for getting me "inside" the population I wanted to study. Building rapport with respondents in the course of an interview, I would ask at the end for the names of others who might take part. Snowball sampling is a kind of nonprobability sampling that is useful for theoretical development, especially when knowledge about a particular subject is lacking.

It is often criticized for its empirical generalizability about an entire population yet can be useful for theoretical generalizability (Small 2009).

My sample is relatively homogeneous in terms of educational attainment and employment status. Many respondents were involved in the same professional and social networks.[2] About half of them are connected to each as friends and acquaintances or because they are affiliated with the same organizations. This later became empirically and theoretically useful in considering how immigrant-origin individuals are marginalized owing to race and ethnicity, regardless of class or socioeconomic status. I was not initially focused on the middle-class segment, but from my first interviews, I remember being struck by how upward mobility (in socioeconomic status and educational and professional accomplishments) had not altered experiences of exclusion in France. I further refined questions for subsequent interviews based on previous interviews and interactions.

I do not generalize the entire second-generation maghrébin population (or the second-generation immigrant population as a whole). I also acknowledge that the Parisian metropolitan region is not representative of all of France, and the focus on the former may shape my discussion. Yet I believe the theoretical findings of this research (namely, the denial of cultural citizenship to nonwhite minorities on racial and ethnic grounds) have implications for second-generation minority populations in other contexts. In other words, I have sought theoretical generalizability, if not empirical generalizability (Small 2009).

INTERVIEWS AND PARTICIPANT OBSERVATION

I built rapport with my respondents mostly because of my French language skills and an awareness of French society I had gained by having lived there previously. Interview questions addressed a variety of topics related to the North African second-generation: identity; social networks; employment experiences; family history and parental background; relationship to parents' country of origin; educational experiences; political views; perceptions of racism, discrimination, and marginalization; and religious beliefs and identities. I conducted interviews in French and digitally recorded them, unless respondents requested otherwise. I realized I had interviewed enough people, or reached the point of saturation (Small 2009), when discernible patterns and themes emerged from our interviews. A native French-speaking transcriber later transcribed them. Though I am fluent in French, she was crucial to making sure I did not miss anything as a nonnative speaker. I analyzed the interviews in French and translated them myself during the writing process. All names and identifying information have been changed in accordance with the Institutional Review Board's Human Subjects guidelines.

In addition to these interviews with forty-five individuals, I also conducted about nine months of participant observation and field research with my respondents and other individuals, spending time with respondents' families and attending various community and networking events, such as panel discussions. My ties to the Nanterre Association allowed me to supplement interviews with participant observation there. Association directors offered to help me make connections for potential interviewees in exchange for volunteer work (eight of my respondents were in some way affiliated with the association). This social and educational community organization was founded in 1994 by five residents who grew up in the Petit Nanterre neighborhood, a public-housing complex. Petit Nanterre is an impoverished neighborhood and considered a *zone à urbaniser en priorité* by the French government.[3] The association's employees, volunteers, and the population it serves are mostly North African and sub-Saharan African immigrant-origin individuals. In addition to my many interactions with them, I also taught English classes to elementary school, high school, and college students, as well as working adults. My experiences at the association were invaluable, allowing me to participate in the everyday lives of the population I was studying. I became very attached to the many individuals I met there.

NEGOTIATING IDENTITY IN THE FIELD

Ethnographers have long reflected on how their own social position and identity affects field research. Some have said that interactions with respondents may be thought of as "construction sites" (Cordell and Hartmann 2007) in which similarities and differences in social location cause the constant negotiation and renegotiation of identities on both sides (Horowitz 1986; Lacy 2008; Venkatesh 2002).

The interactions between the two parties inform the analytical process (Horowitz 1986; May and Pattillo-McCoy 2000), and reveal "localized systems of meaning" (Venkatesh 2002, 103). Research participants sometimes view ethnographers as strangers; the curiosity of respondents, and the questions it generates, tell ethnographers a great deal about what is important to their subjects (Horowitz 1986). Venkatesh discusses the "social production of the ethnographer"; that is, the roles assigned to him by his informants in his fieldwork on Chicago's South Side and the importance of their perceptions of his research and his role as a field-worker. Horowitz (1986, 410) says this is best considered as "interactional matters based on processes of continuing negotiation between the researcher and the researched." The social position or identity of the researcher thus shapes how participants see the researcher and how an ethnographer perceives or interprets the research setting (May and Pattillo-McCoy 2000).

Such processes also have implications for the negotiated boundaries between insiders and outsiders in field research and the similarities and differences between researcher and "researched." In her ethnographic study of middle-class black Americans in the suburbs of Washington, D.C., Karyn Lacy (2008) discusses how ethnographers must bargain with participants to ensure their cooperation. As an African American, she found this particularly challenging in the "cross-racial fieldwork" she conducted with white middle-class residents of the communities in which she was interested. Though she herself was middle-class, and also a graduate student at an elite university, her African American identity was most salient in interactions with uncooperative white respondents. In such contexts, participants "may rely on either pervasive stereotypes or personal experiences with members of these groups as an indicator of how the ethnographer will interact with them" (2). In my case, respondents undoubtedly had prior exposure to Americans and black Americans, either personally, through the media, or in some other way, and that exposure may have shaped their perceptions of me.

Differences in citizenship and nationality add another layer of negotiations between insiders and outsiders when researching across national contexts. In her research on symbolic boundaries in France and the United States, Michèle Lamont describes how her identity as both French Canadian and an American professor shaped the interview process: "People were more prone to explain their taken-for-granted assumptions, not knowing the extent to which I might, or might not, be familiar with their culture" (1992, 18–19). This is similar to what Caitlin Killian (2002) experienced researching maghrébin-immigrant women adapting to French society and what Paula Pickering (2007) experienced in her fieldwork with minorities in Bosnia. In Pickering's case, this was particularly challenging in a context where ethnicity is considered a sensitive subject.

OUTSIDER STATUS: AN AMERICAN IN FRANCE

My own experience mirrored that of researchers who have conducted qualitative research in other countries (Killian 2002, Lamont 1992, Pickering 2007). As an American, I was an outsider to those I sought to study. Participants often assumed I was not knowledgeable about French society and history or maghrébin culture, and I was lectured on the history of French colonialism in the Maghreb, for example, as a result. Still, such interactions illustrated how maghrébin-origin individuals understand their place in French society.

My outsider status also exposed my naiveté. When first making connections with various organizations, I once used the slang term for an Arab, *beur*, and was immediately made aware of its inappropriateness and pejorative connotations. One of my respondents, Mourad, a thirty-year-old of Algerian origin, explained that the issue is not so much that *beur* is offensive, but that it implies that one is neither an immigrant nor French but in between, whereas most children of maghrébin immigrants just want to be thought of as French. This contrasts with his (and his maghrébin friends') parents, for whom the term felt more apt. This proved to be a huge insight for understanding the plight of racial and ethnic minorities in France, and how they simply want to considered as French as anyone else. However, I do not know if my blunder would have been so easily excused if potential participants had thought me more knowledgeable about France.

The individuals with whom I worked assumed, merely by virtue of my American citizenship, that I could exercise power and influence on their behalf. At the Nanterre Association, people often thought I could facilitate their travel to the United States, either for work or school, through whatever connections they supposed I had (see Pickering 2007). This caused me to reflect on my status as an American citizen—apart from any other identity I have. As all research involves power relations (Ali 2006), I realized I needed to be conscious of how being American is read or understood by potential participants.

Such assumptions and stereotypes had also arisen during my first extended stay in Paris, in 2000, when I lived with a French family as a part of a junior year abroad program. I encountered negative perceptions of Americans, which was heightened after the contested presidential election of George W. Bush that November. When I returned to Paris in fall 2008 to conduct the fieldwork for this book, there was a different energy, as many in France—across racial and ethnic backgrounds—were excited about the prospect of a Barack Obama presidency. Conducting research during Barack Obama's presidential campaign often led to conversations with respondents about race and racism, upward mobility, and multiculturalism and diversity that might not have otherwise occurred without my prompting. That I was an African American who had moved to Paris from Chicago immediately connected me to this other African-American with ties to Chicago. Many potential respondents were curious about my perspective on Barack Obama and the prospect of his election as the first black president of the United States. Was I excited about him, too? What did it mean to me and other African Americans? My conversations with respondents were also illustrative of the ways in which they thought about racial and ethnic representation. Many maghrébin-origin individuals identified with Obama and were excited about what his presidency would mean for racial and ethnic minorities in France, demonstrating how individuals marginalized based on race and ethnic origin could connect to racial and ethnic minority populations elsewhere. Many reflected on the similarities and differences between racial and ethnic minorities in France and in the United States.

I was repeatedly asked how I became interested in the maghrébin second generation. My status as an American complicated my attempt to blend in with others—I did not deny I was American, but I did not remind others of it, either. I quickly realized that I was considered an expert on all things American. Everyone at the Nanterre Association seemed to know me as "Jean, the American," before I had even spoken with them. Mamadou, of Algerian origin and one of the directors of the association, told me that news travels fast in this community—everyone knows when something new has happened—in this case, my arrival as an American volunteer at the center. People could tell that I was not French, sometimes even without speaking: "Oh, it's obvious you're not from here . . . but I get that you want to be discreet," he said. This resembles the experience of Natasha Warikoo (2011), who in her research in London high schools found that students often asked her questions about the United States and American culture, allowing her to build rapport with her participants.

INSIDER STATUS: BEING A RACIAL AND ETHNIC MINORITY IN FRANCE

While I was an outsider in some ways, many respondents perceived me as an insider, as we shared a status as racial and ethnic minorities (see also Khanna 2011). In interactions with them, they often invoked aspects of my personal biography, whether to point out likenesses or differences in our two identities. I discuss later the implications of this shared racial and ethnic minority status for studying race and ethnicity from a different national context.

Conducting research during the campaign and eventual election of Barack Obama led to many discussions that might not have otherwise occurred. While I was conscious of not imposing an American-style understanding of race and ethnicity on the French context, some respondents invoked such a conception. Throughout my interviews, respondents made many connections and references to race and African American identity and culture. For example, one respondent began our conversation by repeatedly asserting that, although race is a big problem in the United States, it was not a big problem in France (and this was before I mentioned race or racism). He then went on to enumerate the ways in which he has been treated differently from others simply because he is maghrébin.

I also sensed there were moments when being a nonwhite American helped generate trust with potential respondents. A director at the Nanterre Association, not long after we'd met, said that if I ever needed a place to live, I could stay in one of the apartments in the public housing complex affiliated with the organization. I was surprised by his openness, despite our only recent acquaintance, and wondered whether his trust stemmed from the fact that I am visibly African American and a woman.

IMPLICATIONS FOR INTERSECTIONS OF IDENTITY AND RESEARCH

Before I moved to Paris to conduct fieldwork, I was warned to be careful not to impose an American-style understanding of race and ethnicity on the French context, and not interpret my observations based on my own experiences as a black woman. However, what I learned in my research and have shown here is that the researcher's identity is not an impediment to ethnographic research. Rather, significant insights can be gained from how participants engage and perceive that identity.

This became particularly salient when conducting research related to race and difference across national contexts. I was often asked why I did not conduct research on racial and ethnic minorities in the United States. And there were questions as to whether, as a member of a racial and ethnic minority group myself, I could objectively study race and marginalization. Would I naturally see race and racism through my own filter, rather than understanding race and other phenomena through the lens of those individuals under study? Yet this misses how minorities in another national context understand race and racism for themselves, and ignores the connections they make with racial and ethnic minorities in other countries. Other scholars have reflected on the potential complications of studying race in France from an American perspective. I agree with Keaton et al. (2012), who posit that speaking of race in France does not imply importing American-style constructs of race and ethnicity in the analysis.[4] My experiences parallel those of minority researchers studying race within the United States, whose findings are filtered through their racial and ethnic identity but not the research itself (Trusdell 2013; Young 2008). For example, Young discusses how he can paint "a more compassionate, rather than intensely critical, portrait" of African American men as an African American man himself (2008, 200).

While researchers are never "ideologically free" (Keaton 2006), I remained vigilant, to the degree possible, about not imposing my own understandings on my respondents. In short, I believe that qualitative researchers should not fear the implications of their identities and social locations for the research process, including their relationships with the "researched." Rather, we should embrace them as integral to understanding the totality of individuals' lives.

NOTES

PREFACE: BLACK GIRL IN PARIS

1. The title to this preface is taken from Shay Youngblood's novel *Black Girl in Paris*, about a black girl's pilgrimage to Paris in the 1980s and her reflections on Langston Hughes, James Baldwin, Josephine Baker, and other African-American luminaries who had spent time in the city.

1. NORTH AFRICAN ORIGINS IN AND OF THE FRENCH REPUBLIC

1. Manual Valls tweeted this in response in May 2015 to Robert Ménard, mayor of Béziers in the south of France, who claimed that he counted the number of Muslim children in town based on whether they had Muslim names (AFP 2015).

2. Gare du Nord, in the tenth arrondissement, is one of the main train stations in Paris and connects to the subway system. The surrounding neighborhood is known for the presence of African immigrants and their descendants.

3. Nadine Morano, in an interview on the television program *Le Supplément*, on the Canal+ cable network, in May 2016. Les Républicains is a center-right political party formed in 2015, when former president Nicolas Sarkozy renamed the Union pour un movement populaire (UMP).

4. All names and identifying information have been changed in the interest of confidentiality per Human Subjects guidelines, by the Institutional Review Board.

5. When I began my research, I was initially surprised and confused about why respondents would want to meet at Starbucks (where I conducted about a third of my interviews and meetings). Besides the fact that they are ubiquitous in Paris, I later realized that many respondents assumed that all Americans like Starbucks and likely they just wanted to make sure I was comfortable.

6. When I indicate that someone is of a certain origin, I mean that he or she is a child of an immigrant from that particular country. In addition, I use *maghrébin* (the French-language term for those from the Maghreb, the former French colonies countries of Tunisia, Morocco, and Algeria) and North African interchangeably. Many respondents also used the term *arabe* interchangeably with maghrébin and North African.

7. By assimilated, I am referring to the process or processes by which racial and ethnic minorities "come to share a common culture and to gain equal access to the opportunity structure of society" (Zhou 1997, 70). Language assimilation, socioeconomic attainment, and increasing rates of intermarriage are all commonly seen as evidence for contemporary assimilation (Alba and Nee 2003).

8. French Republicanism frames the French nation as one in which "only individuals are citizens, citizens are equal, and therefore all individuals are equal citizens" and "ethnic, regional, or religious categorizations are ignored" (Bertossi 2007, 3). Furthermore, there can be "no intermediate bodies between the state and the citizens. . . . As soon as the prior existence of these groups is acknowledged, there is nothing to prevent them from being considered minorities that are impossible to absorb" (Amselle 2003, 114). Part of the fear of *communautarisme* (communitarianism)—see note 9 below for a definition of the term—in France is a fear that it may result in the lack of any nation-based cohesion and community. Many of the questions concerning the meaning of French Republicanism center on the tension between universality and particularity (Schnapper et al. 2003).

9. *Communautarisme* is the often-feared idea in France that groups based on identity will only settle and interact among themselves, rather than integrating into society and being a part of the French national community (Fernando 2014). Multiculturalism is seen to lead to the fragmentation of society along identity lines, as in the United States, for example (Chabal 2015). This sentiment was often mentioned in my interviews as respondents considered the implications of different models of identity politics.

10. For an elaborated definition of *laïcité* see Gunn (2004) and Weill (2006). While secularism is not an exact translation of *laïcité*, I follow the trend of other scholars who use the terms interchangeably for simplicity's sake (Kastoryano 2002, 2004).

11. This 1905 law withdrew state official recognition and financial support from religions while also guaranteeing citizens the right to form private religious associations (Bauberot 2009; Laurence 2001; Scott 2007).

12. Over the years, several exceptions to this rule have been made, allowing the French state to, among other things, subsidize private religious schools and the building of mosques, recognize religious holidays, and create Muslim state organizations (Bowen 2006; Laurence 2001).

13. Chabal (2015) rightly critiques Noiriel for his separating out of immigration from colonialism in this regard.

14. Wright (2004) further argues that blacks are framed as "other" so that whites can maintain superiority in Western culture and that Europe is more generally tied to blackness as a permanent "othered" category.

15. "The case of differential status in the French colonies offers an example of a breach in the continuity of the universalist principle. It demonstrates that, in the colonial context, the Republic made distinctions between individuals on the basis of their belonging to a specific group considered as ethnically different. Furthermore, post-colonial immigrants who came

to France in the second half of the 20th century carried this complex system of status with them" (Kastoryano and Escafré-Dublet 2012, 29).

16. In *Black Skin, White Masks* (1967), Frantz Fanon describes the relations between the white colonizers and the black colonized and its impact on racism in French Algeria. Colonized Algerians internalized the cultural values of the French colonizers and therefore began to see themselves as inferior to their colonizers. This was originally published in 1952 in French as *Peau noire, masques blancs*. I elaborate on Fanon in chapter 5.

17. Unlike later periods of migration, prewar immigrant workers from the Maghreb did not permanently settle in France (Kaya 2009).

18. In 1945 the Haut Comité consultatif de la population et de la famille (High Committee for Population and Families) was created by de Gaulle to formulate immigration policies that were more favorable to groups considered more easily assimilated (often Europeans). Those policies never officially adopted (Derderian 2004; Lyons 2013). In 1946 the Office national d'immigration was founded. In 1958 the Fonds d'action sociale (Social Action Fund) was created to provide social services to immigrant workers (Amara 2006; Bleich 2004; Derderian 2004; Simon 1998).

19. I do not have space here to fully capture the horrific nature of the Algerian War of Independence (Chabal 2015; Dubois 2010). The Paris massacre of October 17, 1961, in which the police repressed Algerians, including drowning them in the Seine, is one example. France did not acknowledge the conflict as a war until 1999. Other scholars have also detailed how the memory of this conflict and its suppression has been reinforced throughout France, particularly as it concerns descendants of Algerian migrants (Silverstein 2008). In my own findings, respondents who are not children of Algerian immigrants but instead children of Tunisian or Moroccan immigrants similarly identified the brutal conflict between France and Algeria over its independence as an example of how France has long disregarded nonwhite individuals.

20. I use the term *white French* or *white* throughout this book to refer to Français de souche, or those of white native French-European origin, though I recognize that *white* is not an official term in French society. I am also following the lead of many respondents who use the term *white*. Even though much of the extant literature uses the term *native French*, I use the term *white* since children of immigrants born in France are also native French people.

21. While I do not discuss migration from former French colonies in sub-Saharan Africa, including Senegal and the Ivory Coast, nor the descendants of this postcolonial migration in this book, there were similar increases in migrants from these regions in the postcolonial period (Bass 2014; Bleich 2001; Hargreaves 2003).

22. Some scholars argue that the spatial relationship between Paris and its banlieues is emblematic of the spatial relations between France and the colonial Maghreb (see Silverstein 2008; Stovall 2003).

23. The government also considered suspending family reunification, but that was considered a right in 1976 (Kirszbaum et al. 2009).

24. Barou (2014) notes how many of the immigration-related policies were influenced by racist ideologies.

25. Bleich refers to this as "antiracism without races" (2003, 50). As racism is framed as more of an individual act, the 1972 law targeted hate speech more than direct discrimination. This at least partially explains how the satirical publication *Charlie Hebdo* has been

charged multiple times for hate speech against Muslims and other groups. The collection of statistics based on race and ethnicity was reminiscent of the Vichy regime and generated opposition. The 1990 Gayssot law extended the 1972 law, by among other measures, establishing an annual report by the National Commission on Human Rights (Bleich 2001; Bleich 2004).

26. Mitterand's *politique de la ville* (urban policy program) targeted social integration in *zones urbaines sensibles* (poor urban neighborhoods, or ZUSs) without mentioning race and ethnicity (Barou 2014). For example, a 1989 law created *zones d'éducation prioritaire* (educational priority zones, or ZEPs) to increase educational resources for students from disadvantaged regions (Calvès 2004; Dikeç 2007; Simon 1998). A 1991 law was passed to prevent residential concentration based on ethnic origin (though Republicanism did not permit use of the term *ethnic origin*) (Dikeç 2007). In 1999, in response to growing evidence of discriminatory behavior, then-interior minister Jean-Pierre Chevenevent established the Commission départementale d'accès à la citoyenneté (Departmental Commission for Access to Citizenship, or CODAC) in each *département* of France to monitor cases of discrimination. However, it had no significant impact (Hargreaves 2004). The debate over *discrimination positive* (affirmative action) also illustrates the complications in addressing issues related to ethnic origin in public policy and government programs (Bleich 2008; Sabbaugh 2002).

27. A 2001 report by the Haut Conseil à l'intégration (High Council on Integration, or HCI) distinguished between being "of Muslim culture" and "of Muslim religion" based on how often Muslims pray in mosques; it estimates that there are about one million Muslims "of Muslim religion" and about three million Muslims "of Muslim culture" (Bowen 2004c; HCI 2001). As of 2007, 33 percent of people from Muslim families are believing and practicing Muslims and 38 percent are believing Muslims. About 35 percent of French Muslims live in the Parisian metropolitan region (Sebian 2007). In terms of practices, 61 percent of French Muslims pray every day; 23 percent attend mosque every Friday; 70 percent fast during Ramadan; and 62 percent only consume meat that is halal. Praying daily and going to the mosque on Fridays are the most discriminating distinctions between believing and practicing Muslims. Praying every day and going to the mosque on Fridays are the most discriminating distinctions between believing and practicing Muslims (IFOP 2009). Recent research has distinguished between an Islam en France (Islam in France) and an Islam de France (Islam of France) meaning "a simple presence of Muslims and their practices visible in France" versus "an Islam that is expressed and developed within national institutions, assuming its freedom from 'foreign' influences, especially those of the homeland" (Kastoryano 2004, 82). This perspective focuses on how Muslim practice is constructed, adapted, and influenced by the French context (Bowen 2004b, 2004c, 2009; Fernando 2005; Gray 2008; Roy 1994).

28. When considering the ratios of regular mosque participation to regular church participation, French Muslims are as secularized as other French people (Hargreaves et al. 2007; Kuru 2008; Laurence and Vaisse 2006). According to a 1999 study, about 18 percent of second-generation Muslim immigrants attend mosque regularly, about 28 percent attend mosque sometimes, and about 54 percent never attend mosque (Penn and Lambert 2009).

29. A 2006 Pew report found that French Muslims are equally likely to identify as French (about 42 percent) as they are to identify as Muslim (about 46 percent) (Barou 2014). A 2007 Gallup poll similarly found that, while Muslims in Paris are more likely to

define religion as an important part of their lives than the Parisian population as a whole, that does not prevent them from identifying with being French (Nyiri 2007).

30. These changing demographics had political implications. For example, in the 1980s, and continuing into present society, the Front National (National Front), a Far Right political party led by Jean-Marie Le Pen, became increasingly popular and portrayed North African and sub-Saharan African immigrants as eroding French society (Fysh and Wolfreys 2003).

31. According to the ministry's website, promoting French identity included the following: "both our historical heritage and the future of our national community. Article 1 of the Constitution of the Fifth Republic states that 'France is a Republic—indivisible, laic [secular], democratic and social. She ensures equality in front of the law of all citizens, without distinction of origin, race or religion.' The promotion of our identity constitutes a response to communitarianism and aims at preserving our nation's equilibrium. Immigration, integration, and national identity are complementary and very closely linked. Because of her own identity, which she can be proud of, France had the means to integrate immigrants who respect our values and can organize immigration in a confident way."

32. Official communications from the Ministry of Immigration, Integration, National Identity and Codevelopment emphasized the following questions: What does it mean to you to be French today? What do issues of diversity mean for our national identity? What are the elements, symbols, and values of French national identity? What is the role of the French nation? Why should we welcome and/or integrate foreigners into our Republic and our national community? What is the relationship among national, local, and European identities? What is the relationship between national identity and globalization? How can national identity be better celebrated?

33. For example, activist and journalist Rokhaya Diallo (Diallo et al. 2012), a child of Senegalese immigrants, wrote in Le Monde: "The national identity 'debate' questions only the identity of certain French who are a little too tan. The endless debates on secularism scrutinize those of us who are unfortunate enough to be Muslim. Nicolas Sarkozy's Grenoble speech—whose objective was to strip targeted French of their nationality, as if it were an option—the difficulties we are confronted with in simply renewing an ID card if one of our ancestors is linked to a foreign country. All the above have created an enormous identity insecurity for us."

34. I use the term postcolonial immigrants here to distinguish between immigrants to France who are attached to its colonial history and immigrants from countries without a colonial relationship with it.

35. Many Algerians fought for France during World War I, though they had no citizenship rights and military service at that time was tied to French citizenship (Cornell and Hartmann 2007; Silverstein 2008). Moreover, according to Tetreault: "During the colonial period, French citizenship by colonial African subjects could often only be obtained when individuals renounced Islam, indicating a bias against religious and racialized difference" (2013, 533).

36. Moreover, "while Muslim Algerians gained French citizenship with the adoption of the Constitution of the Fifth Republic in 1958, a racialized distinction in legal status and representation was maintained. After independence, Algerian citizenship superseded French legal belonging, with nationality replacing racial-cum-religious status in setting divides between populations" (Silverstein 2008, 28).

37. In 1985 the Front National and the Rassemblement pour la République (RPR, a former right-wing political party associated with former president Jacques Chirac) began the process of revising the *code de la nationalité* to restrict the citizenship of those born in France of noncitizen parents (Silverman 1992). The Méhaignerie law, passed in 1993, amended the *code de la nationalité* to end the automatic acquisition of citizenship to children of immigrants (Silverstein 2008; Thomas 2007).

38. According to the Haut Conseil à l'intégration (High Council on Integration, or HCI), integration refers to a reciprocal process between the immigrant and the host society that incorporates immigrants and their children while also maintaining social cohesion in "construction of a society that brings [its citizens] together around shared principles (liberty of thought and conscience, equality between men and women) as they are expressed in equal rights and common responsibilities" (Chabal 2015, 91; see also Tetreault 2013).

39. There is a debate in France over whether to collect statistics on ethnic origin. As categorization is seen to promote differentiation among citizens, the absence of such statistics is often seen as protection against racism and discrimination. The 2007 Hortefeux law proposed that data related to race and ethnicity should be gathered to monitor discrimination. It was later ruled unconstitutional (it also involved stricter requirements for naturalization related to family unification (Bass 2014). See Begag (2007), Bleich (2004), Escafré-Dublet and Simon (2011), Maxwell (2009), Ringelheim (2009), Sabbaugh (2008) Simon (2008), and Simon and Clement (2006) for more on the debate regarding ethnic statistics.

40. Concerning immigrant-origin individuals across generations, as of 2000, 7.3 percent of the French population (including those born overseas and those who have acquired French nationality) has origins in the North African nations of Morocco, Algeria, and Tunisia (Lamont et al. 2002; Préteceille 2008; Thomas 2007).

41. While I follow the convention of research on immigration in the United States in using the terms *second generation* and *second-generation immigrants*, I recognize their problematic nature. Constant (2009) notes that applying the term *immigrant* to the second generation implies that their immigrant status is inherited. Throughout my research, the various terms I found used for this population include *issus de l'immigration* (people of immigrant background), *enfants d'immigrées* (children of immigrants), *secondes générations* (second generations), *descendants d'immigrées* (descendants of immigrants), *jeunes d'origine maghrébine qui sont nés en France* (youth of maghrébin origin who were born in France), *franco-maghrébins, jeunes ethniques* (ethnic youth), and *descendants des peuples colonisés* (descendants of colonized peoples). See Begag (2007) for more on terminology as it relates to this population.

42. I discuss my own experience with this term in the methodological appendix.

43. A 1999 survey of second-generation immigrants aged sixteen to twenty-five from Britain, France, and Germany found that 31 percent of second-generation maghrébin immigrants perceived discrimination at school and 35 percent of second-generation maghrébin immigrants reported experiencing racism (Penn and Lambert 2009).

44. Those who appeared to be of sub-Saharan African or Caribbean origin were six times more likely than whites to be stopped (OSI 2009).

45. As of 2008, about 21 percent of children of immigrants lived below the poverty line, in contrast to about 10 percent for children of French citizens and 28 percent for immigrants overall. The gap between children of European immigrants and children of French citizens

is narrower than the gap between children of African immigrants (including North African and sub-Saharan African) and children of French citizens (Lombardo and Pujol 2011).

46. First-generation Moroccan and Tunisian immigrant men had a 24.6 percent unemployment rate, and women had a 26.1 percent unemployment rate. Among second-generation Moroccan and Tunisian immigrants (ages 18–40), 19.4 percent of men and 21.7 percent of women were unemployed. First-generation Algerian immigrant men had a 29.6 percent unemployment rate and women 30.5 percent. Among second-generation Algerian immigrants (ages 18–40), 23.2 percent of men were unemployed and 22.3 percent of women were unemployed. Those of Italian, Spanish, and Portuguese origin had lower unemployment rates. First-generation Spanish and Italian immigrant men had an unemployment rate of 10.7 percent, while women had an unemployment rate of 13.8 percent. Among second-generation Spanish and Italian immigrants (ages 18–40), 10.3 percent of men were unemployed and 13.5 percent of women were unemployed. Among first-generation Portuguese immigrants, men had an unemployment rate of 9.8 percent, while women had a 10.2 percent unemployment rate. Among second-generation Portuguese immigrants (ages 18–40), 14.3 percent of men and 16 percent of women were unemployed (Meurs et al. 2006).

47. The HCI was created in 1990, and in a report it defined integration as "not midway between assimilation and insertion, but a specific process where the active participation in the national society of varied and different elements is encouraged" (Barou 2014, 649)

48. In fact, according to a meta-analysis of field experiments of hiring discrimination, France has a higher rate of hiring discrimination than the United States, Great Britain, Netherlands, Canada, Belgium, Sweden, and Germany. Whites receive about 80 percent more callbacks than nonwhites. Compared to other groups, North African–origin individuals are discriminated against the most (Quillian et al. 2016).

49. Per the Institut national d'études démographiques (National Institute of Demographic Studies, or INED), the mainstream refers to "persons living in France who are not immigrants and who do not have an immigrant parent. This group includes French persons born abroad and their children, including colonial repatriates and their children born in metropolitan France. It also includes the adult grand-children of immigrants" (Shon 2011).

50. Such African American professionals continually face an inability to fit in, exclusion from the "club," low expectations, shattered hopes, faint praise, coping fatigue, identity troubles, self-censorship and silence, and guilt by association (Cose 1994).

51. As Neckerman et al. (1999) show, the experiences of middle-class immigrants in the United States are often like those of the black middle-class, particularly in terms of navigating discrimination and conforming to white middle-class society. Their "minority culture of mobility" "draws on available symbols, idioms, and practices to respond to distinctive problems of being middle-class and a minority" (949). However, this framework exists in a context of multiple options for identity based on race, ethnicity, and national origin. In this book, I explore how this interplay among race, ethnicity, and middle-class status plays out in a context of limited identity options.

52. In response to their marginalized status, affected groups develop an altered worldview, indigenous organizations and leaders, and a comprehensive framing of their marginalization.

53. "It is this peculiar sensation, this double-consciousness, this sense of always looking at one's self through the eyes of others, of measuring one's soul by the tape a world that looks

on in amused contempt and pity. One ever feels his twoness—an American, a Negro; two souls, two thoughts, two unreconciled strivings; two warring ideals in one dark body, whose dogged strength alone keeps it from being torn asunder" (DuBois [1903] 1994, 3).

54. Here I am also informed by Guinier and Torres' (2002, 16) framing of race, which "both reinforces hierarchies of power and simultaneously camouflages those hierarchies," in considering the multiplicative ways that race structures society.

55. As I later discuss, some respondents can cross symbolic boundaries around race and ethnicity owing to their lighter skin color or a traditionally French sounding name, which make their North African origins less apparent to others.

56. Here I am informed by Vilna Bashi Treitler (2013) regarding how ethnic groups exist on a racial hierarchy.

57. I am also informed by Wimmer's (2013) call for an all-encompassing definition of ethnicity, which does not treat race as fundamentally different from ethnicity.

58. Ethnic identities can vary in terms of the degree to which they shape social life. For example, thick ethnic identities comprehensively organize social life, and thin ethnic identities minimally organize social life (Cornell and Hartmann 2007). Ethnic and racial identities are constructed and continually negotiated in various contexts or "construction sites" (170). (Lacy [2007] distinguishes between private versus public construction sites.)

59. We can see this in the United Kingdom, as evidenced by Hall's (2004) ethnography on working-class second-generation Sikh immigrants in London, which reveals how becoming middle-class British citizens involves reconciling their sense of being Sikh, Indian, and Asian. This is also evident in the United States. Sharma's (2010) ethnography of middle-class second-generation South Asians reveals how these "desis" adopt a diasporic ethnicity, as they invoke conceptions of black identities and blackness in how they self-identify.

60. Research reveals a typology of ethnic self-identifications, including those based on ethnic origin, those based on the nation, and a hyphenated identity (Ajrouch 2004; Chong 1998; Eid 2008; Labelle 2004; Rumbaut 1996; Song 2010; Waters 1999; and Zéphir 2001). For example, Waters' (1999) examination of second-generation West Indian immigrants in New York delineates three paths for identity construction—a black American identity, an ethnic American identity with some distancing from black Americans, and an immigrant identity outside of racial and ethnic categories. Waters' typology reflects how individuals who are read by others as black come to understand and make sense of the black-white racial divide in America. Zéphir's (2001) research on second-generation Haitian immigrants in New York similarly emphasizes how immigrant families socialize their children and that children understand American race relations as the process in which second-generation individuals develop their ethnic identity. In other words, the degree of their "Haitianness" depends on a multitude of factors, revealing the heterogeneity of ethnic identity among second-generation populations.

61. Moreover, Goldberg (2006) argues that when race is mentioned in Europe, it is at the level of embarrassment, as a reference to the past, as in the case of the Holocaust.

62. Lamont and Molnar (2002, 168) define symbolic boundaries as "conceptual distinctions made by social actors to categorize objects, people, practices, and even time and space. . . . Symbolic boundaries also separate people into groups and generate feelings of

similarity and group membership." Symbolic boundaries become social boundaries when there is a consensus about their meaning and "take on a constraining character and pattern social interaction in important ways," including "identifiable patterns of social exclusion or class or racial segregation" (169). Boundaries have "both a categorical and social or behavioral dimension. The former refers to acts of social classification and collective representation, the latter to everyday networks of relationships that result from individual acts of connecting and distancing" (Wimmer 2013, 9). Boundaries are marked through everyday interactions that privilege particular groups over others. Moreover, Alba explains how social and symbolic boundaries affect immigrant-origin individuals: "In all immigration societies, the social distinction between immigrant and second generations, on the one hand, and natives, on the other, is . . . in a sense, a fault line along which other differences and distinctions pile up" (2005, 41).

63. I am also informed here by Bloemraad (2015, 60), who clarifies how citizenship boundaries work: "If citizenship is a boundary demarcation between those 'inside' and 'outside' the membership circle, that boundary is not a single wall, but rather a series of fences that can be more or less inclusive, and which can overlap our cut across each other."

64. I build upon Stephen Castles' (1997) notion of differential exclusion, in which immigrants and their descendants are incorporated into certain areas of society (such as the labor market) but not others (i.e., political participation). Regarding France, he argues that the Republican model "appears to be purely political, yet it brings culture in through the back door. There is no room for cultural diversity or for formation of ethnic communities" (9). In this sense, cultural citizenship extends the notion of multicultural citizenship, which is opposed to universal citizenship and recognizes that formal equality through citizenship rights can mask actual disadvantage and that therefore difference needs to be recognized and accommodated (Bloemraad 2015; Castles 1997; Joppke 2001). Thus, additional rights should be given to particular groups (Kymlicka 1995). My notion of cultural citizenship differs from this, in that I am not arguing for a differentiated citizenship, nor for different kinds of citizenship rights to be applied, but rather for recognition of the nonlegal dimensions upon which citizenship is based (Beaman 2016b).

65. British sociologist T. H. Marshall (1950) first referred to citizenship as a status accorded to full members of a community.

66. For example, Cohen (2010) discusses the second-class citizenship of African Americans, and Berry and Junn (2015) discuss the citizenship of racial and ethnic minorities, particularly Asian Americans and Latinos, as "silent citizenship."

67. Or as Étienne Balibar (2004) argues, reinforcing a "virtual European apartheid" in which anyone connected to immigration is always seen as an immigrant.

68. While I have an almost even number of men and women in my respondent sample, I do not explicitly use gender as a variable of analysis in this study, primarily because the experiences of my respondents did not vary substantially by gender.

69. Most of my respondents with dual citizenship are of Algerian origin (including three respondents who were born in Algeria and immigrated to France as babies).

70. See the INSEE (2003) report *Nomenclature des professions et catégories socioprofessionnelles des emplois salariés d'entreprise.*

71. I also made contacts for potential interviews at these events.

2. GROWING UP FRENCH? EDUCATION, UPWARD MOBILITY, AND CONNECTIONS ACROSS GENERATIONS

1. This history is somewhat distinct from other maghrébin families because there was no arranged marriage (Begag 2007; Gray 2008).

2. It is worth noting the history of assimilation through French education for rural, regional populations who were considered culturally distinct in the nineteenth century. I thank Deborah Reed-Danahay for this insight (Reed-Danahay 1996).

3. Fernando (2014) refers to schoolteachers as "guardians of the Republican school."

4. Diana particularly takes issue with the terms *les issus de l'immigration* (persons of immigrant background) and *l'intégration* (integration).

5. The three phases of the French educational system are *école primaire* (elementary school), for ages 6–11; *collège* (secondary school), for ages 11–15; and lycée (high school), for ages 15–18. Educational attainment levels in France are typically referenced in terms of the *baccalauréat*, or *bac*, exam (taken by lycée graduates, it is a prerequisite for higher education) and the number of years of school post-*bac* ("*bac* plus 7," for example, means a student has passed the *bac* exam and has seven years of postsecondary education). There are three types of *bac* exam—general, technology, and vocational (students choose a track in high school that leads to one of these *bac* exams). The university system is divided between public universities and the prestigious *grandes écoles* (including the École nationale d'administration [ENA], Institut d'études politiques de Paris [Sciences Po], and the École des hautes études en sciences sociales [EHESS]); public universities admit all *bac* graduates. See Brinbaum and Kieffer 2005 and Brinbaum and Kieffer 2009.

6. One notable and recent exception is Sciences Po, which has an affirmative action-style program for students from *zones d'éducation prioritaires* (ZEPs), areas considered educationally disadvantaged. This has been heavily debated and critiqued (Sabbaugh 2002; Sabbaugh 2011).

7. University of Paris 8, University of Paris 1, and University of Paris 2 are all public universities connected to the Paris-Sorbonne university system.

8. The full names of these universities are as follows: École polytechnique; École nationale des ponts et chaussées; École supérieure des sciences économiques et commerciales; and École des hautes études commerciales.

9. For more on how an education at Sciences Po and other *grandes écoles* translates to a higher social status, see Bourdieu (1984) and Draelants and Darchy-Koechlin (2011).

10. See the Human Rights Watch report *The Root of Humiliation: Abusive Identity Checks in France* (HRW 2012) and the Open Society Institute report *Profiling Minorities: A Study of Stop-and-Search Practices in Paris* (OSI 2009) for more information on this.

3. MARGINALIZATION AND MIDDLE-CLASS BLUES: RACE, ISLAM, THE WORKPLACE, AND THE PUBLIC SPHERE

1. One example was how some middle-class respondents framed and understood the 2005 banlieue uprisings as the only resort for their working-class and impoverished counterparts many of whom are unemployed and underemployed.

2. On October 27, 2005, two teenagers—one of Tunisian origin and the other of Malian origin—were electrocuted in an electricity substation as they fled police in the Clichy-sous-Bois

banlieue. They were apparently trying to avoid the constant police identity checks targeted at youths. A few days later, police shot a tear-gas grenade into a local mosque and refused to apologize. These events led to uprisings, which spread in banlieues throughout France for about three weeks. See Balibar (2007), Echchaibi (2007), Koff and Duprez (2009), and Schneider (2008) for an overview of the vast literature on the causes of these uprisings.

3. See Bremner (2005), Bell (2005), Body-Gendrot (2007), Bowen (2006); Canet et al. (2008), Haddad and Balz (2006), Smith (2005a, 2005b), and Snow et al. (2007).

4. This was seen in the media and popular discourse surrounding the treatment of African Americans by the police in the death of Sandra Bland in Hampstead, Texas, and Michael Brown and the ensuing uprisings in Ferguson, Missouri (Beaman 2015b).

5. This is the case in France, as evidenced most recently in the aftermath of the massacre at the offices of the satirical magazine *Charlie Hebdo* in January 2015, when many anti-Muslim incidents and attacks occurred (Beaman 2015c).

6. Here I follow Brubaker (2013, 6), who cautions that "people who identify as Muslims (like those who identify with any other religion) do not identify *only* or *always* as Muslims, and they may not identify *primarily* as Muslims, though some of course do [italics in the original]."

7. Religious identity, as Eid (2008) describes it, encompasses familiarity with beliefs, observation of religious practices, and a sense of belonging to one's religious culture.

8. A 2009 UNICEF report on children of immigrants found that many second-generation Muslims practice Islam in way that could be considered tolerant, inclusive, and largely secular (Kirszbaum, Brinbaum, and Simon 2009).

9. Mourad further explained that this apartment was too small to rent out, according to French law. The landlord, also an attorney, would have known that his attempt to do so was illegal.

10. Furthermore, as Silverstein (2008) has shown, residents from the *cités* are considered immigrants even when they are not.

11. One example of this euphemistic coding is in territorial affirmative action. According to Calvès (2004, 222), "in communities where problems and tensions tend to be translated in the language of race, the very categories of territorial affirmative action (young zone residents, ZEP pupils) do convey racialized denotations that are unambiguously perceived as such by institutional as well as local social actors. An implicit consensus filters the geographical criteria through the sifter of various religious, ethnic, and phenotypical denominations."

12. Shon (2011) states that, as of 2008, 42 percent of migrants from North Africa, sub-Saharan Africa, and Turkey live in the 10 percent of neighborhoods with the highest unemployment rate. This number drops to 35 percent for children of these immigrant groups, pointing to a moderate intergenerational residential mobility.

13. Hicham clarified that the old mayor was reprimanded for abuse of power and is currently fighting these charges in court. I should also note that, while some of the HLM complexes will be demolished, Hicham and others signed an agreement with the current mayor that reduced the number of units to be demolished and would increase the number of housing units in the *cité*.

14. Sherwood (2009) highlights how the prominence of North African culture in Marseille sets it apart from other French cities, and that residents' identification with Marseille supersedes other identities and identifications.

15. For more on housing discrimination, see Bonnal et al. (2012), Shon and Verdugo (2014), and Simon and Heath (2013).

4. FRENCH IS, FRENCH AIN'T: BOUNDARIES OF FRENCH IDENTITY

1. See Ernest Renan's 1882 *Qu'est-ce qu'une nation? et autres essais politiques*.

2. I thank Marcus Anthony Hunter for this suggestion.

3. According to the Institut national de la statistique et des études économiques (National Institute of Statistics and Economic Studies, or INSEE), as of 2013, foreigners (individuals of foreign nationality born outside France) make up about 6.4 percent of the total French population and immigrants about 8.9 percent of the total French population.

4. Sarkozy is the child of a Hungarian immigrant father and a French mother. I discuss later in this chapter how his Hungarian origins do not stigmatize him in the same way my respondents's maghrébin origins do.

5. For more on inequalities in the French school system, see Brinbaum and Kieffer (2009), Brinbaum and Lutz (forthcoming), d'Appollonia (2009), and Van Zanten (1997).

6. Still, some respondents (about 13.5 percent) do not invoke their North African origins or French citizenship and instead adopt an abstract identity (such as "citizen of the world") or one based on where they grew up in France. For these individuals, being French and being maghrébin are not the most significant aspects of their identity.

7. By *consciousness*, I am referring to the "meaning people give to their acts through the symbols, norms, and ideological forms they create" (P. H. Collins 1989, 746).

8. In fact, more than a few respondents noted how their parents had them celebrate Christmas when they were children so they would not stand out.

9. It is important to note that, while banlieues are often a catchall for residential disadvantage (Hargreaves 2007), from a demographic standpoint, they are heterogeneous (Oberti 2007). Neuilly-sur-Seine and Orsay, for example, where fewer immigrant-origin individuals live, are not characterized as socioeconomically disadvantaged.

10. This correlates with large-scale studies of the maghrébin second generation, such as Simon (2012).

5. BOUNDARIES OF DIFFERENCE: CULTURAL CITIZENSHIP AND TRANSNATIONAL BLACKNESS

1. Yade is a conservative French politician who emigrated from Senegal to France when she was eight years old.

2. I think my visible identity as a black American was invoked as a way to get at my closeness with or proximity to the people I was studying. I discuss this further in the methodological appendix.

3. Individuals reject what is "available to them and [reach] out for those less-known samples, including aspects of South Asian and African diasporic formations in England and the Caribbean. In not being a biological concept tied to ancestry that is imputed upon

individuals, 'desi' becomes a racialized construct selected by some South Asians" (Sharma 2010, 27).

4. James Baldwin, in his 1955 essay "Encounter on the Seine: Black Meets Brown," observes the nuances of race and racism in Paris, where African American expatriates were appreciated in France but Algerians were not.

5. This is also reminiscent of how some African Americans consider themselves more American than white Americans because the labor of their ancestors built the United States.

6. Brown discusses how the French census, in its refusal to collect racial and ethnic statistics, is an instrument of racial and ethnic exclusion.

CONCLUSION: SACRIFICED CHILDREN OF THE REPUBLIC?

1. See http://www.bbc.com/news/world-europe-30767929.

2. See http://www.nytimes.com/2015/01/08/world/europe/charlie-hebdo-paris-shooting. html). See also https://www.nytimes.com/2015/03/19/world/europe/dieudonne-mbala-mbala-french-comedian-convicted-of-condoning-terrorism.html?_r=o.

3. Note how the French government has extended this state of emergency six times to November 2017 (http://www.bbc.com/news/world-europe-40105183), which makes it the longest state of emergency in France since the Algerian War of Independence. Under a state of emergency, the police can execute searches without a warrant, among other measures.

4. See http://www.nytimes.com/2016/07/16/world/europe/nice-france-truck-attack-what-we-know.html and https://www.nytimes.com/2016/07/16/world/europe/attack-in-nice-france-represents-terrorisms-new-reality.html?action=click&contentCollection=Europe&module=RelatedCoverage&region = Marginalia&pgtype=article.

5. See http://www.nytimes.com/2016/08/27/world/europe/france-burkini-ban.html.

6. The title of this section is borrowed in part from William Julius Wilson's *The Declining Significance of Race: Blacks and Changing American Institutions* (1980), although I argue that race and ethnicity remain significant in understanding France's past and present society.

7. See http://www.nytimes.com/2015/05/22/opinion/a-lingering-injustice-in-france.html?_r = o.

8. See http://www.nytimes.com/2016/09/20/world/europe/france-minorities-assimilation. html?emc=edit_tnt_20160926&nlid=43222843&tntemailo=y&_r=o.

9. By *identity politics*, I am referring to how culture and identity are constructed to various political ends. As Hill and Wilson articulate, "Identity politics refers mainly to the 'top down' processes whereby various political, economic, and other social entities attempt to mold collective identities, based on ethnicity, race, language, and place, into relatively fixed and 'naturalized' frames for understanding political action and the body politic" (2003, 2).

10. See http://redux.slate.com/cover-stories/2017/01/the-death-of-adama-traore-has-become-frances-ferguson.html.

11. The inspiration for the title of my conclusion comes from an article by activist and journalist Rokhaya Diallo, "Zyed et Bouna: Enfants sacrifiés de la République" (Zyed and Bouna: Sacrificed children of the Republic), about the death of two adolescents that led to the 2005 uprisings; see http://www.regards.fr/web/Zyed-et-Bouna-enfants-sacrifies-de.

METHODOLOGICAL APPENDIX: ANOTHER INSIDER:
DOING RACE FROM/IN ANOTHER PLACE

1. I included three respondents in my sample who were not born in France because they immigrated when they were two years of age or younger. They self-identified as children of immigrants or second-generation immigrants. Other scholars define the second generation by their place of socialization and primary schooling (see Noiriel 1996), and I felt confident including them in my sample. All of them were naturalized French citizens.

2. Small (2009) has noted that another critique of snowball sampling is that respondents are more likely to know each other or even "constitute a social network" which might be "more biased" than random sampling. He challenges this by showing how random sampling involves the bias of nonresponse, meaning that only those individuals who are willing to participate are interviewed. Furthermore, he argues that samples may be considered "a set of cases with particular characteristics that, rather than being 'controlled away', should be understood, developed, and incorporated" (14) into researchers' analytical understanding.

3. According to INSEE, as of 1999, about 86 percent of neighborhood housing is public housing.

4. I also want to challenge the idea that an American understanding of race and ethnicity is completely divorced from the European one, particularly when considering the history of slavery and colonialism in both Europe and the United States (Goldberg 2006).

REFERENCES

AFP (Agence France-Presse). 2015. "French Mayor Attacked for Counting Schoolchildren with 'Muslim Names.'" *The Guardian*, May 5. https://www.theguardian.com/world/2015/may/05/french-mayor-attacked-for-counting-schoolchildren-with-muslim-names.

Ajrouch, Kristine J. 2004. "Gender, Race, and Symbolic Boundaries: Contested Spaces of Identity among Arab American Adolescents." *Sociological Perspectives* 47 (4): 371–91.

Alba, Richard. 2005. "Bright vs. Blurred Boundaries: Second-Generation Assimilation and Exclusion in France, Germany, and the United States." *Ethnic and Racial Studies* 28 (1): 20–49.

Alba, Richard, and Nancy Foner. 2015. *Strangers No More: Immigration and the Challenges of Integration in North America and Western Europe*. Princeton, NJ: Princeton University Press.

———. 2016. "Integration's Challenges and Opportunities in the Wealthy West." *Journal of Ethnic and Migration Studies* 42 (1): 3–22.

Alba, Richard, and Victor Nee. 2003. *Remaking the American Mainstream: Assimilation and Contemporary Immigration*. Cambridge, MA: Harvard University Press.

Alba, Richard, and Roxane Silberman. 2002. "Decolonization Immigrations and the Social Origins of the Second Generation: The Case of North Africans in France." *International Migration Review* 36 (4): 1169–93.

Alba, Richard, and Mary C. Waters, eds. 2011. *The Next Generation: Immigrant Youth in a Comparative Perspective*. New York: New York University Press.

Ali, Suki. 2006. "Racializing Research: Managing Power and Politics?" *Ethnic and Racial Studies* 29 (3): 471–86.

Ali, Syed. 2008. "Understanding Acculturation among Second-Generation South Asian Muslims in the United States." *Contributions to Indian Sociology* 42 (3): 383–411.

Amara, Fadela. 2006. *Breaking the Silence: French Women's Voices from the Ghetto*. Oakland: University of California Press.

Amiraux, Valérie, and Patrick Simon. 2006. "There are No Minorities Here: Cultures of Scholarship and Public Debate on Immigrants and Integration in France." *International Journal of Comparative Sociology* 47 (3–4): 191–215.

Amselle, Jean-Loup. 2003. *Affirmative Exclusion: Cultural Pluralism and the Rule of Custom in France*. Ithaca, NY: Cornell University Press.

Anderson, Benedict. 1991. *Imagined Communities: Reflections on the Origins of Nationalism*. London: Verso.

Anderson, Elijah. 2015. "The White Space." *Sociology of Race and Ethnicity* 1 (1): 10–21.

Avenel, Cyprien. 2007. *Sociologie des "quartiers sensibles."* Paris: Armand Colin.

BBC News Services. 2017. "France Using State of Emergency Against Peaceful Protests, Amnesty Says." May 31. http://www.bbc.com/news/world-europe-40105183.

Baldwin, James. 1955. "Encounter on the Seine: Black Meets Brown." In *Notes of a Native Son*, 101–16. Boston: Beacon Press.

Balibar, Étienne. 2004. *We, the People of Europe? Reflections on Transnational Citizenship*. Princeton, NJ: Princeton University Press.

———. 2007. "Uprisings in the *Banlieues*." *Constellations* 14 (1): 47–71.

Barou, Jacques. 2014. "Integration of Immigrants in France: A Historical Perspective." *Identities: Global Studies in Culture and Power* 21 (6): 642–57.

Barth, Fredrik. l969. *Ethnic Groups and Boundaries: The Social Organization of Culture Difference*. London: Allen & Unwin.

Bass, Loretta E. 2014. *African Immigrants in Another France: Sub-Saharan African Immigrants in France*. New York: Palgrave Macmillan.

Bauberot, Jean. 2009. "*Laïcité* and the Challenge of Republicanism." *Modern and Contemporary France* 17 (2): 189–98.

Beaman, Jean. 2012. " 'But Madame, We Are French Also': Being Middle Class, North African, and Second-Generation in France." *Contexts* 11 (3): 46–51.

———. 2015a. "Boundaries of Frenchness: Cultural Citizenship and France's Middle-Class North African Second Generation." *Identities: Global Studies in Culture and Power* 22 (1): 36–52.

———. 2015b. "From Ferguson to France." *Contexts* 14 (1): 65–67.

———. 2015c. "Qui est Ahmed? Understanding Race, Racism, and French Muslims in the Wake of Charlie Hebdo," *Migration and Citizenship* 3 (2): 14–18.

———. 2016. " 'As French as Anyone Else': Islam and the North African Second Generation in France." *International Migration Review* 50 (1): 41–69.

———. 2016b. "Citizenship as Cultural: Towards a Theory of Cultural Citizenship." *Sociology Compass* 10 (10): 849–57.

Begag, Azouz. 1990. "The 'Beurs': Children of North-African Immigrants in France: The Issue of Integration." *Journal of Ethnic Studies* 18 (1): 1–14.

———. 2007. *Ethnicity and Equality: France in the Balance*. Lincoln: University of Nebraska Press.

Bell, David A. 2003. *The Cult of the Nation in France: Inventing Nationalism, 1680–1800*. Cambridge, MA: Harvard University Press.

———. 2005. "The Shorn Identity: How the French Forgot How to Assimilate." *The New Republic*, November 28.

Belmessous, Hacène. 2007. "Les minorisés de la République: La discrimination au logement des jeunes générations d'origine immigrée." Le centre de ressources politique de la ville en Essonne. Essonne, France. http://www.crpve91.fr/Lutte_contre_les_discriminations/ Productions_du_CRPVE/pdf/Publication_minorises.pdf.

Benia, Mouss. 2009. "Où trouver l'Obama français?" Le Monde, January 31. http://www. lemonde.fr/idees/article/2009/01/31/ou-trouver-l-obama-francais-par-mouss-benia-acteur-et-ecrivain_1149056_3232.html#.

Berry, Justin A., and Jane Junn. 2015. "Silent citizenship among Asian Americans and Latinos: Opting Out or Left Out?" Citizenship Studies 19 (5): 570–90.

Bertossi, Christophe. 2007. Distant Neighbors: Understanding How the French Deal with Ethnic and Religious Diversity. London: Runnymede Trust.

Beydoun, Khaled A. 2013. "The French Kiss 'Race' Goodbye." Al Jazeera, June 2. http://www. aljazeera.com/indepth/opinion/2013/06/20136273349196523.html.

Bilefsky, Dan, and Maia de la Baume. 2015. "Terrorists Strike Charlie Hebdo Newspaper in Paris, Leaving 12 Dead." New York Times, January 7. https://www.nytimes. com/2015/01/08/world/europe/charlie-hebdo-paris-shooting.html.

Bleich, Erik. 2001. "Race Policy in France." Brookings U.S.-France Analysis Series. Washington, DC: Brookings Institution. https://www.brookings.edu/articles/ race-policy-in-france/.

———. 2003. Race Politics in Britain and France: Ideas and Policymaking Since the 1960s. Cambridge: Cambridge University Press.

———. 2004. "Anti-Racism without Races: Politics and Policy in a 'Color-Blind' State." In Race in France: Interdisciplinary Perspectives on the Politics of Difference, edited by H. Chapman and L. L. Frader, 162–88. New York: Berghahn Books.

———. 2006. "Constructing Muslims as Ethno-Racial Outsiders in Western Europe." European Studies Newsletter 36: 1, 3–7.

———. 2008. "From Republican Citizens to 'Young Ethnics' in the 'Other France'? Race and Identity in France and the United States." French Politics 6 (2): 166–77.

———. 2009. "Where Do Muslims Stand on Ethno-Racial Hierarchies in Britain and France? Evidence from Public Opinion Surveys, 1988–2008." Patterns of Prejudice 43: 379–400.

Bloemraad, Irene. 2015. "Theorizing and Analyzing Citizenship in Multicultural Societies." The Sociological Quarterly 56 (4): 591–606.

Body-Gendrot, Sophie. 1993. "Migration and Racialization of the Postmodern City in France." In Racism, the City, and the State, edited by M. Cross and M. Keith, 77–92. London: Routledge.

———. 2007. "Urban Riots or Urban Violence in France?" Policing 1 (4): 416–27.

Bohlen, Celestine. 2016. "France Fears Becoming Too 'Anglo-Saxon' in Its Treatment of Minorities." New York Times, September 19. https://www.nytimes.com/2016/09/20/world/ europe/france-minorities-assimilation.html?emc=edit_tnt_20160926&nlid=43222843& tntemailo=y&_r=0.

Boittin, Jennifer Anne. 2012. " 'Among Them Complicit'? Life and Politics in France's Black Communities, 1919–1939." In Africa in Europe: Studies in Transnational Practice in the Long Twentieth Century, edited by E. Rosenhaft and R. Aitken, 55–75. Liverpool: Liverpool University Press.

Boittin, Jennifer Anne, and Tyler Stovall. 2010. "Who Is French?" *French Historical Studies* 33 (3): 349–56.

Bonilla-Silva, Eduardo. 2013. *Racism without Racists: Color-Blind Racism and the Persistence of Racial Inequality in America.* Lanham, MD: Rowman & Littlefield.

Bonilla-Silva, Eduardo, and Sarah Mayorga. 2011. "On (Not) Belonging: Why Citizenship Does Not Remedy Racial Inequality." In *State of White Supremacy: Racism, Governance, and the United States,* edited by M.-K. Jung, J. H. Costa Vargas, and E. Bonilla-Silva, 77–92. Palo Alto, CA: Stanford University Press.

Bonnal, Liliane, Rachid Boumahdi, and Pascal Favard. 2012. "Nonexpected Discrimination: The Case of Social Housing in France." *Applied Economics Letters* 19 (18): 1909–16.

Borrel, Catherine, and Patrick Simon. 2005. "L'origine des Français." In *Histoires de familles, histoires familiales: Les résultats de l'enquête Famille de 1999,* edited by C. Lefèvre and A. Filhon, 425–41. Cahiers de l'INED, no. 156. Paris: INED.

Bouamama, Saïd. 2009. *Les classes et quartiers populaires: Paupérisation, ethnicisation et discrimination.* Paris: Éditions du Cygne.

Bourdieu, Pierre. 1984. *Distinction: A Social Critique of the Judgment of Taste.* Cambridge, MA: Harvard University Press.

Bowen, John R. 2004a. "Does French Islam Have Borders? Dilemmas of Domestication in a Global Religious Field." *American Anthropologist* 106 (1): 43–55.

———. 2004b. "Muslims and Citizens: France's Headscarf Controversy." *Boston Review,* February/March, 31–35. http://bostonreview.net/world/john-r-bowen-muslims-and-citizens.

———. 2004c. "Pluralism and Normativity in French Islamic Reasoning." In *Remaking Muslim Politics,* edited by R. Hefner, 326–46. Princeton, NJ: Princeton University Press.

———. 2006. *Why the French Don't Like Headscarves: Islam, the State, and Public Space.* Princeton, NJ: Princeton University Press.

———. 2008. "Republican Ironies: Equality and Identities in French Schools." In *Just Schools: Pursuing Equality in Societies of Difference,* edited by M. Minow, R. A. Shweder, and H. R. Markus, 204–24. New York: Russell Sage Foundation.

———. 2009. *Can Islam Be French? Pluralism and Pragmatism in a Secularist State.* Princeton, NJ: Princeton University Press.

Breeden, Aurelien. 2015. "Dieudonné M'bala M'bala, French Comedian, Convicted of Condoning Terrorism." *New York Times,* March 18. https://www.nytimes.com/2015/03/19/world/europe/dieudonne-mbala-mbala-french-comedian-convicted-of-condoning-terrorism.html.

Bremner, Charles. 2005. "Outrage as Paris Burns and French Riots Spread." *The Times,* November 7.

Brettell, Caroline B., and Deborah Reed-Danahay. 2012. *Civic Engagements: The Citizenship Practices of Indian and Vietnamese Immigrants.* Palo Alto, CA: Stanford University Press.

Brinbaum, Yaël, and Annick Kieffer. 2005. "D'une génération à l'autre, les aspirations éducatives des familles immigrées: Ambition et persévérance." *Éducation & formations* 72: 53–75.

———. 2009. "Trajectories of Immigrants' Children in Secondary Education in France: Differentiation and Polarization." *Population* 64 (3): 561–610.

Brinbaum, Yaël, and Amy Lutz. Forthcoming. "Examining Educational Inequalities in Two National Systems: A Comparison of the North African Second Generation in France and the Mexican Second Generation in the United States." *Journal of Ethnic and Migration Studies.*

Brown, Jacqueline Nassy. 2009. "The Racial State of the Everyday and the Making of Ethnic Statistics in Britain." *Social Text* 27 (1): 11–36.

Brubaker, Rogers. 1992. *Citizenship and Nationhood in France and Germany.* Cambridge, MA: Harvard University Press.

——. 2009. "Ethnicity, Race, and Nationalism." *Annual Review of Sociology* 35: 21–42.

——. 2013. "Categories of Analysis and Categories of Practice: A Note on the Study of Muslims in European Countries of Immigration." *Ethnic and Racial Studies* 36 (1): 1–8.

Brutel, Chantal. 2015. "Populations française, étrangère et immigrée en France depuis 2006." *INSEE Focus*, no. 38.

Burawoy, Michael. 1998. "The Extended Case Method." *Sociological Theory* 16 (1): 4–33.

Cadge, Wendy, and Elaine H. Ecklund. 2007. "Immigration and Religion." *Annual Review of Sociology* 33: 359–79.

Cain, Artwell. 2010. "Ambiguous Citizenship as Impediment to Social Mobility in the Netherlands: The Case of Afro-Caribbean Dutch." *Journal of Contemporary Thought* 32: 141–56.

Calvès, Gwénaële. 2004. "Color-Blindness at a Crossroads in Contemporary France." In *Race in France: Interdisciplinary Perspectives on the Politics of Difference*, edited by H. Chapman and L. L. Frader, 219–26. New York: Berghahn Books.

Campt, Tina. 2005. *Other Germans: Black Germans and the Politics of Race, Gender, and Memory in the Third Reich.* Ann Arbor: University of Michigan Press.

Canet, Raphaël, Laurent Pech, and Maura Stewart. 2008. "France's Burning Issue: Understanding the Urban Riots of November 2005." https://ssrn.com/abstract=1303514.

Carter, Prudence. 2005. *Keepin' It Real: School Success beyond Black and White.* Oxford: Oxford University Press.

Cartrite, Britt. 2009. "Minority Language Policy in France: Jacobinism, Cultural Pluralism, and Ethnoregional Identities." In *Culture and Belonging in Divided Societies*, edited by M. H. Ross, 128–50. Philadelphia: University of Pennsylvania Press.

Castles, Stephen. 1997. "Multicultural Citizenship: A Response to the Dilemma of Globalisation and National Identity?" *Journal of Intercultural Studies* 18 (1): 5–22.

Cesari, Jocelyne. 2002. "Islam in France: The Shaping of a Religious Minority." In *Muslims in the West: From Sojourners to Citizens*, edited by Y. Y. Haddad, 36–51. New York: Oxford University Press.

Chabal, Emile. 2015. *A Divided Republic: Nation, State and Citizenship in Contemporary France.* Cambridge: Cambridge University Press.

Chapman, Herrick, and Laura L. Frader. 2004. "Race in France." Introduction to *Race in France: Interdisciplinary Perspectives on the Politics of Difference*, edited by H. Chapman and L. L. Frader, 1–19. New York: Berghahn Books.

Chong, Kelly H. 1998. "What It Means to Be Christian: The Role of Religion in the Construction of Ethnic Identity and Boundary among Second-Generation Korean Americans." *Sociology of Religion* 59 (3): 159–286.

Clerge, Orly. 2014. "Balancing Stigma and Status: Racial and Class Identities among Middle-Class Haitian Youth. *Ethnic and Racial Studies* 37 (6): 958–77.

Cohen, Cathy J. 1999. *The Boundaries of Blackness: AIDS and the Breakdown of Black Politics.* Chicago: University of Chicago Press.

——. 2010. *Democracy Remixed: Black Youth and the Future of Politics.* Oxford: Oxford University Press.

Collins, Patricia Hill. 1986. "Learning from the Outsider Within: The Sociological Significance of Black Feminist Thought." *Social Problems* 33 (6): S14–S32.

——. 1989. "The Social Construction of Black Feminist Thought." *Signs: Journal of Women in Culture and Society* 14 (4): 745–73.

Collins, Sharon M. 1983. "The Making of the Black Middle Class." *Social Problems* 30 (4): 369–82.

Constant, Fred. 2009. "Talking Race in Color-Blind France: Equality Denied, 'Blackness' Reclaimed." In *Black Europe and the African Diaspora*, edited by D. C. Hine, T. D. Keaton, and S. Small, 145–60. Urbana: University of Illinois Press.

Cooper, Frederick. 2014. *Citizenship between Empire and Nation: Remaking France and French Africa, 1945–1960.* Princeton, NJ: Princeton University Press.

Cornell, Stephen E., and Douglas Hartmann. 2007. *Ethnicity and Race: Making Identities in a Changing World.* Thousand Oaks, CA: Pine Forge Press.

Cose, Ellis. 1994. *The Rage of a Privileged Class.* New York: Harper Collins.

Cowell, Alan. 2009. "France Tries to Define Frenchness." *New York Times*, November 14. http://www.nytimes.com/2009/11/14/world/europe/14iht-letter.html.

Crul, Maurie, and John H. Mollenkopf. 2012. *The Changing Face of World Cities: Young Adult Children of Immigrants in Europe and the United States.* New York: Russell Sage Foundation.

Cuba, Lee, and David M. Hummon. 1993. "A Place to Call Home: Identification with Dwelling, Community, and Region." *The Sociological Quarterly* 34 (1): 111–31.

d'Appollonia, Ariane Chebel. 2009. "Race, Racism, and Anti-Discrimination in France." In *The French Fifth Republic at Fifty: Beyond Stereotypes*, edited by S. Brouard, A. M. Appleton, and A. G. Mazur, 267–85. London: Palgrave Macmillan.

Deitch, Elizabeth A., Adam Barsky, Suzanne Chen, Arthur P. Brief, and Jill C. Bradley. 2003. "Subtle yet Significant: The Existence and Impact of Everyday Racial Discrimination in the Workplace." *Human Relations* 56 (11): 1299–1324.

Delanty, Gerard. 2002. "Two Conceptions of Cultural Citizenship: A Review of Recent Literature on Culture and Citizenship." *The Global Review of Ethnopolitics* 1 (3): 60–66.

Derderian, Richard L. 2004. *North Africans in Contemporary France: Becoming Visible.* New York: Palgrave Macmillan.

Diallo, Rokhaya. 2015. "Zyed et Bouna: Enfants Sacrifiés de la République." *Regards* (Spring): 62. http://www.regards.fr/web/Zyed-et-Bouna-enfants-sacrifies-de.

Diallo, Rokhaya, Faïza Guen, Alice Diop, Disiz, Maboula Soumahoro, Ridan, Sid Rouis, Marc Chebsun, Fatou Diome, Ofer Bronchtein, and Gilles Sokoudjou. 2012. "Français d'origine étrangère, nous refusons d'être la variable d'ajustement de l'élection présidentielle" *Le Monde*, May 4. http://www.lemonde.fr/idees/article/2012/05/04/francais-d-origine-etrangere-nous-refusons-d-etre-la-variable-d-ajustement-de-l-election-presidentielle_1695522_3232.html.

Dikeç, Mustafa. 2007. *Badlands of the Republic: Space, Politics, and Urban Policy*. Malden, MA: Blackwell Publishing.

Draelants, Hugues, and Brigitte Darchy-Koechlin. 2011. "Flaunting One's Academic Pedigree? Self-presentation of Students from Elite French Schools." *British Journal of Sociology of Education* 32 (1): 17–34.

Dubois, Laurent. 2010. *Soccer Empire: The World Cup and the Future of France*. Oakland: University of California Press.

DuBois, W. E. B. (1903) 1994. *The Souls of Black Folk: Essays and Sketches*. Mineola, NY: Dover Publications.

 Γιλιλιλιιι, ινιιθιι. 2007. "Republican Betrayal: Beur FM and the Suburban Riots in France." *Journal of Intercultural Studies* 28 (3): 301–16.

Edwards, Brent Hayes. 2003. *The Practice of Diaspora: Literature, Translation, and the Rise of Black Internationalism*. Cambridge, MA: Harvard University Press.

Eid, Paul. 2008. *Being Arab: Ethnic and Religious Identity Building among Second Generation Youth in Montreal*. Montreal: McGill-Queen's University Press.

ENAR (European Network Against Racism). 2014. "Racism and Discrimination in Employment in Europe: ENAR Shadow Report 2012–2013." Brussels: ENAR.

Erlanger, Steven. 2008. "After U.S. Breakthrough, Europe Looks in Mirror." *New York Times*, November 11. http://www.nytimes.com/2008/11/12/world/europe/12europe.html.

———. 2009. "France Debates Its identity, but Some Ask Why." *New York Times*, November 28. http://www.nytimes.com/2009/11/29/world/europe/29identity.html?rref=collection%2F byline%2Fsteven-erlanger&action=click&contentCollection=undefined&region=stream &module=stream_unit&version=search&contentPlacement=1&pgtype=collection.

———. 2010. "French 'Identity' Debate Leaves Public Forum." *New York Times*, February 8. http://www.nytimes.com/2010/02/09/world/europe/09france.html?rref=collection%2 Fbyline%2Fsteven-erlanger&action=click&contentCollection=undefined&region=stre am&module=stream_unit&version=search&contentPlacement=1&pgtype=collection.

Escafré-Dublet, Angéline, and Riva Kastoryano. 2012. "Tolerance in French Political Life." Accept-Pluralism Policy Brief no. 15. Florence, Italy: Robert Schuman Centre for Advanced Studies, European University Institute.

Escafré-Dublet, Angéline, and Patrick Simon. 2011. "Ethnic Statistics in Europe: The Paradox of Colorblindness." In *European Multiculturalisms: Cultural, Religious, and Ethnic Challenges*, edited by A. Triandafyllidou, T. Modood, and N. Meer, 213–37. Edinburgh: Edinburgh University Press.

Esman, Milton. 2009. *Diasporas in the Contemporary World*. Malden, MA: Polity Press.

Essed, Philomena. 1991. *Understanding Everyday Racism: An Interdisciplinary Theory*. Sage Series on Race and Ethnic Relations 2. Newbury Park, CA: Sage Publications.

Euro-Islam.info. "Islam in France." http://www.euro-islam.info/country-profiles/france/.

Fanon, Frantz. 1967. *Black Skin, White Masks*. New York: Grove Press.

Favell, Adrian. 2001. *Philosophies of Integration: Immigration and the Idea of Citizenship in France and Britain*. New York: Palgrave Macmillan.

Feagin, Joe R. 1991. "The Continuing Significance of Race: Antiblack Discrimination in Public Places." *American Sociological Review* 56 (1): 101–16.

Feldblum, Miriam. 1999. *Reconstructing Citizenship: Politics of Nationality, Reform, and Immigration in Contemporary France*. Albany: State University of New York Press.

Fernando, Mayanthi. 2005. "The Republic's 'Second Religion': Recognizing Islam in France." *Middle East Report* 235: 12–17.

———. 2009. "Exceptional Citizens: Secular Muslim Women and the Politics of Difference in France." *Social Anthropology* 17 (4): 379–92.

———. 2014. *The Republic Unsettled: Muslim French and the Contradictions of Secularism.* Durham, NC: Duke University Press.

Ferroukhi, Ismaël. 2004. *Le grand voyage (The Great Journey)* (film). New York: Film Movement.

Fisher, Max. 2016. "Attack in Nice, France, Represents Terrorism's New Reality." *New York Times,* July 15. https://www.nytimes.com/2016/07/16/world/europe/attack-in-nice-france-represents-terrorisms-new-reality.html?action=click&contentCollection=Europe&module=RelatedCoverage&region = Marginalia&pgtype=article.

Fleischmann, Fenella, Karen Phalet, Karen Neels, and Patrick Deboosere. 2011. "Contextualizing Ethnic Educational Inequality: The Role of Stability and Quality of Neighborhoods and Ethnic Density in Second-Generation Attainment." *International Migration Review* 45 (2): 386–425.

Foner, Nancy, and Richard Alba. 2008. "Immigration Religion in the U.S. and Western Europe: Bridge or Barrier to Inclusion?" *International Migration Review* 42 (2): 360–92.

Frazier, E. Franklin. 1957. *Black Bourgeoisie: The Book That Brought the Shock of Self-Revelation to Middle-Class Blacks in America.* New York: Free Press.

Fysh, Peter, and Jim Wolfreys. 2003. *The Politics of Racism in France.* New York: Palgrave Macmillan.

Gafaïti, Hafid. 2003. "Nationalism, Colonialism, and Ethnic Discourse in the Construction of French Identity." In *French Civilization and its Discontents: Nationalism, Colonialism, Race,* edited by T. Stovall and G. Van Den Abbeele, 189–211. Lanham, MD: Lexington Books.

García-Sánchez, Inmaculada M. 2013. "The Everyday Politics of 'Cultural Citizenship' among North African Immigrant School Children in Spain." *Language and Communication* 33: 481–99.

Gay, Roxane. 2014. "The Price of Black Ambition." *VQR* 90 (4). http://www.vqronline.org/essays-articles/2014/10/price-black-ambition.

Germain, Felix. 2016. "Mercer Cook and the Origins of Black French Studies." *French Politics, Culture, and Society* 34 (1): 66–85.

Ghorashi, Halleh, and Ulrike M. Vietan. 2012. "Female Narratives of 'New' Citizens' Belonging(s) and Identities in Europe: Case Studies from the Netherlands and Britain." *Identities: Global Studies in Culture and Power* 19 (6): 725–41.

Gieryn, Thomas F. 2000. "A Space for Place in Sociology." *Annual Review of Sociology* 26: 463–96.

Gilroy, Paul. 1991. *There Ain't No Black in the Union Jack: The Cultural Politics of Race and Nation.* Chicago: University of Chicago Press.

Glenn, Evelyn Nakano. 2011. "Constructing Citizenship: Exclusion, Subordination, and Resistance." *American Sociological Review* 76 (1): 1–24.

Goldberg, David Theo. 2006. "Racial Europeanization." *Ethnic and Racial Studies* 29 (2): 331–64.

Gobineau, Arthur de. (1853) 1915. *Essai sur l'inégalité des races humaines* (Essay on the Inequality of the Human Races). Translated by Adrian Collins. London: William Heinemann.

Grabar, Henry. 2017. "France's Ferguson." *Slate.com*, February 1. https://slate.com/cover-stories/2017/01/the-death-of-adama-traore-has-become-frances-ferguson.html.

Gray, Doris H. 2008. *Muslim Women on the Move: Moroccan Women and the French Women of Moroccan Origin Speak Out.* Plymouth, UK: Lexington Books.

Green, Nancy L. 2007. "Of Croissants and Couscous: National Identity after the French Elections." *Dissent Magazine* (Fall). https://www.dissentmagazine.org/article/of-croissants-and-couscous-national-identity-after-the-french-elections.

Gregg, Robert. 1998. "The New African American Middle Class." *Economic and Political Weekly*, 33 (46): 2933–938, November 14, 1998.

Guinier, Lani, and Gerald Torres. 2002. *The Miner's Canary: Enlisting Race, Resisting Power, Transforming Democracy.* Cambridge, MA: Harvard University Press.

Gunn, T. J. 2004. "Religious Freedom and *Laïcité*: A Comparison of the United States and France." *Brigham Young University Law Review* (2): 419–506.

Haddad, Yvone Yazbeck, and Michael J. Balz. 2006. "The October Riots in France: A Failed Immigration Policy or the Empire Strikes Back?" *International Migration* 44 (2): 23–34.

Hajjat, Abdellali. 2013. *La marche pour l'égalité et contre le racisme.* Paris: Éditions Amsterdam.

———. 2015. "Reflections on the January 2015 Killings and Their Consequences." *Migration and Citizenship* 3 (2): 7–14.

Hajjat, Abdellali, and Marwan Mohammed. 2013. *Islamophobie: Comment les élites françaises fabriquent le "problème musulman."* Paris: Éditions La Découverte.

Hall, Kathleen D. 2004. "The Ethnography of Imagined Communities: The Cultural Production of Sikh Ethnicity in Britain." *Annals of the American Academy of Political and Social Science* 595: 108–21.

Hall, Stuart. 1991. "Old and New Identities, Old and New Ethnicities." In *Culture, Globalization, and the World System: Contemporary Conditions for the Representation of Identity*, edited by A. D. King, 44–68. Minneapolis: University of Minneapolis Press.

Hargreaves, Alec G. 1996. "A Deviant Construction: The French Media and the '*Banlieues*.'" *Journal of Ethnic and Migration Studies* 22 (4): 607–18.

———. 1998. "The Beurgeoisie: Meditation or Mirage?" *Journal of European Studies* 28 (1): 89–102.

———. 2003. "The Contribution of North and Sub-Saharan African Immigrant Minorities to the Redefinition of Contemporary French Culture." In *Francophone Postcolonial Studies: A Critical Introduction*, edited by C. Forsdick and D. Murphy, 145–54. New York: Hidden Education Publishers.

———. 2004. "Half-Measures: Anti-Discrimination Policy in France." In *Race in France: Interdisciplinary Perspectives on the Politics of Difference*, edited by H. Chapman and L. L. Frader, 227–45. New York: Berghahn Books.

———. 2007. *Multi-Ethnic France: Immigration, Politics, Culture, and Society.* London: Routledge.

Hargreaves, Alec G., J. Kelsay, and S. B. Twiss. 2007. *Politics and Religion in France and the US.* Lanham, MD: Rowman and Littlefield.

Harvey Wingfield, Adia. 2011. *Changing Times for Black Professionals.* New York: Routledge.

———. 2013. *No More Invisible Man: Race and Gender in Men's Work.* Philadelphia: Temple University Press.

HCI (Haut Conseil à l'intégration). 2001. "Islam dans la République." Paris: Documentation française.

Hill, Jonathan, and Thomas Wilson. 2003. "Identity Politics and the Politics of Identities." *Identities: Global Studies in Culture and Power* 10 (1): 1–8.

Hine, Darlene Clark, Trica Danielle Keaton, and Stephen Small, eds. 2009. *Black Europe and the African Diaspora.* Urbana: University of Illinois Press.

Horowitz, Ruth. 1986. "Remaining an Outsider: Membership as a Threat to Research Rapport." *Urban Life* 14 (4): 409–30.

Hout, Michael. 1986. "Opportunity and the Minority Middle Class: A Comparison of Blacks in the United States and Catholics in Northern Ireland." *American Sociological Review* 51 (2): 214–23.

HRW (Human Rights Watch). 2012. "The Root of Humiliation: Abusive Identity Checks in France." Paris: HRW.

Ichou, Mathieu, and Marco Oberti. 2014. "Le rapport à l'école des familles déclarant une origine immigrée: Enquête dans quatre lycées de la banlieue populaire." *Population* 69 (4): 617–57.

Imoagene, Onoso. 2012. "Being British vs. Being American: Identification among Second-Generation Adults of Nigerian Descent in the U.S. and U.K." *Ethnic and Racial Studies* 35 (12): 2152–73.

IFOP (Institut français d'opinion publique). 2009. "Enquête sur l'implantation et l'évolution de l'Islam de France." Paris: IFOP.

INSEE (Institut national de la statistique et des études économiques). 2003. *Nomenclature des professions et catégories socioprofessionnelles des emplois salariés d'entreprise PCS-ESE.* Paris: INSEE. https://www.insee.fr/fr/metadonnees/pcsese2003/categorie SocioprofessionnelleAgregee/1.

Jackson, John L. 2001. *Harlemworld: Doing Race and Class in Black America.* Chicago: University of Chicago Press.

Jiménez, Tomás R. 2010. "Affiliative Ethnic Identity: A More Elastic Link between Ethnic Ancestry and Culture." *Ethnic and Racial Studies* 33 (10): 1756–775.

Joppke, Christian. 2001. "Multicultural Citizenship: A Critique." *European Journal of Sociology/Archives Européennes de Sociologie* 42 (2): 431–47.

Judge, Harry. 2004. "The Muslim Headscarf and French Schools." *American Journal of Education* 111 (1): 1–24.

Kasinitz, Philip, John H. Mollenkopf, and Mary C. Waters, eds. 2004. *Becoming New Yorkers: Ethnographies of the New Second Generation.* New York: Russell Sage Foundation.

Kastoryano, Riva. 2002. *Negotiating Identities: States and Immigrants in France and Germany.* Princeton, NJ: Princeton University Press.

———. 2004. "Race and Ethnicity in France." In *Social Inequalities in Comparative Perspective,* edited by F. Devine and M. C. Waters, 66–88. Malden, MA: Blackwell Publishers.

———. 2006. "Territories of Identities in France." In *Riots in France.* Brooklyn, NY: Social Sciences Resource Council. http://riotsfrance.ssrc.org/Kastoryano.

Kastoryano, Riva, and Angéline Escafré-Dublet. 2012. "France." In *Addressing Tolerance and Diversity Discourses in Europe: A Comparative Overview of 16 European Countries,* edited by R. Zapata-Barrero and A. Triandafyllidou, 27–47. Barcelona: Barcelona Centre for International Affairs.

Kaya, Ayhan. 2009. *Islam, Migration, and Integration: The Age of Securitization*. London: Palgrave Macmillan.

Keaton, Trica Danielle. 2006. *Muslim Girls and the Other France: Race, Identity Politics, and Social Exclusion*. Bloomington: Indiana University Press.

———. 2009. " 'Black (American) Paris' and the 'Other France': The Race Question and Questioning Solidarity." In *Black Europe and the African Diaspora*, edited by D. C. Hine, T. D. Keaton, and S. Small, 95–118. Champaign: University of Illinois Press.

———. 2010. "The Politics of Race-Blindness: (Anti) Blackness and Category-Blindness in Contemporary France." *Du Bois Review: Social Science Research on Race* 7 (1): 103–31.

Keaton, Trica Danielle, T. Denean Sharpley-Whiting, and Tyler Stovall, eds. 2012. *Black France/France Noire: The History and Politics of Blackness*. Durham, NC: Duke University Press.

Kelley, Robin D. G. 1995. "Race and Racism: A Symposium." *Social Text* 42: 1–52.

Kepel, Gilles, Leyla Arslan, and Sarah Zouheir. 2011. *Banlieue de la République*. Paris: Institut Montaigne.

Khanna, Nikki. 2011. "Ethnicity and Race as 'Symbolic': The Use of Ethnic and Racial Symbols in Asserting a Biracial Identity." *Ethnic and Racial Studies* 34 (6): 1049–67.

Killian, Caitlin. 2002. "Culture on the Weekend: Maghrébin Women's Adaptation in France." *International Journal of Sociology and Social Policy* 22 (1–3): 75–105.

Kirszbaum, Thomas, Yaël Brinbaum, and Patrick Simon. 2009. "The Children of Immigrants in France: The Emergence of a Second Generation." Innocenti Working Paper 2009–13, UNICEF Innocenti Research Centre, Florence, Italy.

Kiwan, Nadia. 2009. *Identities, Discourses, and Experiences: Young People of North African Origin in France*. Manchester, UK: Manchester University Press.

Klausen, Jytte. 2008. *The Islamic Challenge: Politics and Religion in Western Europe*. Oxford: Oxford University Press.

Kleinman, Julie. 2016. " 'All the Daughters and Sons of the Republic'? Producing Difference in French Education." *Journal of the Royal Anthropological Institute* 22 (2): 261–78.

Koff, Harlan, and Dominique Duprez. 2009. "The 2005 Riots in France: The International Impact of Domestic Violence." *Journal of Ethnic and Migration Studies* 35 (5): 713–30.

Kokoreff, Michel. 2003. *La force des quartiers: De la délinquance à l'engagement politique*. Paris: Payot.

Kuru, Ahmet T. 2008. "Secularism, State Politics, and Muslims in Europe." *Comparative Politics* 41 (1): 1–20.

Kymlicka, Will. 1995. *Multicultural Citizenship*. Oxford: Oxford University Press.

Labelle, Micheline. 2004. "The 'Language of Race,' Identity Options, and 'Belonging' in the Quebec Context." In *Social Inequality in Comparative Perspective*, edited by F. Devine and M. C. Waters, 39–65. Malden, MA: Blackwell Publishers.

Laborde, Cécile. 2008. *Critical Republicanism: The Hijab Controversy and Political Philosophy*. Oxford: Oxford University Press.

Lacy, Karyn R. 2004. "Black Spaces, Black Places: Strategic Assimilation and Identity Construction in Middle-Class Suburbia." *Ethnic and Racial Studies* 27 (6): 908–30.

———. 2007. *Blue-Chip Black: Race, Class, and Status in the New Black Middle Class*. Oakland: University of California Press.

———. 2008. "When Ethnographers Fail: Lessons from Cross-Race Fieldwork in Middle-Class Suburbia." Unpublished manuscript, University of Michigan, Ann Arbor.

Lamont, Michèle. 1992. *Money, Morals, and Manners: The Culture of the French and American Upper-Middle Class.* Chicago: University of Chicago Press.

———. 1995. "National Identity and National Boundary Patterns in France and the United States." *French Historical Studies* 19 (2): 349–65.

———. 2000. "The Rhetorics of Racism and Anti-Racism in France and the United States." In *Rethinking Comparative Cultural Sociology: Repertoires of Evaluation in France and the United States,* edited by M. Lamont and L. Thévenot, 25–55. Cambridge Cultural Studies. Cambridge, UK: Cambridge University Press.

———. 2002. *The Dignity of Working Men: Morality and the Boundaries of Race, Class, and Immigration.* Cambridge, MA: Harvard University Press.

Lamont, Michèle, and Virag Molnar. 2002. "The Study of Boundaries in the Social Sciences." *Annual Review of Sociology* 28: 167–95.

Lamont, Michèle, Ann Morning, and Margarita Mooney. 2002. "Particular Universalisms: North African Immigrants Respond to French Racism." *Ethnic and Racial Studies* 25 (3): 390–414.

Landry, Bart, and Kris Marsh. 2011. "The Evolution of the New Black Middle Class." *Annual Review of Sociology* 37: 373–94.

Lapeyronnie, Didier. 2008. *Ghetto urbain: Ségrégation, violence, pauvreté en France Aujourd'hui.* Paris: Robert Laffont.

Lareau, Annette. 2015. "Cultural Knowledge and Social Inequality." *American Sociological Review* 80 (1): 1–27.

Laurence, Jonathan. 2001. "Islam in France." Washington, DC: Brookings Institution.

Laurence, Jonathan, and Justin Vaisse. 2006. *Integrating Islam: Political and Religious Challenges in Contemporary France.* Washington, DC: Brookings Institution Press.

LePoutre, David. 1997. *Coeur de banlieue: Codes, rites, et langage.* Paris: Éditions Odile Jacob.

Leveque, Thierry, Crispian Balmer, and Mark Trevelyan. 2009. "French Minister Tells Muslims to Speak Properly." Reuters, December 15. http://www.reuters.com/article/us-france-minister-muslims-idUSTRE5BE3KC20091215.

Lieberman, Robert C. 2004. "A Tale of Two Countries: The Politics of Color-Blindness in France and the United States." In *Race in France: Interdisciplinary Perspectives on the Politics of Difference,* edited by H. Chapman and L. L. Frader, 189–216. New York: Berghahn Books.

Logan, John R., and Harvey L. Molotch. 1987. *Urban Fortunes: Political Economy of Place.* Berkeley: University of California Press.

Lombardo, Philippe, and Jérôme Pujol. 2011. "Le niveau de vie des descendants d'immigrés." In *Les revenus et le patrimoine des ménages,* 73–81. Paris: INSEE.

Lorde, Audre. 2007. *Sister Outsider: Essays and Speeches.* Berkeley, CA: TenSpeed Press.

Lowe, Lisa. 1996. *Immigrant Acts: On Asian American Cultural Politics.* Durham, NC: Duke University Press.

Lutz, Amy, Yaël Brinbaum, and Dalia Abdelhady. 2014. "The Transition from School to Work for Children of Immigrants with Lower-Level Educational Credentials in the United States and France." *Comparative Migration Studies* 2 (2): 227–54.

Lyons, Amelia. 2013. *The Civilizing Mission in the Metropole: Algerian Families and the French Welfare State during Decolonization*. Palo Alto, CA: Stanford University Press.

Maier, Sylvia. 2004. "Multicultural Jurisprudence: Muslim Immigrants, Culture, and the Law in France and Germany." Paper presented at the Council for European Studies Conference, Chicago.

Marsh, Kris, Jr., William A. Darity, Philip N. Cohen, Lynne M. Casper, and Danielle Salters. 2007. "The Emerging Black Middle Class: Single and Living Alone." *Social Forces* 86 (2): 735–62.

Marshall, T. H. 1950. "Citizenship and Social Class." In *Class, Citizenship and Social Development*. Chicago: University of Chicago Press.

Maurin, Éric. 2004. *Le ghetto français: Enquête sur le séparatisme social*. Paris: Éditions du Seuil.

Maxwell, Rahsaan. 2009. "Pour en finir avec un faux débat: Les statistiques ethniques." *En Temps Réel*, cahier 40.

Maxwell, Rahsaan, and Erik Bleich. 2014. "What Makes Muslims Feel French?" *Social Forces* 93 (1): 155–79.

May, Reuben A. Buford, and Mary Pattillo-McCoy. 2000. "Do You See What I See? Examining a Collaborative Ethnography." *Qualitative Inquiry* 6 (1): 65–87.

McCrone, David, and Frank Bechhofer. 2010. "Claiming National Identity." *Ethnic and Racial Studies* 33 (6): 921–48.

Meer, Nasar. 2010. *Citizenship, Identity, and the Politics of Multiculturalism: The Rise of Muslim Consciousness*. Basingstoke, UK: Palgrave Macmillan.

Meurs, Dominique, Ariane Pailhé, and Patrick Simon. 2005. "Immigrés et enfants d'immigrés sur le marché du travail: Une affaire de génération?" In *Histoires de familles, histoires familiales*, edited by C. Lefèvre and A. Filhon, 461–82. Cahiers de l'INED, no. 156. Paris: INED.

——. 2006. "The Persistence of Intergenerational Inequalities linked to Immigration: Labor Market Outcomes for Immigrants and their Descendants in France." *Population* 61: 645–82.

Mills, C. Wright. (1951) 2002. *White Collar: The American Middle Classes*. Oxford: Oxford University Press.

Murray, Graham. 2006. "France: The Riots and the Republic." *Race & Class* 47 (4): 26–45.

Ndiaye, Pap. 2008. *La condition noire: Essai sur une minorité française*. Paris: Editions Calmann-Lévy.

Neckerman, Kathryn M., Prudence Carter, and Jennifer Lee. 1999. "Segmented Assimilation and Minority Cultures of Mobility." *Ethnic and Racial Studies* 22 (6): 945–65.

New York Times. 2015. "A Lingering Injustice in France." May 21. http://www.nytimes.com/2015/05/22/opinion/a-lingering-injustice-in-france.html?_r = 0.

——. 2016. "Truck Attack in Nice, France: What We Know, and What We Don't." July 7. https://www.nytimes.com/2016/07/16/world/europe/nice-france-truck-attack-what-we-know.html.

Noiriel, Gérard. 1996. *The French Melting Pot*. Minneapolis: University of Minnesota Press.

Nyiri, Zsolt. 2007. "European Muslims Show No Conflict between Religious and National Identities." Princeton, NJ: Gallup Organization.

Oberti, Marco. 2007. "The French Republican Model of Integration: The Theory and Cohesion and the Practice of Exclusion: Some Sociological Reflections after the Riots in

France." Translated by B. Shevenaugh. OSC Notes & Documents 2007–02. Paris: Observatoire sociologique du changement.

Omi, Michael, and Howard Winant. 1994. *Racial Formation in the United States: From the 1960s to the 1990s*. New York: Routledge.

Ong, Aihwa. 1996. "Cultural Citizenship as Subject-Making." *Current Anthropology* 37 (5): 737–62.

OSI (Open Society Institute). 2009. *Profiling Minorities: A Study of Stop-and-Search Practices in Paris*. New York: OSI.

Pandey, Gyanendra. 2009. "Can There Be a Subaltern Middle Class? Notes on African American and Dalit History." *Public Culture* 21 (2): 321–42.

Pattillo, Mary. 2007. *Black on the Block: The Politics of Race and Class in the City*. Chicago: University of Chicago Press.

Pattillo-McCoy, Mary. 1998. "Church Culture as a Strategy of Action in the Black Community." *American Sociological Review* 63 (6): 767–84.

———. 1999. *Black Picket Fences: Privilege and Peril among the Black Middle Class*. Chicago: University of Chicago Press.

Peabody, Sue, and Tyler Stovall, eds. 2003. *The Color of Liberty: Histories of Race in France*. Durham, NC: Duke University Press.

Penn, Roger, and Paul Lambert. 2009. *Children of International Migrants in Europe: Comparative Perspectives*. New York: Palgrave Macmillan.

PRC (Pew Research Center). 2013. *Second-Generation Americans: A Portrait of the Adult Children of Immigrants*. Washington, D.C.: PRC.

Pickering, Paula M. 2007. *Peacebuilding in the Balkans: The View from the Ground Floor*. Ithaca, NY: Cornell University Press.

Portes, Alejandro, and Rubén G. Rumbaut. 2001. *Legacies: The Story of the Immigrant Second Generation*. Oakland: University of California Press.

Portes, Alejandro, and Min Zhou. 1993. "The New Second Generation: Segmented Assimilation and Its Variants." *Annals of the American Academy of Political and Social Science* 530 (1): 74–96.

Portes, Alejandro, Erik Vickstrom, and Rosa Aparicio. 2011. "Coming of Age in Spain: The Self-Identification, Beliefs, and Self-Esteem of the Second-Generation." *British Journal of Sociology* 62 (3): 387–417.

Préteceille, Edmond. 2008. "La ségrégation ethno-raciale a-t-elle augmenté dans la métropole parisienne?" Paris: Observatoire sociologique du changement.

Quillian, Lincoln, Ole Hexel, Devah Pager, Arnfinn Midtbøen, Fenella Fleischmann, and Anthony Heath. 2016. "Discrimination in American and European Labor Markets: An International Meta-Analysis of Field Experiments." Paper presented at the American Sociological Association Annual Meeting, Seattle, August.

Raveaud, Maroussia. 2008. "Culture-Blind? Parental Discourse on Religion, Ethnicity, and Secularism in the French Educational Context." *European Educational Research Journal* 7 (1): 74–88.

Reed-Danahay, Deborah. 1996. *Education and Identity in Rural France: The Politics of Schooling*. Cambridge, UK: Cambridge University Press.

Renan, Ernest. (1887) 1992. *Qu'est-ce qu'une nation? et autres essais politiques*. Paris: Presses Pocket.

Rey, Henri. 1996. *La peur des banlieues*. Paris: Presses de la Fondation nationale des sciences politiques.

Ribert, Évelyne. 2006. *Liberté, égalité, carte d'identité: Les jeunes issus de l'immigration et l'appartenance nationale*. Paris: Éditions La Découverte.

Riggs, Marlon. 1994. *Black Is . . . Black Ain't* (film). San Francisco: Independent Television Service.

Ringelheim, Julie. 2009. "Collecting Racial or Ethnic Data for Antidiscrimination Policies: A U.S.-Europe Comparison." *Rutgers Race and the Law Review* 10 (1): 39–142.

Rojas-García, Georgina. 2013. "Transitioning from School to Work as a Mexican 1.5er: Upward Mobility and Glass-Ceiling Assimilation among College Students in California." *Annals of the American Academy of Political and Social Science* 648 (1): 87–101.

Rosaldo, Renato. 1994. "Cultural Citizenship in San Jose, California." *PoLAR* 17 (2): 57–64.

Roy, Oliver. 1994. "Islam in France: Religion, Ethnic Community or Social Ghetto?" In *Muslims in Europe*, edited by B. Lewis and D. Schnapper, 54–66. London: Pinter Publishers.

Rumbaut, Rubén G. 1996. "Ties that Bind: Immigration and Immigrant Families in the United States." In *Immigration and the Family: Research and Policy on U.S. Immigrants*, edited by A. Booth, A. C. Crouter, and N. Landal, 3–45. Mahwah, NJ: Lawrence Erlbaum.

Sabbagh, Daniel. 2002. "Affirmative Action at Sciences Po." *French Politics, Culture & Society* 20 (3): 52–64.

———. 2008. "The Collection of Ethnoracial Statistics: Developments in the French Controversy." New York: French-American Foundation.

———. 2011. "Affirmative Action in Comparative Perspective." *Daedalus* 140 (2): 109–20.

Sayad, Abdelmalek. 2004. *The Suffering of the Immigrant*. Cambridge, UK: Polity Press.

Schnapper, Dominique, Pascale Krief, and Emmanuel Peignard. 2003. "French Immigration and Integration Policy: A Complex Combination." In *The Integration of Immigrants in European Societies: National Differences and Trends*, edited by F. Heckmann and D. Schnapper, 15–44. Forum Migration 7. Stuttgart: Lucius and Lucius.

Schneider, Cathy Lisa. 2008. "Police Power and Race Riots in Paris." *Politics & Society* 36 (1): 133–59.

Scott, Joan Wallach. 2007. *The Politics of the Veil*. Princeton, NJ: Princeton University Press.

Sharma, Nitasha Tamar. 2010. *Hip Hop Desis: South Asian Americans, Blackness, and a Global Race Consciousness*. Durham, NC: Duke University Press.

Shelby, Tommie. 2002. "Foundations of Black Solidarity: Collective Identity or Common Oppression?" *Ethics* 112 (2): 231–66.

Sherwood, Seth. 2009. "Marseille Sways to a Maghreb Rhythm." *New York Times*, June 26. http://www.nytimes.com/2009/07/26/travel/26next.html.

Shon, Jean-Louis Pan K. 2010. "The Ambivalent Nature of Ethnic Segregation in France's Disadvantaged Neighborhoods." *Urban Studies* 47 (8): 1603–23.

———. 2011. "Residential Segregation of Immigrants in France: An Overview." *Population & Sociétés*, no. 477.

Shon, Jean-Louis Pan Ké, and Gregory Verdugo. 2014. "Forty Years of Immigrant Segregation in France, 1968–2007: How Different Is the New Immigration?" Bonn, Germany: Institute for the Study of Labor.

Silberman, Roxane. 2011. "The Employment of Second Generations in France: The Republican Model and the November 2005 Riots." In *The Next Generation: Immigrant Youth in a Comparative Perspective*, edited by R. Alba and M. C. Waters, 283–316. New York: New York University Press.

Silberman, Roxane, Richard Alba, and Irène Fournier. 2007. "Segmented Assimilation in France? Discrimination in the Labor Market against the Second Generation." *Ethnic and Racial Studies* 30 (1): 1–27.

Silverman, Maxim. 1992. *Deconstructing the Nation: Immigration, Racism, and Citizenship in France*. London: Routledge.

Silverstein, Paul. 2008. "Thin Lines on the Pavement: The Racialization and Spatialization of Violence in Postcolonial (Sub)Urban France." In *Gendering Urban Space in the Middle East, South Asia, and Africa*, edited by K. Ali and M. Rieker, 169–206. New York: Palgrave Macmillan.

Simon, Patrick. 1998. "Ghettos, Immigrants, and Integration: The French Dilemma." *Netherlands Journal of Housing and the Built Environment* 13 (1): 41–61.

———. 1999. "Nationality and Origins in French Statistics: Ambiguous Categories." *Population: An English Selection* 11: 193–220.

———. 2003. "France and the Unknown Second Generation." *International Migration Review* 37 (4): 1091–1119.

———. 2008. "The Choice of Ignorance: The Debate on Ethnic and Racial Statistics in France." *French Politics, Culture & Society* 26 (1): 7–31.

———. 2012. *French National Identity and Integration: Who Belongs to the National Community?* Washington, DC: Migration Policy Institute.

Simon, Patrick, and Martin Clément. 2006. "Comment décrire la diversité des origines en France ? Une enquête exploratoire sur les perceptions des salariés et des étudiants." *Populations & Sociétés*, no. 425.

Simon, Patrick, and Anthony Heath. 2013. "Discrimination against Immigrants: Measurement, Incidence and Policy Instruments." In *International Migration Outlook 2013*, 191–230. Paris: OECD.

Skrenty, John D. 2014. *After Civil Rights: Racial Realism in the New American Workplace*. Princeton, NJ: Princeton University Press.

Small, Mario Luis. 2009. " 'How Many Cases Do I Need?': On Science and the Logic of Case Selection in Field-Based Research." *Ethnography* 10 (1): 5–38.

Smith, Candis Watts. 2014. *Black Mosaic: The Politics of Black Pan-Ethnic Diversity*. New York: New York University Press.

Smith, Craig G. 2005a. "Rioting Spreads in Paris Suburbs as Angry Youths Burn More Cars." *New York Times*, November 4. http://www.nytimes.com/2005/11/04/world/europe/rioting-spreads-in-paris-suburbs-as-angry-youths-burn-more.html.

———. 2005b. "Immigrant Rioting Flares in France for Ninth Night." *New York Times*, November 5. http://www.nytimes.com/2005/11/05/world/europe/immigrant-rioting-flares-in-france-for-ninth-night.html?_r=0.

Smith, Michelle. 2006. "Blackening Europe/Europeanising Blackness: Theorising the Black Presence in Europe." *Contemporary European History* 15 (3): 423–39.

Snow, David, Rens Vliegenthart, and Catherine Corrigall-Brown. 2007. "Framing the French Riots: A Comparative Study of Frame Variation." *Social Forces* 86 (2): 385–415.

Song, Steve. 2010. "Finding One's Place: Shifting Ethnic Identities of Recent Immigrant Children from China, Haiti and Mexico in the United States." *Ethnic and Racial Studies* 33 (6): 1006–31.

Stearns, Peter N. 1979. "The Middle Class: Toward a Precise Definition." *Comparative Studies in Society and History* 21 (3): 377–96.

Stébé, Jean-Marc. 2007. *La crise des banlieues: Sociologie des quartiers sensibles*. Paris: Presses Universitaires de France.

Stolcke, Verena. 1995. "Talking Culture: New Boundaries, New Rhetorics of Exclusion in Europe." *Current Anthropology* 36 (1): 1–24.

Stovall, Tyler. 1996. *Paris Noir: African Americans in the City of Light*. New York: Houghton Mifflin.

———. 2003. "From Red Belt to Black Belt: Race, Class, and Urban Marginality in Twentieth-Century Paris." In *The Color of Liberty: Histories of Race in France*, edited by S. Peabody and T. Stovall, 351–369. Durham, NC: Duke University Press.

———. 2006. "Race and the Making of the Nation: Blacks in Modern France." In *Diasporic Africa: A Reader*, edited by M. Gomez, 200–218. New York: New York University Press.

Stovall. 2009. "No Green Pastures: The African Americanization of France." In *Black Europe and the African Diaspora*, edited by D.C. Hine, T.D. Keaton, and S. Small, 180–197. Urbana, IL: University of Illinois Press.

Tatum, Beverly Daniel. 1997. *"Why Are All the Black Kids Sitting Together in the Cafeteria?" and Other Conversations about Race*. New York: Basic Books.

Tetreault, Chantal. 2013. "Cultural Citizenship in France and Le Bled among Teens of Pan-Southern Immigrant Heritage." *Language & Communication* 33 (4): 532–43.

Thomas, Dominic. 2007. *Black France: Colonialism, Immigration, and Transnationalism*. Bloomington: Indiana University Press.

Tin, Louis-Georges. 2008. "Who Is Afraid of Blacks in France? The Black Question: The Name Taboo, the Number Taboo." *French Politics, Culture, and Society* 26 (1): 32–44.

Tissot, Sylvie. 2007. "The Role of Race and Class in Urban Marginality: Discussing Loïc Wacquant's Comparison between the USA and France." *City* 11 (3): 364–69.

———. 2008. " 'French Suburbs': A New Problem or a New Approach to Social Exclusion?" CES Working Papers Series 160, European Studies Center, University of Pittsburgh.

Tomaskovic-Devey, Donald, Melvin Thomas, and Kecia Johnson. 2005. "Race and the Accumulation of Human Capital across the Career: A Theoretical Model and Fixed Effects Application." *American Journal of Sociology* 111(1): 58–89.

Treitler, Vilna Bashi. 2013. *The Ethnic Project: Transforming Racial Fiction into Ethnic Factions*. Palo Alto, CA: Stanford University Press.

Tribalat, Michèle. 2004a. "An Estimation of the Foreign-Origin Populations of France in 1999." *Population* 59 (1): 49–80.

———. 2004b. "The French 'Melting Pot': Outdated—or in Need of Reinvention?" In *Reinventing France: State and Society in the Twenty-First Century*, edited by S. Milner and N. Parsons, 127–42. French Politics, Culture and Society Series. New York: Palgrave Macmillan.

Truong, Fabien. 2015. *Jeunesses françaises: Bac + 5 made in banlieue*. Paris: Éditions La Découverte.

Truesdell, Nicole. 2013. "Researching Race While Being Raced: Reflections on Race Politics in Anthropology." In "Confronting Race & Racism," *Anthropologies*, no. 18, May 24.

Urry, John. 1973. "Towards a Structural Theory of the Middle Class." *Acta Sociologica* 16 (3): 175–87.

Vallejo, Jody Agius. 2013. *Barrios to Burbs: The Making of the Mexican American Middle Class.* Palo Alto, CA: Stanford University Press.

Van Laer, Koen, and Maddy Janssens. 2011. "Ethnic Minority Professionals' Experiences with Subtle Discrimination in the Workplace." *Human Relations* 64 (9): 1203–27.

Van Zanten, Agnes. 1997. "Schooling Immigrants in France in the 1990s: Success or Failure of the Republican Model of Integration?" *Anthropology and Education Quarterly* 28 (3): 351–74.

Vega, Judith, and Pieter Boele van Hensbroek. 2010. "The Agendas of Cultural Citizenship: A Political-Theoretical Exercise." *Citizenship Studies* 14 (3): 245–57.

Venel, Nancy. 2004. *Musulmans et citoyens.* Paris: Presses Universitaires de France.

Venkatesh, Sudhir. 2002. " 'Doing the Hustle': Constructing the Ethnographer in the American Ghetto." *Ethnography* 3 (1): 91–111.

Voas, David, and Fenella Fleischmann. 2012. "Islam Moves West: Religious Change in the First and Second Generations." *Annual Review of Sociology* 38: 525–45.

Volpp, Leti. 2000. "Blaming Culture for Bad Behavior." *Yale Journal of Law & the Humanities* 12 (1): 89–116.

———. 2007. "The Culture of Citizenship." *Theoretical Inquiries in Law* 8 (2): 571–602.

Wacquant, Loïc J. D. 1991. "Making Class: The Middle Class(es) in Social Theory and Social Structure. In *Bringing Class Back In: Contemporary and Historical Perspectives*, edited by S. G. McNall, R. F. Levine, and R. Fantasia, 39–54. Boulder, CO: Westview Press.

———. 2007. *Urban Outcasts: A Comparative Sociology of Advanced Marginality.* Cambridge, UK: Polity Press.

Warikoo, Natasha Kumar. 2004. "Cosmopolitan Ethnicity: Second-Generation Indo-Caribbean Identities." In *Becoming New Yorkers: Ethnographies of the New Second Generation*, edited by P. Kasinitz, J. H. Mollenkopf and M. C. Waters, 361–91. New York: Russell Sage Foundation.

———. 2011. *Balancing Acts: Youth Culture in the Global City.* Berkeley: University of California Press.

Waters, Mary C. 1990. *Ethnic Options: Choosing Identities in America.* Berkeley: University of California Press.

———. 1999. *Black Identities: West Indian Immigrant Dreams and American Realities.* Cambridge, MA: Harvard University Press.

Waters, Mary C., Van C. Tran, Philip Kasinitz, and John H. Mollenkopf. 2010. "Segmented Assimilation Revisited: Types of Acculturation and Socioeconomic Mobility in Young Adulthood." *Ethnic and Racial Studies* 33 (7): 1168–93.

Weber, Max. (1922) 2013. *Economy and Society.* Edited by G. Roth and C. Wittich. 2 vols. Oakland, CA: University of California Press.

Weill, Nicolas. 2006. "What's in a Scarf? The Debate on *Laïcité* in France." *French Politics, Culture & Society* 24 (1): 59–73.

Weiner, Melissa F. 2012. "Towards a Critical Global Race Theory." *Sociology Compass* 6 (4): 332–50.

Weir, Margaret. 1993. "Race and Urban Poverty: Comparing Europe and America." *Brookings Review* 11 (Summer): 22–27.

White, Elisa Joy. 2012. *Modernity, Freedom, and the African Diaspora: Dublin, New Orleans, Paris*. Bloomington: Indiana University Press.

Wieviorka, Michel. 1992. *La France raciste*. Paris: Éditions du Seuil.

Wilder, Gary. 2007. "Thinking through Race, Confronting Republican Racism." Paper presented at Racing the Republic: Ethnicity and Inequality in France in American and World Perspective conference, University of California, Berkeley, September.

Wilson, William Julius. 1980. *The Declining Significance of Race: Blacks and Changing American Institutions*. Chicago: University of Chicago Press.

Wimmer, Andreas. 2013. *Ethnic Boundary Making: Institutions, Power, Networks*. Oxford: Oxford University Press.

Winant, Howard. 2001. *The World Is a Ghetto: Race and Democracy since World War II*. New York: Basic Books.

Wihtol de Wenden, Catherine, and Rémy Leveau. 2001. *La Beurgeoisie: Les trois âges du mouvement associatif civique issu de l'immigration*. Paris: CNRS Éditions.

Wright, Michelle. 2004. *Becoming Black: Creating Identity in the African Diaspora*. Durham, NC: Duke University Press.

———. 2006. "Postwar Blackness and the World of Europe." *Österreichisches Zeitschrift für Geschichtswissenschaften* 17 (2): 113–22.

Wu, Frank H. 2001. "Profiling Principle: The Prosecution of Wen Ho Lee and the Defense of Asian Americans." *UCLA Asian Pacific American Law Journal* 7: 52–56.

X, Malcolm, and Alex Haley. 1965. *The Autobiography of Malcolm X*. New York: Grove Press.

Yade, Rama. 2007. *Noirs de France*. Paris: Calmann-Lévy.

Young, Alford A., Jr. 2006. *The Minds of Marginalized Black Men: Making Sense of Mobility, Opportunity, and Future Life Chances*. Princeton, NJ: Princeton University Press.

——— 2008. "White Ethnographers on the Experiences of African-American Men: Then and Now." In *White Logic, White Methods: Racism and Methodology*, edited by T. Zuberi and E. Bonilla-Silva, 179–202. Lanham, MD: Rowman and Littlefield.

Zéphir, Flore. 2001. *Trends in Ethnic Identification among Second-Generation Haitian Immigrants in New York City*. Westport, CT: Bergin & Garvey.

Zhou, Min. 1997. "Growing Up American: The Challenge Confronting Immigrant Children and Children of Immigrants." *Annual Review of Sociology* 23: 63–95.

Zhou, Min, and Jennifer Lee. 2007. "Becoming Ethnic or Becoming American? Reflecting on the Divergent Pathways to Social Mobility and Assimilation among the New Second Generation." *DuBois Review: Social Science Research on Race* 4 (1): 189–205.

Zolberg, Aristide R., and Long Litt Woon. 1999. "Why Islam Is Like Spanish: Cultural Incorporation in Europe and the United States." *Politics & Society* 27: 5–38.

INDEX

affirmative action, 9; *discrimination positive*, 116; territorial, 9, 122n6, 123n11

African Americans, 69, 84, 86, 88, 90, 102, 125n5; black president, 28, 86–87, 109–10; code-switching and behavior-switching, 78; cultural citizenship denied to, 41, 101; "double consciousness," 18, 76, 119–20n53; hyphenated and combined identity, 76; Malcolm X, 1, 86, 90, 91; media portrayals, 86, 123n4; middle-class professionals, 16, 119nn50,51; in Paris, ix–x, 25, 28, 95, 105–6, 109–10, 113n1, 125n4; researcher identities, 26, 105–11, 124n2; second-class citizenship, 121n66; transnational blackness, 86, 88; West Indian immigrants and, 120n60

African diaspora, 27, 84, 85, 87–92. *See also* African Americans; ethnic origin

age, of respondents, 25

Alba, Richard, 14–15, 121n62

Algeria: colonial, 8, 11, 116n16, 117nn35,36; ethnic origin, 1–2, 8, 11, 25, 35–37, 45, 73–81, 121n69; Fanon, 88, 115n16; War of Independence, 1–2, 8, 36, 39, 115n19, 125n3

alienation: between two cultures, 79–81. *See also* otherness

Arabic language, 25, 36, 37, 40, 45, 79

Asian origin: Americans, 24, 76, 88, 120n59, 121n66; "desis," 88, 120n59, 124–25n3; Sikhs in London, 22, 120n59

assigned blackness, 89

assigned identity, 27, 75, 82–83

assigned otherness, 4–6, 34, 36, 41, 67, 100

assimilation, 4, 17, 48, 53, 100–101, 114n7; cultural, 48; French education, 122n2; and hyphenated and combined identity, 76; and integration, 11–12, 98–99, 101, 119n48; *laïcité*, 7; partial, 24–25; structural, 48

The Autobiography of Malcolm X, 1, 86

banlieues, 8–9, 25, 56–60, 124n9; Nanterre, 26, 55 *fig*, 58; Paris isolated from, 58, 115n22; respondents, 25, 57; uprisings (2005), 46, 59, 86, 98–99, 106, 122–23nn1,2, 125n11

Benna, Zyed, 99, 125n11

Besson, Eric, 11

beur, 12, 109

beurgeoisie, 14

bidonvilles (shantytowns), 8

Black Girl in Paris, ix–x, 113n1

Black Is . . . Black Ain't (Riggs), 69

blackness, 28, 92; assigned, 89; in France, 20; otherness, 85–86, 88–89, 91, 114n14; "social uniform," 88; thick, 90; thin, 86, 90; transnational, 27, 84–92. *See also* African Americans; race/ethnicity

Bouhlel, Mohamed Lahouaiej, 94

boundaries, 120–21n62; both French and maghrébin identities, 66–83, 98; citizenship, 22–23, 32–33, 121n63; of difference, 27, 31–32, 84–92; around French identity, 4–5, 7, 11,

147

identity (*continued*)
125n5; assigned versus asserted, 27, 75, 82–83; British, 76, 91; hyphenated and combined, 67, 71, 75–79; Marseilles, 61–62, 123n14; multiculturalism and, 7, 69, 71, 114n9, 121n64; Muslim, 49–52, 123n6; politics based on, 7, 44, 69, 71, 85, 90, 99, 114n9, 125n9; "public identities," 63; religious, 123n7; researchers, 26, 105–11, 124n2. *See also* cultural citizenship (denial of); ethnic origin; French identity

"imagined community," France's, 3, 18, 83

"immigrant shadow," 69

immigration, 6, 8–9, 117n34; economic, 1, 9, 25; policies, 9, 101, 115n18; political, 1–2; population percentage, 6, 10; postcolonial immigrants, 1, 11, 115n21, 117n34; terminology, 117n34, 118n41. *See also* ethnic origin; second-generation immigrants

income, North African second generation compared with whites, 13

INED (Institut national d'études démographiques/National Institute of Demographic Studies), 13, 119n49

INSEE (Institut national de la statistique et des études économiques/National Institute of Statistics), 6, 9, 13, 124n3, 126n3

insiders, 4, 16–18, 22, 69, 105, 108–9, 110, 120n63

integration, 117n31, 118n38, 119n48; and assimilation, 11–12, 98–99, 101, 119n48; uprisings and, 98–99

interviews, 107–8. *See also* respondents

Islam. *See* Muslims

Islamophobia, 49–50, 94–95, 101

Kassovitz, Mathieu, 93

Keaton, Trica Danielle, 89–90, 111

Kelley, Robin, 93

Killian, Caitlin, 109

Kouachi, Saïd and Chérif, 93–94

Lacy, Karyn R., 63, 108, 120n58

laïcité, 7, 114n10. *See also* secularism

Lamont, Michèle, 22, 108–9, 120–21n62; *The Dignity of Working Men: Morality and the Boundaries of Race, Class, and Immigration*, 20–21

Landry, Bart, 15–16

Latinos, United States, 23, 24, 41, 48, 121n66

Lee, Bruce, 1, 91

LeMaire, Bruno, 66

Le Pen, Marine, 28

Lorde, Audre, 4

maghrébin origin. *See* ethnic origin; North African second generation

mainstream, defined, 14–15, 119n49

Malcolm X, 1, 86, 90, 91

Marche des Beurs/March for Equality and against Racism, 9

marginalization, 119n52; class and socioeconomic status, 20; and identity, 72; in middle-class, 3, 6, 14–18, 43–65, 97; of Muslims, 10, 22, 49–53; race/ethnicity, 3, 4–6, 8, 14–24, 27, 43–65, 82–83, 89–92, 95–101. *See also* cultural citizenship (denial of)

Marseilles, identity, 61–62, 123n14

Marsh, Kris, 15–16

M'Bala M'Bala (Dieudonné), 94

media portrayals, 86, 98–99, 106, 123n4

Merabet, Ahmed, 94, 101

methodology, 25, 105–11, 126

Meurs, Dominique, 13–14

middle-class, 2, 3–4, 6, 42, 67–68, 95, 119n51; alienation between two cultures, 80; "cultural brokers," 41, 43–44; exclusion within, 16, 99; marginalized, 3, 6, 14–18, 43–65, 97; measurement of, 15, 25; "subaltern," 16. *See also* professional work

Mills, C. Wright, 15

Ministère de l'immigration, de l'intégration de l'identité nationale et du développement solidaire (Ministry of Immigration, Integration, National Identity and Codevelopment), 10–11, 117n32

Mitterrand, François, 9, 71, 116n26

Morano, Nadine, 1, 93

Morocco: colonization, 8; ethnic origin, 25, 74–75, 78

multiculturalism, 7, 69, 71, 114n9, 121n64

Muslims, 10, 116–17; believing or practicing, 2, 10, 50–52, 123n8; burkini, 94–95; as descriptive terminology, 12; difference based on, 10, 49–53; exclusion based on race/ethnicity, 9, 10, 21–22, 44, 49–55, 95; French identity, 10, 52–53, 116–17n29; hate speech against, 116–17n25; identity as, 49–52, 123n6; Islamic extremism, 94; Islamophobia toward, 49–50, 94–95, 101; privacy of religion, 2, 49, 51–53; terrorist associations, 94; United Kingdom, 76; workplace, 53–55

Nanterre, 26, 55 *fig*, 58

Nanterre Association, 26, 58, 86–87, 107–8, 109, 110

nation, 7, 11, 19, 85. *See also* ethnic origin; French identity

Ndiaye, Pap, *La condition noire: Essai sur une minorité française* (The black condition: Essay on a French minority), 20, 47, 86, 90, 91–92
Nee, Victor, 14–15
Netherlands, 6, 101
Noiriel, Gérard, 7–8
North African second generation, 3–6, 9, 12–14, 36 3/, 0/*9n, ... f ri assigned otherness, 4–6, 34, 36, 41, 67, 100; "citizen outsiders," 4, 17, 95, 105; "cultural brokers," 31, 41, 43–44; dual education, 30–38; educational status, 13–14, 15, 17, 25; hyphenated and combined identity, 67, 71, 75–79; terminology, 118n41. *See also* cultural citizenship (denial of); difference; ethnic origin; marginalization; middle-class

Obama, Barack, 28, 82, 86–87, 90, 109–10
otherness: alienation between two cultures, 79–81; assigned, 4–6, 34, 36, 41, 67, 100; *banlieues*, 57; blackness, 85–86, 88–89, 91, 114n14; colonialism and, 8; "forever foreigners," 34; "perpetual foreigners," 24–25, 63; schools as sites of, 33. *See also* difference
outsiders, 4, 16–18, 22, 69, 105–7, 108–10, 120n63; "citizen outsiders," 4, 17, 95, 105

Pandey, Gyanendra, 16
parents of respondents: Christmas celebrations, 77, 124n8; educational status, 25; influence on respondents, 34–38, 45–46, 77–78, 81; labor force participation, 25; mixed-race, 25; respondents' differences from, 46, 77–78, 109
Paris: African Americans in, ix–x, 25, 28, 95, 105–6, 109–10, 113n1, 125n4; *banlieues* isolated from, 58, 115n22; metropolitan region, 5 *map*; Muslims, 116–17n29; researcher, ix–x, 25, 28, 105–7, 109–10; respondents, 25
participant observation, 26, 107–8
"perpetual foreigners," 24–25, 63
Petit Nanterre, 107–8
Pickering, Paula, 109
Place de la République, 96 *fig*
Le Point, 68 *fig*
police, 122–23n2; and race/ethnicity, 13, 40, 86, 99–103, 118n44, 123n4
politics, 9; Far Right, 20, 28, 101, 117n30, 118n37; identity, 7, 44, 69, 71, 85, 90, 99, 114n9; 125n9; immigration based on, 1–2; Les Républicains, 1, 93, 113n3. *See also* French Republicanism

population: immigrant-origin, 6, 10, 12, 118n40, 124n3; Muslim, 10
presidents: black, 28, 86–87, 109–10; Sarkozy, 10–11, 72, 81–82, 87, 90, 113n3, 117n33; United States, 28, 82, 86–87, 90, 101, 109–10. *See also* United States
private sphere, of religion, 2, 7, 49, 51–53
professional work, 13, 15, 25–26; and race-based marginalization, 15, 16, 119n50; respondents, 25–26, 47, 107
public sphere: "doing race/ethnicity," 69; domain of exclusion, 44, 63, 101; religion, 7

race/ethnicity, 92, 95, 98–103, 111, 120, 125n6; American vs. European understanding, 111, 126n4; ban on statistics based on, 9; boundaries around, 19, 21–22, 91; census and, 9, 12, 19, 69, 106, 125n6; consciousness, 20, 22, 60, 75–76, 85–86, 89, 92; cultural racism, 21; European embarrassment about, 120n61; French colonial code, 88, 115–16n15; and French identity, 3, 4, 8, 13, 18, 47–83, 89, 91, 92, 97–100; German citizenship based on, 11, 82; hate speech, 116–17n25; insider-outsider position, 16–18, 105, 108–9, 110; "making race," 89; marginalization based on, 3, 4–6, 8, 14–24, 27, 43–65, 82–83, 89–92, 95–101; middle-class, 15–16, 119n51; and nation, 19, 85; nonwhite markers, 19; Obama election and, 110; otherness based on, 4–6, 8, 18, 85–86, 88–89; place and, 56; police and, 13, 40, 86, 99–103, 118n44, 123n4; privacy of, 69; "racial common-sense," 18; Republicanism and, 7–8, 9, 18–22, 69, 95, 97, 100, 106, 121n64; researcher and interviewees, 26, 105–11; terminology, 12, 114n6, 118n41; thick and thin identities, 86, 90, 120n58; transnational, 27, 84–92; white French identity, 18, 21, 70, 115n20. *See also* African Americans; blackness; differential treatment based on race/ethnicity; ethnic origin; racial project
racial project: France's, 6, 18–22, 24, 48, 56–57, 83, 85. *See also* cultural citizenship (denial of)
religion: French Republicanism, 2, 7, 49, 51–53; identity, 123n7; "lived religion perspective," 49. *See also* Muslims
Renan, Ernest, 7, 66
Les Républicains, 1, 93, 113n3
Republicanism. See French Republicanism
research, 25–26, 105–7
researchers: identity, 26, 105–11, 124n2; Paris, ix–x, 25, 28, 105–7, 109–10; participant observation, 26, 107–8

CPSIA information can be obtained
at www.ICGtesting.com
Printed in the USA
LVOW10s0236240917
549802LV00001B/1/P

9 780520 294264